A HISTORY

OF

COOPER COUNTY,

Missouri,

From the first visit by White Men, in February, 1804, to the 5th day of July, 1876.

BY HENRY C. LEVENS AND NATHANIEL M. DRAKE.

ST. LOUIS:
PERRIN & SMITH, STEAM BOOK AND JOB PRINTERS, 701 WASHINGTON AVENUE,
1876.

This volume was reproduced from
An 1884 edition located in the
Publisher's private library,
Greenville, South Carolina

All rights reserved. No part of this publication
may be reproduced, stored in a retrieval system,
transmitted in any form, posted on to the web
in any form or by any means without the
prior written permission of the publisher.

Please direct all correspondence and orders to:

www.southernhistoricalpress.com
or
SOUTHERN HISTORICAL PRESS, Inc.
PO BOX 1267
375 West Broad Street
Greenville, SC   29601
southernhistoricalpress@gmail.com

Originally published: Chicago & Louisville, 1884
Reprinted with New Material by:
Southern Historical Press, Inc.
Greenville, SC 2017
New Material Copyright 2017 by
Southern Historical Press, Inc.
Greenville, SC
ISBN #0-89308-895-1
All rights Reserved.

CONTENTS.

	PAGE.
Correspondence,	5
Introduction,	7
Dedication,	10

CHAPTER I.
History of Boone's Lick Country, from the First Visit by White Men to the Organization of Howard County, . . 11

CHAPTER II.
History of Boone's Lick Country, continued, . . . 20

CHAPTER III.
History of Boone's Lick Country, continued, . . 29

CHAPTER IV.
Organization of Howard County, ... 39

CHAPTER V.
Organization of Cooper County, ... 48

CHAPTER VI.
History of Cooper County, ... 56

CHAPTER VII.
History of Cooper County, continued, . . . 64

CHAPTER VIII.
History of Cooper County, continued, . . . 68

CHAPTER IX.
Political History of Cooper County, ... 72

CHAPTER X.
War History of Cooper County, ... 87

CHAPTER XI.
War History of Cooper County, continued, . . . 96

CHAPTER XII.
Character, Manners and Customs of the Early Settlers of Cooper County, ... 119

CHAPTER XIII.
Different Towns in Cooper County, . . . 126

CONTENTS.

CHAPTER XIV.
Different Townships in Cooper County, ... 142

CHAPTER XV.
Early History of Different Townships, ... 157

CHAPTER XVI.
Early History of Different Townships, continued, . . 177

CHAPTER XVII.
Biographies of some of the Old Citizens, which were not placed in the History of the Townships in which they lived, . 196

CHAPTER XVIII.
Celebration of July Fourth, 1876, at Boonville. Poem by H. A. Hutchison, ... 203

CHAPTER XIX.
Present Boundaries of Cooper County, Population, etc., etc., . 210

CHAPTER XX.
Complete List of State Officers who served from the Organization of the State to the present time, ... 215

CHAPTER XXI.
Complete List of County Officers who have served from the Organization of the County to the present time, . . . 221

Those to Whom we are under Obligations for Assistance, . 228

Abstracts. 229-231

HISTORY OF COOPER COUNTY.

The following correspondence explains itself:

BOONVILLE, Mo., June 5, 1876.

Messrs. H. C. LEVENS and N. M. DRAKE:

GENTLEMEN—We are making arrangements for celebrating the 100th Anniversary of the Declaration of Independence, and in order to do so with credit to our people, we propose to enlist the cordial efforts of our citizens. Knowing your thorough acquaintance with the history of Cooper county, we respectfully solicit a contribution from you in conformity to a resolution of Congress and proclamation of the President, to be read upon the above occasion, at least such portions as you may deem of special interest to our people. We are aware that we are asking a great deal to be done in so short a time, but the circumstances, we think, justifies the appeal, and our confidence in your willingness to respond favorably.

Awaiting an early reply, we have the honor to remain with sentiments of high respect.

Very truly yours,

F. W. LUDWIG, } Spec'l Com.
H. M. CLARK,

BOONVILLE, Mo., June 8, 1876.

Messrs. F. W. LUDWIG and H. M. CLARK:—

GENTLEMEN—Yours of 5th inst., requesting us to write a short history of Cooper county, &c., received. In reply would say, that we will comply with your request to the best of our ability. Very Respectfully,

HENRY C. LEVENS,
N. M. DRAKE.

INTRODUCTION.

In compliance with a resolution of Congress, and the Proclamation of the President of the United States, the Committee of Invitation for the Celebration of the "Centennial" 4th day of July, requested us to write a brief historical sketch of Cooper county, Missouri, to which we, with considerable mistrust, as to our ability to meet the expectations of the people, consented, and undertook to perform.

After reading the same on that occasion, the multitude there assembled, unanimously passed a resolution, offered by Maj. Henry M. Clark, Chairman of said Committee, requesting us to complete said history, and have the same published in book or pamphlet form, which has accordingly been done.

This book contains, among other items of interest, viz:

1st. The history of the "Boone's Lick Country," from the time it was first visited by white Americans to the organization of Cooper county.

2d. The general history of the county of Cooper from the time of its organization, to the 5th day of July, 1876.

3d. The Political History of the County, containing the names of all of the voters at the first election for delegates to Congress on the 2d day of August, 1819, who lived within the present limits of the county; and, also, the names of the candidates for office at several of the early elections and the number of votes given.

4th. The war history of the county,

5th. A short biographical sketch of some of the most prominent early settlers.

6th. A description of the first churches, and schools, ministers of the gospel and school teachers, showing that the first school was taught upon a log in the open air, and the names of the pupils attending the same.

7th. A list of all of the State and County officers elected and appointed, from the formation of the State and county government to the 4th day of July, 1876; their terms of office, when the same commenced and when expired.

8th. A table showing the progress of schools, the taxable wealth and taxes at different periods and other useful statistics, in regard to the advancement of the county.

9th. A description of each post office in the county, and a separate history of the City of Boonville and the different towns.

10th. A brief history of each township, with the names of a number of its earliest settlers, from the best information which could be obtained from the records, and the recollections of the old citizens still living. A large majority of those mentioned were here and voted at the August election, in 1820, and but few are included, who arrived subsequent to that date. These lists are, we think, in the main correct, but some of the early settlers have, no doubt, been omitted, for the want of proper information. It will be noticed that the histories of some of the townships are more full and complete than others, their citizens having taken more interest in giving the desired information.

We expect our history to be severely criticised by some, but they must bear in mind, that it is a difficult and laborious task to write a detailed history, reaching over a period of sixty-six years, when there are so few of the old settlers now living from whom information could be obtained.

Neither could any other history, written previous to this one be found, which could be used as a guide.

We have, merely in a plain old-fashioned style, recorded the facts, as they were learned from others, and from the State and county records. We undertook the task, not because we thought that we could perform it better than any one else, but because we felt that it should be done, and no one else showed a disposition to put his shoulder to the wheel.

For these and other reasons, we have undertaken this responsible duty, hoping that our efforts, in that behalf, may meet the expectations of a generous public; and that the following pages may be the means of perpetuating the memories of at least some of those who braved the dangers of the savage foe, and whose privations and toil were the means of opening to civilization one of the most productive and best counties, upon which the sun has ever shone. Many of them, whose remains are sleeping in the sacred soil of old Cooper have been long since entirely forgotten, and all recognize the fact that this should not be.

We should honor their memories, and imitate their virtues, their moral courage and their heroic bravery. We have few such men among us now. Those glorious days of simplicity have passed away, and only the memory of them remains. We live during the fast age of steamboats, railroads and telegraphs. Whether these things have increased our happiness and prosperity is left to others to determine.

But one thing is certain, and that is, the fact that crime has increased to an alarming extent. The records of our county show that no person was indicted or punished for crime, during the twelve years subsequent to its first settlement. This proves that the first settlers were, with hardly an exception, honest men and law abiding citizens.

Hoping that our efforts, in this behalf, will be the means of accomplishing some good, we are,

Very Respectfully, Your Obedient Servants,
HENRY C. LEVENS,
N. M. DRAKE.

DEDICATION.

To Captain SAMUEL COLE and MRS. JENNIE DAVIS, his sister, the only two persons now living in Cooper county, who were among the first company of settlers who put their feet upon its sacred soil—this work is respectfully dedicated. May they live long, and be forever blessed, and may their latter days be as peaceful and happy as their former ones have been honorable and glorious.

HISTORY OF BOONE'S LICK COUNTRY.

From the First Visit by White Men to the Organization of Howard County.

CHAPTER I.

BOUNDARIES of the Boone's Lick Country.—Derivation of the Name.—First Visit by White Men.—Second Visit.—Third Visit.—First Salt Manufactured in County.—First regular Settlement in Boone's Lick Country.—First Settlement in Cooper County.—Aspect of the Savages.

All of the present State of Missouri, lying west of Cedar Creek, and north and west of the Osage river, and extending to the territorial line on the west and north, was, for many years, known as the "Boone's Lick Country." The first settlers, who came here, knew it only by that name.

It received its name from a place called "Boone's Lick," in what is now Howard county, situated about eight miles northwest of New Franklin, near the Missouri river. This place was visited by Daniel Boone at a very early time, but the exact date is not known. Here Boone found several large salt springs, and, as such places were always resorted to by deer and other game, he often hunted in the neighborhood.

Although it has always been stated, as a *surmise*, that Daniel Boone once resided at this Lick, and afterwards, within the present county of Cooper, yet it has been impossible to find anything authentic upon the subject; and, as Samuel Cole, a member of the first white family, which settled in the present limits of Cooper county, says emphatically, that Daniel Boone never lived farther west than St. Charles county, the conclusion is inevitable, that these histories are mistaken, when they make the statement, that he was the first settler in the "Boone's Lick Country."

The first Americans, of whom we have any definite knowledge, who were ever in this portion of the State, were Ira P. Nash, a deputy United States surveyor, Stephen Hancock, and Stephen Jackson, who came up the Missouri river, in the month of February 1804, and located a claim, on the public lands, in Howard county, nearly opposite the mouth of the Lamine river. They remained there until the month of March, in the same year, employing their time in surveying, hunting and fishing; and in the month of March they returned to their homes, which were situated on the Missouri river, about 25 miles above St. Charles.

While Nash and his companions were in Howard county, they visited "Barclay's and Boone's Licks;" also a trading-post, situated about 2 miles northwest of Old Franklin, kept by a white man by the name of Prewitt. The existence of this trading-post, and the fact that "Barclay's and Boone's Licks" had already received their names, from the white persons who visited them, shows conclusively, that this portion of the country had been explored, even before this, by white Americans. But no history makes mention of this trading-post, or of Prewitt; hence we are unable to determine when he came to the "Boone's Lick Country," how long he remained, and where he went when he left; but he, evidently, left before the year 1808, as, when Benjamin Cooper moved to what is now Howard county, in that year, there was then no settlement in this part of the State.

In July, 1804, Ira P. Nash, in company with William Nash, James H. Whitesides, William Clark, and Daniel Hubbard, again came into what is now Howard county, and surveyed a tract of land near the present site of Old

Franklin. On this second trip, Ira P. Nash claimed that, when he came up the river the February before, he had left a compass in a certain hollow tree, and started out with two companions to find it, agreeing to meet the balance of the company the next day at Barclay's Lick, which he did accordingly, bringing the compass with him, thus proving beyond a doubt, that he had visited the country before this time.

Lewis and Clarke, on their exploring expedition across the Rocky Mountains, and down the Columbia river to the Pacific ocean, arrived at the mouth of the Bonne Femme, in Howard county, on the 7th day of June 1804, and camped for the night. When they arrived at the mouth of the "Big Moniteau Creek," they found a point of rocks, covered with hieroglyphic paintings, but the large number of rattlesnakes which they found there, prevented a close examination of the place. Continuing their way up the river, they arrived at the mouth of the Lamine river on the 8th of the same month, and on the 9th at Arrow Rock.

When they returned from their journey in 1806, after having successfully accomplished all the objects for which they were sent out, they passed down the Missouri river and camped, on the 18th of September, in Howard county, opposite the mouth of the Lamine river. And, as they journeyed down the river on that day, they must have passed the present site of Boonville early on the morning of the 19th of September, 1806.

The next evidence we have, of any white persons being in the "Boone's Lick Country," is the following:

In 1807, Nathan and Daniel M. Boone, sons of old Daniel Boone, who lived with their father in what is now St. Charles county, about 25 miles west of the city of St. Charles, on the Femme Osage Creek, came up the Missouri river, and manufactured salt at "Boone's Lick," in Howard county. After they had manufactured a considerable amount, they shipped it down the river to St. Louis where they sold it. It is thought by many that this was the first instance of salt being manufactured in what was at that time a part of the Territory of Louisiana, now the State of Missouri. Though soon after salt was manufactured in large quantities, "salt licks" being discovered in many parts of the State. Although these were the first white persons who remained for any length of time in the "Boone's Lick Country," yet they were not permanent settlers, as they only came up there to make salt and left as soon as they had finished.

William Christie and John G. Heath came up from St. Louis in 1808, and manufactured salt in what is now Black Water Township, Cooper County. The place is known to this day as "Heath's Salt Lick." He for years afterwards, every summer, made salt at the same place, and was known as the "big salt maker." The salt springs are located on "Heath's Creek," which was also named after him.

Previous to the year 1808, every white American who came to the Boone's Lick Country, came with the intention of only remaining there a short time. Three parties had entered it while on exploring and surveying expeditions; two parties had been to its fine salt licks to make salt, and, no doubt, many of the adventurous settlers living in the eastern part of this State, had often on their hunting expeditions, pierced the trackless forests to the "Boone's Lick Country," but, of course, there is no record of these, hence, those expeditions of which there is a record, are placed as being the first to this part of the country, when, in reality, they may not be.

But in 1808, one adventurous spirit, determined to forsake what appeared to him to be the too thickly settled portion of the State, and move farther west to the more pleasant solitudes of the uninhabited forest. In the Spring of that year, Col. Benjamin Cooper and his family, consisting of his wife and five sons, moved to the "Boone's Lick Country," and located in what is now Howard County, about two miles south-west of "Boone's Lick," in the Missouri river bottom. Here he built him a cabin, cleared a piece of ground and commenced arrangements to make a permanent settlement at that place. But he was not permitted to remain long at his new home. Governor Merriwether Lewis, at that time Governor of the Territory, issued an order directing him to return below the mouth of the Gasconade river, as he was so far advanced into the Indian country, and so far away from protection, that in case of an Indian war he would be unable to protect him. So he returned to Loutre Island, about four miles below the mouth of the Gasconade river, where he remained until the year 1810.

But the rich Territory was not destined to be left forever to the reign of wild beasts or still more savage Indians. Aside from the fact that the character of the men of the early days caused them continually to revolt against living in thickly settled communities, yet the Boone's Lick Country, and especially what is now Cooper County, presented advantages, which those seeking a home where they could find the richest of lands and the most healthful of climate, could not and did not fail to perceive. Its fertile soil promised, with little labor, the most abundant harvests. Its forests were filled with every variety of game, and its streams with all kinds of fish. Is it a wonder, then, that those seeking homes where these things could be found, should select and settle first the rich lands of Cooper and Howard Counties, risking all the dangers from the Indians who lived in great numbers close around them? Two years after the settlement of Benjamin Cooper and his removal to Loutre Island, the first lasting settlement was made in the Boone's Lick Country, and this party was but the forerunner of many others who soon followed, and in little more than one-half of a century have thickly settled one of the richest and most attractive parts of the State of Missouri.

On the 20th of February, 1810, Col. Benjamin Cooper with several others returned to what is now Howard County. They came up on the north side of the Missouri river from Loutre Island, and all of them, except Hannah Cole and Stephen Cole, settled in Howard county, north of the Missouri river. Hannah Cole and Stephen Cole settled in what is now Cooper county; Stephen Cole, about one and one-half miles east of Boonville, in what is now called the old "Fort Field," now owned by J. L. Stephens; and Hannah Cole, in what is now East Boonville, on the big bluff overlooking the river at a point of rocks where a lime kiln now stands. Benjamin Cooper settled in Howard county, in the cabin which he had built two years before, and which had not been disturbed by the Indians, although they occupied all the adjacent country.

When the families of Hannah and Stephen Cole settled in what is now Cooper county, there was no white American living in Missouri west of Franklin county and south of the Missouri river. Those who came with them and settled north of the Missouri river, were their nearest neighbors, but they were most of them two or three miles distance from this side of the river.

The families of the first settlers south of the Missouri river, were composed of the following members: Hannah Cole and her children Jennie, Mattie, Dikie, Nellie, James, Holburt, Stephen, William and Samuel. Stephen Cole and Phoebe, his wife, and their children James, Rhoda, Mark, Nellie and Polly, making seventeen in all, members of the two families who made the first settlement in what is now Cooper county, but what was then an untrodden wilderness. Here they were surrounded on all sides by savages who pretended to be friendly, but who sought every opportunity to steal horses and commit other depredations upon the settlers.

Only four of these children are still alive; they are Dikie, Jennie, Mark and Samuel Cole. Dikie Cole, now Mrs. Dikie Dallias, and Mark Cole, lived in this county for some time, then moved to St. Clair county, where they now reside. Samuel Cole, and Jennie Cole, now Mrs. Jennie Davis, have resided in this county ever since the first settlement by their mother. To Samuel Cole we are indebted for a great deal of the early history of this county, for he was here a long time before any other person now living here, except his sister, came to the county.

When Benjamin Cooper and those who were with him came up the river, there was no road nor anything to guide them through the wilderness. They had to take, as the path in which to travel, any opening which they could find in the thickets which would permit the passage of their wagons and animals. When they arrived at the river, where old Franklin now stands, Hannah and Stephen Cole desiring to cross the river with their families, were compelled to use a large canoe, or "perogue," as it was then called, swimming their horses behind them.

Their only neighbors at that time on this side of the Missouri river, were the Sauk and Fox Indians. The Sauk Indians, under Quashgami, their chief, lived on the Moniteau Creek, in the south part of Cooper county. When the settlers first came here, these Indians professed to be friendly to them, but, as is generally the case with all savages, they stole horses and committed other depredations. During the war of 1812, these Indians took sides with the British against the Americans. After the conclusion of the war, the Sauk Indians were ordered off to Grand river, and from thence to Rock river. Their other chiefs during this time were

Keokuk and Blundo; the latter, one-half French, the others full-blooded Indians.

Samuel Cole states that he often hunted with these chiefs, and found them generally kind and obliging. He was also well acquainted with Blackhawk, who was at that time a common Indian warrior, but who afterwards became a noted chief. The whites at that day, although they well knew the treachery of the Indians, were accustomed to hunt and fish with them; also sometimes to visit them at their villages; yet they always kept on their guard against the wiley savages.

When the settlers first came to this county, wild game of all kinds was very abundant, and was so tame as not to be easily frightened at the approach of white men. This game furnished the settlers with all their meat, and in fact, with all the provisions that they used, for most of the time they had little else than meat. There were large numbers of deer, turkeys, elk and other large animals, and to use the expression of an old settler, "they could be killed as easily as sheep are now killed in our pastures." The settlers spent most of their time in hunting and fishing, as it was no use to plant crops to be destroyed by the wild game. Small game, such as squirrels, rabbits, partridges, &c., swarmed around the homes of the frontiersmen in such numbers, that when they did attempt to raise a crop of any kind, in order to save a part of it, they were forced to kill them in large numbers.

But these inoffensive animals were not the only ones which filled the forests. Such terrible and blood-thirsty wild beasts as the bear and the panther could be seen very often lying in wait for any unwary traveler who ventured near their lairs. Near where the present residence of Washington Adams stands, in the City of Boonville, a panther was one day killed by Samuel Cole which measured eleven feet from the end of its nose to the tip of its tail, and which was thought to have been one of the largest panthers ever killed in the State of Missouri.

Not only were the settlers and their families thus well provided with food by nature, but also their animals were furnished with everything necessary to their well-being. The range was so good during the whole year that their stock lived without being fed at all by their owners. Even when the ground was covered with snow, the animals, taught by instinct, would in a few minutes paw from under the snow enough grass to last them all day. Their only use of corn, of which they planted very little, was to make bread, and bread made of corn was the only kind they ever had.

After the first settlement of what is now Cooper county, the settlers remained here nearly two years without any neighbors nearer than the opposite side of the Missouri river. For nearly two years they encountered alone the dangers of the forest, and lived in peace and quietness, although they at times feared an attack from the Indians who lived south and west of them.

But in the latter part of the year 1811 some more adventurous spirits moved to this side of the river, and began to settle around and near the present site of Boonville. They settled near one another, so that in time of danger they could readily gather at one place. This timely arrival revived the spirits of the settlers, for already could be heard the dim mutterings in the distance, which foreshadowed a long and bloody conflict with the Indians who had been induced by the emissaries of the British government to take sides with that country against the United States of America.

HISTORY OF BOONE'S LICK COUNTRY

CHAPTER II.

Peaceable condition of the "Boone's Lick Country" previous to 1812.—Arrivals in 1811 and 12.—First Fort Built.—Savage Killed.—Removal of the Settlers to Kincaid's Fort.—Killing of Jonathan Todd and Thomas Smith.—Samuel Cole *et. al.* pursued by Indians.—Killing of Samuel Campbell.

Hitherto the life of the settler had been passed in comparative peace and quiet. Supplied by nature with all that he wished to eat or to drink, he had nothing to induce him to labor, except to provide a shelter to cover his family. This completed, he could spend his time in hunting and fishing, and by his pleasant pastime he could provide all the necessaries for those dependent upon him. He had no care about his stock, for in winter, as well as in summer, they were bountifully fed by the grass and other things which grew luxuriantly on every side. And except an occasional encounter with some wild animal, such as a bear or panther, the life of the pioneer was one devoid of incident or excitement.

During the winter of 1811 and the spring of 1812, several families of adventurous frontiersmen came into what is now Cooper county, and settled near the present site of Boonville. The names of those who arrived previous to the commencement of the Indian war, were as follows:

Joseph Jolly, Joseph Yarnell, Gilliard Rupe, Muke Box, Delany Bolin, William Savage, John Savage, James Savage, Walter Burress and David Burress; and these, together with Captain Stephen Cole and Mrs. Hannah Cole, included all who had moved into the "Boone's Lick Country," south of the Missouri River, and west of the Osage river previous to the summer of 1812.

At this time the settlers became satisfied from reports which reached them from time to time, that the Indians were making preparations to attack the settlements along the Missouri river, and they determined to be ready to receive them properly when they did appear. So they soon commenced the building of a fort.

The first fort in the present limits of Cooper county was built by Stephen Cole, his neighbors assisting, in the year 1812, and was called "Cole's" fort. It was situated in the north part of what is now known as the "old fort field," about one and one-half miles east of the City of Boonville, north of the road from Boonville to Rocheport. As soon as it was completed, all the families living around, gathered at the fort for protection from the savages. As their meat consisted entirely of the wild game which they killed, they had to send out parties from day to day to kill it. And it happened that a couple of parties were out hunting when the Indians attacked the fort.

A few months after the fort was built, a band of about four hundred Indians suddenly made their appearance in the neighborhood. When they appeared before the fort, there were two parties out hunting, in one of which were two men by the name of Smith and Savage, who, on their return to the fort, were pursued by the Indians. The savages shot at them several times; in the first fire, Smith was severely wounded, but staggered on to within fifty yards of the fort, where the Indians shot him again, two balls taking effect and hurling him to the ground. As soon as Savage saw him fall, he turned to assist him; but Smith handed him his gun, and told him to save himself, as he knew he was mortally wounded. As the Indians were in close pursuit of them, Savage was forced to leave his unfortunate companion and attempt to make his escape. He reached the fort unhurt, although he had been shot at some twenty-five times. The Indians after having scalped Smith, and barbarously multilated his body, withdrew to the adjacent woods, and laid siege to the fort.

As the Indians who were in pursuit of Savage came in full view of the fort, several of them could have been killed. Indeed, Samuel Cole, who was in the fort at the time, begged his mother to let him shoot an Indian. But she refused, telling him that as the Indians had as yet shown no disposition to fire upon the fort, the inmates did not wish to arouse their anger by killing any of them; hoping that before they did attack, those settlers, who were out hunting, would arrive, and they perhaps get a chance to escape. During the following night the remaining settlers, who were outside of the fort, returned.

The next day the settlers captured a French boat which came up the river loaded with powder and balls, to trade with the Indians at Council Bluffs. They crossed their families and all their stock, furniture, &c., over the river in this boat, to Kincaid Fort, or Fort Hempstead, which was located in what is now Howard county, about one mile from the north end of the great iron bridge over the Missouri river at Boonville. It will be seen from this, that these settlers were not only brave men, but fit to lead an army in time of danger, as when they made this retreat, the fort was surrounded by the Indians on all sides except that protected by the river. And yet in the face of all this they saved everything from the fort.

After they had crossed their families, &c., in the captured boat, and taken possession of the twenty-five kegs of powder and five hundred pounds of balls which the boat contained, the settlers let the Frenchmen return down the river with their boat with the admonition, that if they ever came up the river again with supplies for the Indians, they would hang them, as they could not permit their enemies to thus obtain supplies.

Previous to the capture of this boat and the ammunition with which it was loaded, which was sufficient to last the settlers a long time, Joseph Jolly had supplied them with powder, manufacturing it himself, saltpetre being found in a cave near Rocheport.

The first white men killed by the Indians in the "Boone's Lick Country" were Jonathan Todd and Thomas Smith, who, early in the spring of 1812, had started down the river to pick out a piece of land on which to settle. The Indians attacked them not far from the present line between Howard and Boone counties, and after a long struggle in which several Indians were killed, Todd and Smith were slain. The savages after killing them, cut off their heads and cut out their hearts and placed them by the side of the road on poles.

As soon as the news of the killing of Todd and Smith was brought to the fort, a party of men started out to get their bodies. After they had gone several miles, they captured an Indian warrior who seemed to be watching their movements, and started to take him to the fort alive, in order to get information from him. As they returned after finding the bodies of the settlers, when they arrived within two miles of the fort, the Indian prisoner suddenly broke away from them and attempted to escape. The settlers pursued him about one-half of a mile, when they finding that they could not overtake him and capture him alive, they shot him, killing him instantly.

Immediately after the killing of Todd and Smith, the settlers living on both sides of the Missouri river, being desirous of finding out the true state of affairs, sent out

James Cole and James Davis on a scouting expedition to see whether or not the Indians were really upon the war path. After looking around for some time, and not being able to hear anything of the plans of the savages, they were preparing to return to the fort, when they discovered a large band of Indians in pursuit of them, and directly between them and the fort, in which were their families and friends, unconscious of their danger.

As retreat to the fort was cut off, and they could not withstand the attack of the large body of Indians in the open woods, they started for what was then called Johnson's Factory; a trading post kept by a man named Johnson; it was situated on the Moniteau Creek in what is now Moniteau county, about 200 yards from the Missouri river. They reached the Factory that afternoon and the Indians immediately surrounded the place. As Cole and Davis knew that their friends, at the different forts, would fall an easy prey to the savages, if not warned of their danger in time to prepare for the attack which they seemed certain to make upon the fort, the hardy rangers determined at all hazards to escape and bear the tidings to them. But here the main difficulty presented itself. As long as they remained at the trading post they were safe from the shots of the enemy; but as soon as they left that protection they knew they would be slain.

But knowing the imminent danger of their families and friends, they resolved to make a desperate effort to reach them. So at 12 o'clock that night, they took up a plank from the floor of the "Factory," reached the creek, and finding a canoe, floated down to the river. But just as they reached the river, an unlucky stroke of the paddle against the side of the canoe discovered them to the Indians, who started in pursuit of them in canoes. They pursued the settlers to "Big Lick," now in Cooper county, where, being closely pressed, Cole and Davis turned and each killed an Indian. The Indians then left off pursuit, and the two men reached Cole's Fort in safety, to announce to the settlers, that they were indeed, on the verge of a long and bloody war. From there the melancholy tidings were conveyed to the other forts, and filled the hearts of the settlers with dismay, as they considered how few of them there were, to withstand the attacks of the whole of the Indian nations living around them.

In the summer of 1812, while all the settlers living on the south side of the Missouri river, were at Kincaid's Fort, Samuel Cole, Stephen Cole, and Muke Box, started from the fort on a hunting expedition, crossed the river where Boonville now stands, and penetrated the forest to the Petite Saline Creek. After they had hunted and fished for two days, they were preparing to return upon the third, when they heard firing in the direction of the river, where they had left their canoe. They immediately started toward the river, knowing that the shots were fired by Indians as there was not at that time any white persons except themselves, south of the Missouri river. When they arrived at the residence of Delany Bolin, at or near where the present residence of Mrs. Maria Muir stands, they discovered that a band of Indians was in pursuit of them; and the settlers not knowing their number, but supposing them to be very numerous, immediately separated and took to the woods to meet at the place where they had left their canoe.

When they met there they found the canoe gone, the Indians having stole it. As the Indians were still in hot pursuit of them, they lashed three cottonwood logs together, placed their guns, clothing, &c., upon this raft, swam over, pushing it before them and landed in Howard County, about two and one half miles below the City of Boonville.

That evening they reached the fort in safety, and reported their adventure with the Indians, at the same time advising the inmates of the fort to be prepared for an attack at any time.

Next morning the settlers discovered tracks of the Indians near the fort, and found it had been reconnoitered during the night by a band of eight Indians. They immediately sent to Cooper's & McLean's forts for reinforcements, as there were at that time very few men in the fort, and they supposed that this band of eight was but the scouting party of a large band of Indians. Reinforcements, to the number of 42, soon arrived from the other forts, and they, together with the men belonging to Kincaid's Fort started in pursuit of the Indians, whom they had by this time discovered to be but a small band.

After pursuing them some distance they surrounded them in a hollow, near Monroe's farm, about four miles west of the present site of New Franklin. The Indians concealed themselves in the brush and thickets and behind the timber, and not being able to see them the firing of the settlers was a great deal at random. The fight continued for a long time; four Indians were killed and the remaining four, though badly wounded escaped. None of the settlers were killed and only one, named Adam Woods, was severely wounded, but he afterwards recovered.

Night coming on they were forced to defer the pursuit of the surviving Indians. The next day not satisfied with their work the day before, the rangers started on the trail of the Indians, which was plainly marked with blood.

They followed it to the river and there found the canoe which the savages two days before had stolen from Samuel Cole and his companions. The sides of the canoe were covered with blood, showing that the Indians had attempted to push it into the river, but, on account of being weakened by loss of blood, could not. After hunting them for some time in vain, the party returned to the fort.

In July 1812 some Quapa Indians disguised as Sauks and Foxes, killed a man named Campbell—commonly called "Potter," from his trade, about five miles north-west of Boonville, in Howard county, under the following circumstances: He and a man named Adam McCord, went from Kincaid's Fort to Campbell's home, at the above mentioned place, to tie some flax, which they had been forced to leave longer than they wished, through fear of an attack by the Indians. While they were at work they discovered moccasin tracks around the farm, as though a party of Indians were watching them and seeking a favorable opportunity to slay them. So they started around in order to see whether they had injured anything or not. While they were searching for them, the savages who were concealed in some underbrush, fired upon the party and shot Campbell through the body, killing him almost instantly, but he ran about one hundred yards, climbed a fence, and pitched into the top of a tree which had blown down, and the Indians, though they hunted for his body, never succeeded in finding it. Adam McCord escaped without injury, and going to the fort, reported the death of Campbell, and the circumstances under which he was killed.

Immediately upon his arrival, Col. Benjamin Cooper and Gen. Dodge with a company of about five hundred men, composed of frontiersmen and regular soldiers, started in pursuit of the Indians who numbered one hundred and eighty. The Indians not being able to recross the river, threw up breastworks in order to repel the attack of the soldiers. When Cooper and Dodge appeared before the intrenchments, the Indians after some parley, surrendered themselves as prisoners of war.

After the Indians had surrendered, Col. Cooper and Gen. Dodge had their memorable quarrel in regard to the disposal of the prisoners. Col. Cooper insisted that although they had surrendered as prisoners of war, they, as the murderers of Campbell, were not entitled to protection as such prisoners, and that in accordance with a long established custom of the western country, they should all be hung. But Gen. Dodge insisted that as they had surrendered to him, he being the superior officer, they were entitled to his protection. So fiercely did they quarrel, that at one time the two forces, for Cooper commanded the frontiersmen and Dodge the regulars, came very near having a fight in order to settle the controversy. Finally a peaceful disposition of the matter was made, by Gen. Dodge being permitted to take the prisoners to St. Louis.

HISTORY OF BOONE'S LICK COUNTRY.

CHAPTER III.

Return of the Settlers from the North Side of the River.—Situation of the Settlers for the following Two or Three Years.—Killing of Braxton Cooper, jr., Joseph Still, Wm. McLane, Sarshell Cooper, Samuel McMahan and a Negro Man.—Building of Hannah Cole's Fort. First School Taught in Cooper County.—Fashions, &c., when First Settlement was made.—Territorial Laws extended over the "Boone's Lick Country."

IN the spring of 1813, not having seen any signs of Indians for about three months, and being desirous of raising crops during that year, as they had failed the year before, all of the settlers who had gone to Kincaid's Fort the previous spring, returned to their homes south of the Missouri river. As soon as they arrived they put in their crops of corn, but in order to be advised of the approach of an enemy, they stationed a guard at each corner of the field in which they were at work.

During the following two or three years the settlers were kept continually on the watch against the savages, for every month or two some small band of Indians would suddenly attack and slay some unsuspecting settler who had for the moment forgotten his usual caution, or who feeling secure from attack because the Indians had not appeared for some time, suffered this severe penalty for his negligence. The Indians never after this marched a large band against these settlements, but came in small scouting parties, the members of which had only sufficient courage to shoot down some unsuspecting man, or murder unprotected women and children. They never, except in overwhelming numbers, and then very seldom, made an open attack upon even a lone farmhouse, but stealing up in the darkness of the night they would set fire to the house and slay the inmates as they rushed from their burning dwelling; or as in the case of the killing of Sarshell Cooper, shoot the dreaded enemy of their race, as he sat in the midst of his family.

Is it any wonder, in view of these facts, that when an Indian was captured, 'twas not many minutes before his lifeless body would be hanging from the nearest bough? After all their treachery, woe to the savage who fell into the vengeful hands of the settlers, for they would make short work of him; and they knew they were justified in doing this, for they acted only in self-defense.

During the two or three years following the return of the settlers from Kincaid's Fort, several men were killed by the Indians in the "Boone's Lick Country." The following are the names of all of them of which there is any record; no doubt there may have been some killed whose tragic death has never had a place on the page of history, and which will never be known:

Braxton Cooper, Jr., was killed two miles north-east of the present site of New Franklin, in September, 1813. The Indians attacked him as he was cutting logs to build a house. As he was well armed and a very courageous man, they had a long struggle before the Indians succeeded in killing him. The broken bushes and marks upon the ground showed that the struggle had been very fierce. The settlers who first arrived to take away the body of Cooper, found an Indian's shirt which had two bullet holes in the breast of it, but whether the Indian died or not they never knew. They followed the trail of the Indians for a short distance, but soon lost it, and were forced to abandon the pursuit.

Joseph Still was killed on the Chariton river, in October,

1813, but the cirumstances attending his killing are unknown.

Wm. McLane was killed by the Indians in what is now Howard county, near the present site of Fayette, in October, 1813, under the following circumstances: He, Ewing McLane and four other men, went from McLane's Fort to pick out a piece of land on which some one of them expected to settle. When they arrived at a short distance southwest of the present site of Fayette, they were attacked by a band of about one hundred and fifty Indians. As soon as McLane and his companions saw them, they retreated towards the fort, and just as they were ascending a slant from a long, deep ravine leading to the Moniteau Creek, the Indians fired a volley at them. One shot struck William McLane in the back of the head, and he dropped dead from his horse. After satisfying themselves that he was dead, his remaining companions left his body and continued their retreat to the fort, which they reached in safety. The Indians scalped McLane, cut out his heart and literally hacked him to pieces. As soon as possible, a large party of settlers started out to recover his body, and if possible, to avenge his death; but they found that the Indians had retreated, and left no trace of the direction which they had taken. From the cleared place around the body and the beaten appearance of the earth near, it was supposed that the Indians had, in accordance with their custom, danced their "war dance" there to celebrate their victory. After getting the body they returned sorrowfully to the fort.

Of the many murders committed during the war, none excited so much feeling or caused such a cry of vengeance in the hearts of the frontiersman as the tragic death of Captain Sarshell Cooper, who was the acknowledged leader of the settlers north of the Missouri river. On a dark and stormy night on the 14th day of April, 1814, as Captain Cooper was sitting by his fireside with his family, his youngest child upon his lap, the others playing at different games around the room, and his wife sitting by his side sewing, an Indian warrior crept up to the side of his cabin and picked a hole between the logs just sufficient to admit the muzzle of his gun, the noise of his work being drowned by the storm without. He shot Capt. Cooper, who fell from his chair to the floor, among his horror stricken family, a lifeless corpse. His powers and skill were well known to the Indians whom he had often foiled by these means. He was kind and generous to his neighbors, whom he was always ready to assist in any of their undertakings. Therefore his loss was deeply felt by the settlers whose homes he had defended by his powers, and whose prosperity was owing largely to his advice and counsel.

On the 14th day of December, 1814, a man named Samuel McMahan, living in what is now Lamine township of Cooper county, was killed near Boonville, not far from the present residence of Scott Benedict, under the following circumstances: He had been down to the settlement at Boonville to bring his cattle, as he intended to move down the river, and as he was returning home he came upon a band of Indians who were lying in ambush for some men who were cutting down a bee tree not far away. The savages fired upon him, wounding him and killing his horse. He jumped up after his horse fell, and although severely wounded, ran down a ravine leading to the river. The Indians started in pursuit of him, and as he was weak from the loss of blood, they soon overtook him and killed him, sticking three spears into his back. They afterwards cut off his head and scattered his entrails over the ground. The Indians knowing that the vengeance of the settlers would be sudden and terrible, then scattered, and made their way out of the country the best way they could.

The next day, for the settlers, not knowing the number of the Indians, waited for reinforcements from the opposite side of the river, a party of men went out to get the body of McMahan. James Cole, the brother of Samuel Cole, carried the body before him on his horse, and David McGee brought the head wrapped in a sheep skin. The settlers buried McMahan under the Linn tree, which formerly stood in the centre ring at the old fair grounds. A child of David Buness, which was burned to death, was also buried under this tree.

A negro man named Joe, belonging to Samuel Brown, of Howard county, was killed by the Indians near Mr. Burkhart's farm, about three quarters of a mile east of Estill Station, on the M. K. and T. Railroad.

The above embraces the name of all of the men of whom we have any record, who were killed in the "Boone's Lick Country" during the Indian war, from 1812 to 1815. The peculiar atrocities attending the killing of most of them, makes the stoutest shudder. But they were so common those days, that the settlers did not fear to remain here, although they knew these things might happen to them at any time. Yet they were not daunted by these continued murders, but lived on their lands, making the best defense they could against the Indians.

The next day after the killing of McMahan, all the settlers living near the present site of Boonville, rushed into the house of Hannah Cole, which stood on the Bluff, in what is now "East Boonville," as this place was the most suitable of any near, to defend against an attack of the Indians. All of these men came with their teams, cut down trees, dragged logs to build a fort at that place. They completed the building of the fort in about one week, although all of the men could not work at one time, as it was necessary to station a guard on every side to watch for the approach of the enemy, whom they expected every hour.

The fort was built on the edge of the bluff, and as the bluff was very steep at that point, it was well defended on that side from the Indians. Another reason for building it in that place was because the inmates of the fort could obtain a constant supply of good water from the river. They had a long log running out over the edge of the bluff, and a windlass and rope attached to it, so that it was an easy matter to draw up water, even during an attack of the Indians.

As soon as the fort at Hannah Cole's was completed, the old fort at Stephen Cole's, situated on the bluff near the river, one mile below the new fort, was abandoned, and all the families gathered into the new fort, so as to be a protection to each other.

But this precaution proved to be unnecessary, as the killing of McMahan was virtually the end of the war, in this part of the country, and the settlers had no more open fights with the Indians, although small bands of savages occasionally roamed through the country running off stock, and committing other depredations. The Indians had found out that the men who had pierced the wilderness, and brought their families with them, were ready to lay down their lives in defense of them and their homes, and the savages deserted their hunting grounds, and moved farther west.

Major Stephen Cole, the acknowledged leader of the settlers living south of the Missouri river, survived the war, and after making every effort for their defense, his love of wild adventure led him to become a pioneer in the trade with Santa Fe in 1822. He was killed by the Indians, during the same year, about sixty miles southwest of Santa Fe, on the Rio Grande river. There was also killed at the same time, Stephen Cole, the brother of Samuel Cole.

The first school in the Boone's Lick Country within the

present limits of the county of Cooper, was taught by John Savage, in the year 1813, about one mile east of Boonville, on Lilly's Branch, about one-half of a mile from its mouth. The scholars numbered fifteen children of the settlers living in the neighborhood of Hannah Cole's fort. The names of the scholars who attend the school, were as follows: Benjamin, Delany and William Bolin, Hiram and William Savage, Hess and William Warden, John and William Yarnall, John and William Jolly, Joseph and William Scott, and John and William Rupe. The scholars sat upon one log in the open air, they then having no school house, and the teacher upon another log facing his pupils. The price of tuition was one dollar per month, payable in anything which the settlers had that was worth one dollar. The school progressed very finely under the able management of the teacher who appears to have had some experience in teaching. But it continued only for one month, as it was caused to cease through fears of an attack by the Indians, who about this time commenced a series of depredations upon the settlers, which continued until the year 1815, the close of the war. At this school, where all the surroundings were of the most primitive character, and there was nothing except what was furnished by the kind hand of nature, were planted the first seeds of knowledge in the minds of the young settlers. Here they learned the lessons of honesty and integrity, which even at the present day is a distinguishing characteristic of the generation which grew up at that day.

The next school, of which we have any record, was taught by Abiel Leonard, in the Franklin bottom, near the Bonne Femme Creek, Howard county. Teaching was not congenial to his nature, and it is recorded that he said, the happiest day of his life was when his school closed.

Although many of the settlers were religious persons and

members of the church, there was no regular preaching in the county until the year 1815, yet occasionally service was held by some wandering missionary in the house of some one of the settlers. But in the year 1815, Luke Williams, who afterwards preached at Concord church, held service at Hannah Cole's Fort. Soon after this, a minister named James Savage preached at the fort. The denomination which he represented—the Baptist—was at that time the prevailing one, although every denomination aided in supporting the ministers who preached at the fort, as no one unaided was able to do so. In those days they worked not so much for the success of the *denomination* as for the success of the cause.

When the settlers first came to Cooper county, the women all wore calico dresses, and the men homespun suits of clothes. But the clothes which they brought with them soon wore out, and not having any place at which to buy new ones, they were forced to resort to some expedient to supply the place of the clothes which they were compelled to cast off. For the next few years all the clothes which the settlers had, were made out of knettles.

The low flats along the river, creeks and branches were covered with a thick growth of knettles about three feet high, sometimes standing in patches of twenty acres or more. These were permitted to remain standing until they became decayed in the winter, when they were gathered. They were then broken up, spun into long strings and woven into cloth, from which the garments were made. This would be a very tedious job at the present day, when a ladies dress requires from twenty to thirty yards of cloth, but in those old times five or six yards was as much as was ever put into a dress. Little children usually wore a long leathern shirt over their tow shirt. For several years during the early settlement of this country, the men and women wore garments made out of the same kind of material.

The Territorial laws were not extended over this part of the country until the year 1816. Until which time they had no government or laws except such they themselves made for their own protection, and which, of course, had no effect outside of the boundaries of their narrow Territory. With them, the single distinction was between right and wrong, and they had no medium ground. As the result shows, they really needed no laws or executive officers, for it is a well known fact, that during the early period of this settlement there were no serious crimes committed within its limits. As the men each depended upon the other, and knew that in time of attack by the Indians, their only safety lay in *union*, each endeavored to preserve the good will of his neighbor, and as the best way to obtain the good wishes and assistance of a man, is to act honestly and friendly with him, each did this, and in this way they needed no law, except their own judgments. During the early period of the colony they never had any occasion to punish any one under their law, which was an unwritten one. Although 'tis true, some few crimes were committed, as the nature of man has not entirely changed since then, yet they were uniformly of such a trivial character, as hardly to be worthy to be classed as crimes.

Another reason of the almost entire freedom from crime, was the certainty of punishment. Then there was no "legal technicalities" by which a prisoner could escape. No sooner was the criminal caught and his guilt established—no matter what his crime—than the law-makers took the matter into their own hands, and hung him to the nearest tree.

The following anecdote is related of Mark Cole, son of Stephen Cole, who is still living in St. Clair county, Missouri. One evening, some young ladies visited his father's family at their fort, and remained until pretty late, when they returned home. The road which led to their homes, passed the place where a man had been lately buried; a pen was built around the grave, and covered with logs like a roof, raised about a foot or two from the ground. As most of the persons in those days were superstitious, Mark determined to frighten the young ladies as they passed the grave. So he got a large sheet, and slipping out of the house, went to the grave, no doubt laughing, as there appeared before him a picture of the terror, that his sudden appearance in his strange costume would cause the young ladies, and took his station upon the top of it to await their arrival. But he had not been there long, when suddenly several deep groans issued, seemingly from the bowels of the earth, and the poles on the top of the grave, began to move about, as though the departed spirit was trying to get out, and wreak vengeance upon the profaner of its solitude. Hearing and seeing these things, Mark "did not stand upon the order of his going," but dropping the sheet, he took to his heels, and never stopped until he reached his home, when he fell unconscious upon the door step. He was so badly frightened that he did not fully recover for a month, and even to the present day he will never travel at night alone. The explanation of the noise was very simple, yet the settlers did not let Mark into the secret. One of the men at the fort, who had heard Mark whisper to his brother where he was going, had slipped out of the fort and hastened to the place, just in time to crawl under the poles, and lie down upon the earth, when Mark made his appearance and took his seat.

ORGANIZATION OF HOWARD COUNTY.

CHAPTER IV.

HOWARD COUNTY ORGANIZED.—First Court held in New County, and proceedings of same.—Judge Barton and Stephen Cole Fine one Another for Contempt of Court.—Town of Old Franklin laid off, and Land Office Established There.—Wm. Gibson appointed Constable, and Resigns.—Samuel Cole's Bull Ride.—Joseph Stephens and Family arrive at Boonville.—Visit of Samuel Cole to their Camp.—Discovery of the body of a British Officer Buried in a Mound.

On the 23rd day of January, 1816, that portion of the State of Missouri, lying north and west of the Osage river, and west of Cedar creek, and the dividing ridge between the Mississippi and Missouri rivers, and which formerly had been known as the "Boone's Lick Country," was organized under the territorial laws, and was called "Howard county." Previous to this time, the settlers of this part of the country had made their own laws, and executed them rigorously when occasion demanded, which, it is true, was very seldom. Although the eastern portion of the State, had been, previous to this time, organized into counties; and the territorial laws, by means of the territorial courts, had been extended over them, still the "Boone's Lick Country" had not been sufficiently thickly settled to justify its organization, and the expense of holding terms of court within its limits.

But even during the war with the Indians, the country adjacent to the forts was settled very rapidly, although few ventured to locate, except near enough to reach the fort at the first approach of danger. So that, at the time of the organization of Howard county, it contained a considerable number of settlers, although they lived in what was then called "neighborhoods," so as to be of protection to one another in times of danger from their savage foes.

The act under which the county was organized, located the "seat of justice" at Hannah Cole's fort.

The first court within the territorial limits of Howard county, was held at Hannah Cole's fort, which was situated in what is now "East Boonville;" on the 8th day of July 1816, and discharged, under the territorial laws, all the duties of the circuit, county and probate courts.

The officers of this court were David Barton, Judge; Gray Braynum, Clerk; John G. Heath, Circuit Attorney; and Nicholas S. Burkhart, Sheriff. The attorneys who attended this court, were Edward Bates, Charles Lucus, Joshua Barton, and Lucius Easton.

The following were the proceedings of this first term of the court:

John Muroe was appointed coroner of Howard county, and Benjamin Estill, David Jones, David Kincaid, William Head, and Stephen Cole were appointed commissioners to locate the county seat, which was first located by the territorial legislature at Hannah Cole's fort.

On the 16th day of June, 1816, the above mentioned commissioners settled upon Old Franklin as the most suitable place for the location of the county seat, and to that place the records, documents, &c., were removed, in the year 1817. The county seat remained at Old Franklin until the year 1823, when it was removed to Fayette.

During this term of the court, Maj. Stephen Cole was fined, by Judge Barton, one dollar, for contempt, for misconduct in the presence of the court. Cole objected to paying the fine, but supposing he would be able to retaliate sometime, at last paid it. And his time for retaliation came sooner than he expected. That afternoon, Cole, who was a justice of the peace, organized his court on a log in front of the fort. As Judge Barton was returning from dinner, he stopped in front of Cole and leaned against a tree, watching the proceedings of the justice and smoking his pipe. Cole looked up, and assuming the stern look of insulted dignity, said, "Judge Barton, I fine you one dollar for contempt of my court, for smoking in its presence." Judge Barton smilingly paid his fine, and went to open his own court, acknowledging that he had been beaten at his own game.

The town of Old Franklin was laid off opposite the present site of Boonville, during the year 1816. It was located on fifty acres of land, donated by different individuals for that purpose. It grew very rapidly, soon became very populous, and commanded a large trade. It was for a time the largest and most flourishing town in the State, west of St. Louis, and the starting point for all the Santa Fe traders.

But in the year 1826, the waters of the turbulent Missouri river commenced encroaching upon this beautiful and populous city, and despite the utmost endeavors of its citizens, house after house was swept away, until, in a few years afterwards, the current of the river rolled through her streets, and the whole of the city was engulfed in its hungry waters. Within the last few years, a small village still called "Old Franklin," has sprung up just back of the site of the old town, but not a single house or any other mark remains to suggest to the traveler that he stands near the site of a once large city.

The land office for this district of Missouri was located at Old Franklin, in the year 1818, Gen. Thomas A. Smith was appointed receiver, and Charles Carroll, register. The first land sales west of St. Louis took place here during the year 1818. Great crowds attended this sale from all parts of the State, and lands in every part of the district was sold at that time.

Sometime during the year 1817, William Gibson, now living a short distance east of the City of Boonville, was appointed by the Territorial court constable of that part of Howard county lying south of the Missouri river. His jurisdiction extended from the Missouri river, on the north, to the Osage river on the south. Soon after his appointment, there being some trouble down on the Osage, he was sent there with a warrant for the arrest of the man who had caused the trouble. The distance was between sixty and seventy miles. After arresting the man, he returned to Boonville with his prisoner. As he was on his journey back, having an execution against a man who lived on the road, he stopped at his house and proceeded to levy on the feather beds, as nothing in those days was exempt from levy under execution. But, as soon as he made his purpose known, four women, who were the only persons at home, threatened to give him a thrashing, so he was forced to retire as fast as he could, and return the execution unsatisfied. To add to this, the court only allowed him, for his journey of one hundred and forty miles, which occupied four days, the *magnificent sum of twenty-five cents*. Mr. Gibson thinking the office not quite lucrative enough to justify him in devoting his whole time to its duties, and not wishing to risk his life at the hands of angry women, quietly sent in his resignation, thus furnishing the example of one officer who resigns, although few have the same inducements.

While Samuel Cole was living at his mother's fort in East Boonville, in the year 1817, there was a dance at William Bartlett's boarding house, on the flat near the ferry landing, at the mouth of Ruppe's Branch. Although Samuel wished very much to attend, his mother refused to permit him, as his wardrobe at that time was entirely too limited to permit him to associate with the "elite." He had no pants, his sole garment consisting of a long tow shirt, which reached entirely to his heels. But Samuel, although always, *from his own statement*, an obedient son, was not to be deprived of so great a pleasure, by this, to him, very trivial excuse. So he determined to attend that dance, and then make the best arrangement he could to meet the "wrath to come." Not having any horse, he bridled a tame bull, which was at the fort, and thus mounted, rode up to the door of the house in which they were dancing. After looking in for some time, and by his strange looking steed and attire, attracting a large crowd around him, he drove his bull down to the river, and riding in, he slid back over its haunches, and caught hold of its tail. In this way they swam down the river to Hannah Cole's Fort, when he and his strange companion came out of the water and sought their homes. This story has often been published, but never correctly, as all former accounts represented him as swimming the river to attend a wedding, but our version is *correct*, as it was obtained directly from Samuel Cole himself.

About the 15th day of November, 1817, Joseph Stephens with his large family and several friends, crossed the river where Boonville now stands, and camped near the foot of Main street. The next day after they crossed, Samuel Cole, who was then a boy of sixteen years of age, appeared at their camp and asked Mrs. Stephens if she would like to have some venison. Upon her replying that she would, as she was nearly out of meat, Samuel shouldered his gun and marched off into the woods, telling her to wait a few minutes and he would kill her some. Samuel Cole, at that time, although there was a slight snow on the ground, was bare-footed and bare-headed, his breeches reached only to his knees, the collar of his shirt was open, and he carried an old flint lock rifle. About fifteen minutes after he left the camp, Stephens and his family heard two shots in the direction in which he had gone. Pretty soon Samuel appeared, and told them that he had killed two fine deer, that they must go out and bring them to the camp, as he could not by himself bring in even one of them. So they started out and found the two deer lying on the side of the hill just north of the present residence of William H. Trigg. After they skinned them and cut them up, the party brought them to the camp and presented them to Mrs. Stevens. This shows what little exertion was necessary at that day to obtain meat.

A few days afterwards, Joseph Stephens moved, with his family, to the farm which he had bought about, one-quarter of a mile north of the present site of Bunceton. About Christmas, in the same year, Samuel Cole rode up to Joseph Stephens' camp, and Mrs. Stephens asked him to alight and take dinner. He asked her whether she had any honey, and she told him she had not. He said he could not eat without honey. And although she insistedthat he should remain, he still refused. In the meantime, Larry and Joseph, two of her sons, and a negro man named Basil, came up to the camp carrying their axes, as they had been cutting wood. Samuel turned to them, and told them to go with him and get some honey for dinner. They at first, supposing him to be joking, refused to go. But as he still insisted, they consented. After going some two hundred yards east of the camp, Samuel suddenly stopped, and pointing to a tree, told them to cut it down. The others not seeing anything about the tree that would induce anyone to think that it contained honey, yet willing to accommodate company, cut it down, and it was found filled with nice honey. While they were cutting down this tree, Samuel found another a short distance away, and having cut down this one also, they returned home with six buckets of fine honey, having taken nothing but the clear part. Before he left, Samuel taught them the way in which he found the trees. He told them, that if they would examine the ground around the tree, they would find small pieces of beebread, and occasionally a dead bee. This was an infallible sign of a bee tree. They afterwards, following his direction, searched and found, in a small space, thirteen trees which were filled with honey; and as they had no sugar, this was a great help to them. They sometimes had as much as four hundred pounds of honey on hand at one time.

In the year 1818, Joseph Stevens, who died in 1836, Major Stephen Cole and Wm. Ross, the hatter, started west on a hunting and exploring tour, and traveled as far as the present site of Knob Noster. At that time, all the country west of the present boundary line of Cooper county, was a wilderness, no person living in it. About six miles southeast of the present site of Sedalia, in Pettis county, on the farm now owned by a man by the name of Warren, near Flat Creek, they discovered what appeared to be a large, high and peculiarly shaped Indian mound. They examined it pretty closely, and found on one side that the wolves had scratched an opening into it. After enlarging it, so as to admit them, they beheld a remarkable sight. They found themselves in what resembled a room, about eight feet square, with a ceiling of logs, just high enough to permit a tall man to stand erect. On the side opposite where they had entered, sat an officer dressed in full military uniform, with gold epaulettes upon his shoulders, gold lace fringing every seam of his coat, cocked military hat, knee breeches, lace stockings and morocco slippers. As he sat erect upon a seat hewed out of a log, nothing but the ghastly hue and leathery appearance of his skin would have suggested but that he was alive. By his side stood a heavy gold-headed cane. His features were complete, and his flesh free from decay, though dried to the consistency of leather. The place in which the body was found, was very peculiar. A place about eight feet square and two feet deep had been dug in the earth. The sides had been walled up with sod, until it was high enough for the purpose, reaching several feet above the surface of the ground. The top was then covered with poles, which ran up to a point in the center like the roof of a house. Then the poles and the surrounding walls were covered with sod two or three feet deep, cut from the prairie near by, thus excluding entirely the rain and air. When they left the place, William Ross, being the oldest man of the party, took the cane as a memento, but nothing else was touched.

Who this officer was, from whence he came, what he was doing in this part of the country, what was the cause of his death, and when and by whom he was thus singularly entombed, has not, and perhaps never will be known. But he was supposed, by many, to have been a British officer, who, during the war of 1812, passed around by way of Canada into the Indian country, to incite the Indians against the whites; yet this is only conjecture, though those who discovered his body, account for him in that way.

Soon after this, Joseph Stephens, Sr., now living near Petersburg, on the O. V. & S. K. Railroad, in company with James D. Campbell, went into that part of the country bee hunting, and visited the burial place of this officer. They found that part of the roof had fallen in, and that the wolves had eaten all of the flesh off the body, so that nothing but the skeleton and clothes remained. Joseph Stephens took the epaulettes, as a memento, but nothing else was disturbed. As his mother objected to his keeping the epaulettes, he melted them into a large ball, which was worth fifteen or twenty dollars, as it was solid gold. This description of the burial place, &c., was obtained from the last mentioned Joseph Stephens, and is *correct*, although several different accounts have been published.

The first newspaper published within the present limits of Howard county, was established at Old Franklin, by a gentleman by the name of Nathaniel Patten, in April 1819. This newspaper was called the *Missouri Intelligencer*.

ORGANIZATION OF COOPER COUNTY.

CHAPTER V.

Cooper County Organized.—Its Boundaries.—Present Counties Included in Cooper at the Time of Its Organization.—Seat of Justice Located at Boonville, and Courts to be Held There. The First Court in New County, and its Proceedings.—Proceedings of the Court at the July and November Terms, 1819, and March Term, 1820.

COOPER COUNTY was organized on the 17th day of December, 1818, comprising all that part of what had been Howard county, lying south of the Missouri river.

It was bounded on the north by the Missouri river, on the east and south by the Osage river, and on the west by what was then called the Territorial line.

At the time of its organization, it included the Territory now embraced in the whole of the counties of Cooper, Saline, Lafayette, Jackson, Cass, Henry, Johnson, Pettis, Morgan, Moniteau and Cole; and part of the counties of Bates, St. Clair, Benton, Camden and Miller; eleven whole counties and part of five others.

The act under which Cooper county was organized, located the seat of justice at the town of Boonville. This place was designated as the place for holding court, by the act under which the county was organized, which was adopted by the Legislature, and approved during the year 1818, and entitled an "act establishing a part of Howard county into a separate county, by the name of Cooper." The commissioners to locate the county seat, appointed by the Legislature, were Abel Owens, William Wear, Charles Canale, Luke Williams and Julius Emmons.

HISTORY OF COOPER COUNTY. 49

The first court in the newly organized county of Cooper, was held in the present limits of the City of Boonville, on the first day of March, 1819. It was held at the boarding house of Wm. Bartlett, which was situated on the flat just east of the mouth of Rupe's Branch, near the present site of the "Boonville Furniture Factory." This court, under the Territorial laws of Missouri, exercised the present duties of the County, Probate and Circuit Courts. The duties of these three courts continued to be exercised by this one court until the year 1821, when the duties of the Probate and County Courts were separated from those of the Circuit Court, and a new court, called the "County Court," was organized.

As it was to be supposed that every one would be interested in reading of the actions of the first court, and to compare the mode of procedure with that of the courts of the present day, it has been thought advisable, as being of great interest to the general reader, to insert, at this place, the full proceedings of this first court held in Cooper county after it was organized.

The following are the full proceedings, as appears from the record of the court:

The officers of this first court were, David Todd, Judge; R. P. Clark, Clerk; William McFarland, Sheriff, and John S. Brickey, Prosecuting Attorney.

The grand jury at this term of the court were, Samuel Peters, foreman; Muke Rose, John Savage, James Chambers, Britton Williams, John Roberts, Carroll George, John Davis, James Savage, Clayton Hurt, Joseph Smith, William Gibson, Eli N. Henry, Frederick Houx, Thomas Twentyman, William Noland and Delany Bolin; John Cathey, Zepheniah Bell, Henry Guyer, George Cathey, Daniel Dugan and James Campbell, were summoned on the same jury, but did not appear; process was ordered to be issued, for them to show cause why they should not be fined for their non-appearance.

The commissions of David Todd, as Judge; of William McFarland as Sheriff, and of John S. Brickey, as Prosecuting Attorney, were recorded by the Clerk.

The above named grand jury, after having been sworn, retired and returned into court, when, having nothing to present, they were discharged.

The next day, March 2nd, 1819, the following proceedings were had by the court:

By order of the court, the whole of the county of Cooper was divided into the following five townships: Moreau, Lamine, including all of the present county of Cooper, Arrow Rock, Miami and Tebo.

The following judges of election were appointed, viz:

For Moreau Township.—Wm. Wear, John Verian and John Alexander.

For Lamine Township.—James Bruffee, Robert Wallace and Benjamin F. Hickox.

For Arrow Rock Township.—William Lillard, Benjamin Chambers and James Anderson.

For Miami Township.—John B. Thomas, Joel Estes and John Evans.

For Tebo Township.—Julius Emmons, Gilliard Ruppe and Abel Owens.

The election, at which the foregoing men were to act as judges, was ordered to be held at the following places in each township: at the house of William Bartlett, in Lamine township; at the house of William Cooper, in Arrow Rock township; at the house of Andrew Rupels, in Miami township; at the house of Paul Whitley, in Moreau township, and at the house of Mathew Coxes, in Tebo township.

The following constables were appointed: of Moreau township, Paul Whitley; of Lamine township, John Potter; of Arrow Rock township, Jacob Ish; of Miami township, Elisha Evans; and of Tebo township, Green Macafferty.

Stephen Turley was granted a license to keep a ferry across the Lamine river.

B. W. Levens, Ward and Parker, and George W. Kerr, were granted a license to keep a ferry across the Missouri river, at the present site of Overton.

The following were the rates fixed, by the court, to be charged at B. W. Levens' ferry, viz:

For man and horse, fifty cents; for either, twenty-five cents; for horses and four wheeled wagon, two dollars; for two horses and four wheeled carriage, one dollar; for horned cattle, four cents each; and for meat cattle, two cents each.

William Curtis was appointed under-sheriff of Cooper county.

The first petition for a public road, was presented on this day, by B. W. Levens. It asked for the location of a road leading from Boonville to the mouth of Moniteau Creek. The court appointed Richard Stanford, David Trotter, William George and Benjamin Clark, commissioners, to review the road, as asked for, and report to the court their opinion as to the location, &c., of the same.

Bird Lockhart and George Tompkins, who were appointed to examine as to the qualifications of candidates for the office of county surveyor, having filed their report, the court recommended Wm. Ross to the governor, as a fit subject for said appointment.

The next petition for the location of a public road, was filed by Anderson Reavis on the same day. The road petitioned for, ran from the mouth of the Grand Moniteau to the Boonville and Potosi road. The commissioners appointed to review this road, were Francis Travis, Wm. Lewis and John Savage.

John Potter filed his bond as constable of Lamine township, in the sum of $1,000, with Asa Morgan and William Ross as his securities.

James Bruffee, Benjamin F. Hickox and Robert Wallace were appointed commissioners to superintend the building of the court house.

The court then adjourned until the regular July term.

JULY TERM, 1819.

Monday, July 5th, 1819. The first indictment by the grand jury in Cooper county, was presented on this day. Stanley G. Morgan being then indicted for assault and battery. It then being the law that every offense, however trivial, should be tried by indictment before the Circuit Court.

R. P. Clark, this day, produced his commission as clerk of the Circuit Court of Cooper county; also Peyton R. Hayden was admitted to the bar, as an attorney and counsellor at law.

John Cathey, Henry Guyer, George Cathey and Zepheniah Bell, against whom process was issued at the March term, were each fined one dollar and costs, for contempt of court, for not appearing as grand jurors at the said term, after having been summoned as such.

The first civil suit on record, was an action for debt, brought by George Wilcox against R. P. Clark and Samuel S. Williams, which is entered among the proceedings of this day.

Tuesday, July 6th, 1819.—Jesse McFarland appeared before the court, and took the oath of office as county surveyor. William Bartlett was granted a license to keep a tavern near the mouth of Rupe's Branch, in Boonville.

Wednesday, July 7th, 1819.—Stephen Cole appointed deputy county surveyor of Cooper county.

The first account presented against Cooper county was allowed on this day. It was an account of William Bartlett, for six dollars for the rent of his house, it having been used by the court as a court house. On the same day, four men were fined, by a jury of twelve men, five dollars each, for gambling.

Thursday, July 8th, 1819.—Asa Morgan was granted a license to keep a ferry across the Missouri river at Boonville.

November Term, 1819.—Andrew S. McGirk was enrolled as an attorney and counsellor at law. James Williams was granted a license to keep a ferry across the Osage river, on the road from Boonville to Potosi.

March Term, 1820.—The following men were indicted by the grand jury for swearing, viz: Jesse Mann, Isaac Renfro, William Warden, William Bryant, Thomas Brown, Stephen Tate, John S. Moreland and David Fine. These indictments were afterwards dismissed by the court for want of jurisdiction.

On the 6th day of March, 1820, Abiel Leonard produced his license, and was admitted to the bar; also January 23d, 1821, Hamilton R. Gamble was admitted to the bar.

The following is a list of the attorneys who at this time were enrolled and practicing in this court:

George Tompkins, John S. Brickey, Peyton R. Hayden, Cyrus Edwards, John S. Mitchell, Hamilton R. Gamble, Andrew McGirk, Robert McGavock, Abiel Leonard, John F. Ryland, Arinstedd A. Grundy, Dabney Carr, William J. Redd and John Payne. Among these we find the names of many who afterwards occupied offices of trust in the State of Missouri. Indeed, all of them are noted as being fine lawyers and honorable men.

The following is a copy of the record of the first verdict rendered by a jury in Cooper county. It is taken from the proceedings of the November term, 1819:

UNITED STATES, Plaintiff,
vs.
STANLEY G. MORGAN, Defendant.

This day comes as well the defendant, in discharge of his recognizance, as the prosecuting attorney. Whereupon, the said defendant, being arraigned upon the indictment in this cause, plead not guilty, and, for his trial, put himself upon God and his country, and the circuit attorney also. Whereupon came a jury, viz: Wm. Burk, William Black, Gabriel Fitsworth, Michael Hornbeck, Nicholas Houx, William Reed, Alexander Dickson, David Reavis, Frederick Houx, David McGee and Samuel Peters, who, being elected, tried and sworn, the truth to say, as and upon the issue joined, upon their oaths do say, that the defendant is guilty of assault and battery, whereof he is indicted. Whereupon it is considered by the court, that the said defendant make by the payment of the sum of five dollars and pay the costs hereof, and may be taken, &c.

There was, as shown by the records, but four peddlers and six merchants within the limits of the county of Cooper, during the year 1819.

The total amount of county revenue, on the tax book for 1819, as charged to William Curtis, sheriff, at the July term of this court, was $488.34.

All these terms of court were held at William Bartlett's boarding house, called on the records, the "Tavern of Boonville."

There is embraced in the foregoing, the full proceedings only of the court held on the first and second days of March, 1819; extracts only being made from the other terms of the court referred to, of those proceedings each day which were supposed would be of most interest to the general reader. The proceedings of the court held March 1st, 1819, cover only seventeen pages of a very small record book; for July term, forty-one pages, and for the November term, thirty-three pages. The proceedings of the Circuit Court, *alone*, for the April term, 1876, covers eighty-four pages of the largest record made, which is equal to about 250 pages of record, such as was used for the first court. When it is taken into consideration, also, that the proceedings of the County and Probate Courts, now separate from the Circuit Court, were included in the record of the Circuit Court for 1819, it can easily be perceived what a vast increase has been made in this part of the business of the county.

HISTORY OF COOPER COUNTY.

CHAPTER VI.

First County Court held in Cooper County, and the Proceedings of same.—First and Second Court Houses Built.—Three Attempts to Remove the County Seat from Boonville, and the Causes.—First Church Built in County.—First Baptism in County, and Involuntary Immersion of Jake Simons.—First Schools Taught in County.—Celebration on July 4th, 1820.—The whole Revenue of the County not Sufficient to Support John V. Sharp, a Pauper, &c.

THE first County Court within the county of Cooper, was held on the eighth day of January, 1821, at the house of Robert P. Clark, on the lot where Adam Eckhard now resides, on High street, in the City of Boonville. This court exercised the powers, and performed the duties of the present County and Probate Courts, which had, previous to this time, been under the jurisdiction of the Circuit Court. The County Court continued to perform the duties of both County and Probate Courts, until the year 1847, when, by act of the Legislature, the Probate Court was separated from the County Court, and continues separate to the present time.

James Bruffee, James Miller and Archibald Kavanaugh were the justices of this court, appointed by James McNair, the then Governor of the Territory of Missouri. Robert P. Clark was appointed by the court as its Clerk, and Wm. Curtis, Sheriff.

And on the 9th day of April, 1821, Robert P. Clark produced his commission from the Governor as Clerk of the County Court, during life or good behavior. George Crawford was appointed Assessor, and Andrew Briscoe, Collector of Cooper County.

On the same day, the will of Thomas McMahan, deceased, was probated, it being the first will proven before this court and in this county. Also constables were appointed for the different townships in the county, as follows: Boonville township, John Potter; Lamine township, Bryant T. Nolan; Moniteau township, Martin Jennings, and Clear Creek township, James C. Berry.

George C. Hart was appointed commissioner to run dividing line between Cooper and Saline counties; and B. W. Levens, to run dividing line between Cooper and Cole counties.

The first court house was completed at Boonville, in the year 1823. Previous to that time, the court had either been held at the house of the clerk or at one of the boarding houses. But when Messrs. Morgan and Lucus laid out the town, they donated fifty acres to the county, on condition that the commissioners would locate the county seat at Boonville. As soon as the county seat had been located at Boonville, and part of this land sold by the county, the county court commenced the building of a court house, which was located on the land donated to the county, and in which they could hold court, and also have the offices of the different clerks. It was a small two story brick building, pretty much the style of the present one, although much smaller. It was torn down at the time the present one was built, and some of the brick was used in the construction of the new house.

The present court house, which is situated on the same spot on which the old one was located, was completed in the year 1840. It is a large and commodious two story brick building, situated on a high piece of ground overlooking the river, from the cupalo of which an excellent view can be had of a part of Cooper and Howard counties. It is built upon the old style, and will very likely have to be soon replaced by a new one.

There have been three several attempts to remove the county seat from Boonville.

The first attempt was made in 1832, the second in 1838, and the third in 1842. The first two attempts were caused by some of the citizens wishing to remove the county seat to a more central portion of the county. But they have, it is unnecessary to relate, been unsuccessful, only resulting in creating an ill-feeling between the different portions of the county, which it took years to remove. The third was caused by the excitement resulting from the fight between the militia and an organization of the settlers, known as the "Fantastic Company," which will be more fully described hereafter.

Previous to the year 1817, there were no regular churches in Cooper County, but services were held, from time to time, either in the houses of the settlers, or whenever convenient, in some school house. But in that year the first church in the county was built. It was called "Concord Church," and was located about six miles south of the City of Boonville, near the present residence of John Crawford. Its denomination was Baptist. The first minister who preached there, was Luke Williams, who was also the first regular preacher located in Cooper county.

It has always been stated and believed by many to be the fact, that Concord church was the first church built in Missouri, outside of St. Louis and St. Genevieve, but of the truth of this the authors are not informed, therefore they cannot vouch for same. But is certain, that there could have been but few churches then built in the State, and it is probable that they were all in those two cities, as no neighborhoods in this part of the State were strong enough to be able to build one.

"Old Nebo Church," located about one-half of a mile north of the present site of Bunceton, near the residence of the late Judge L. C. Stephens, at the place where the Dublin school house now stands, was built in 1820. It was built by subscriptions from the settlers; and as there was very little money in circulation in the country, each one contributed his share either in work or materials furnished. William Stevens and Joseph Stevens, Sr., now living near Bunceton, in this county, sawed all the planks for this church; others furnished the shingles and logs; and others still, assisted in putting up the house and other work about it. Its denomination was Baptist. The ministers, who, during the next few years, preached at this church, were Peter Woods, William Jennings, Jacob Chism, Luke Williams and John B. Longan.

This church was very prosperous until about 1826, when there arose a division in it, on account of the difference of sentiment on the question of paying ministers and sending missionaries among the heathen nations. After considerable excitement, and several stormy meetings, the two factions separated. John B. Longan, who was leader of the faction who favored paying the ministers and sending abroad missionaries, drew off a large majority of the members of the congregation, and built a church at Henry Woolery's mill, which was called "New Nebo Church." The opposing faction continued in possession of "Old Nebo Church," and held service regularly in it.

The next churches built, were "Mount Pleasant" and Pisgah, in the south-eastern part of the county, and "New Nebo," at Henry Woolery's mill, the particulars of the building of which, is described above. New Nebo church was afterwards moved about one mile west on to the prairie, and it has always been in a prosperous condition. About this time there was also built a "Cumberland Presbyterian" church, at Lebanon township, of which Finis Ewing was pastor.

The first baptism by immersion took place at "Old Nebo," in the year 1820. At this baptism there happened the following laughable incident: As this was the first thing of the kind that had happened in this part of the country, great crowds of people came from every section of the country, as notice had been given some time before. The banks of the river in which the baptism was to take place, were thronged with people, and many men climbed trees in order to get a good view of the proceedings. One man, by the name of Jake Simons, climbed up a small sappling which stood on the edge of the creek, and which bent over the water with his weight. Another gentleman, by the name of John H. Hutchison, thinking this would be a fine opportunity to have some fun, took out a large pocket knife and commenced cutting away on the tree where it was bent by Simon's weight. Lower and lower bent the tree, weakened by the cutting of the knife, but the victim and those standing near were so engaged in watching the baptism, which, by that time had commenced, that they did not notice this. At last, with one strong blow, the tree was severed, and Simons dropped, with a loud splash, into the water. The crowd shouted and haloed so long and so loud at this, that the minister was almost forced to dismiss the crowd without concluding the exercises. As it was, it took a long time to subdue the confusion which this joke had caused. As soon as Simons, who was a fighter, swam to the shore, he hurled off his coat, and threatened to whip the man who had caused this involuntary ducking. But he did not find out for years who that person was As soon as the excitement had subdued sufficiently to permit it, the baptism was proceeded with, until all the applicants had been immersed. But the remembrance of this incident remains, to this day, fresh in the minds of all of the old settlers, who tell it again and again to their children, as illustrating the fun-loving disposition of the first inhabitants of this country.

The first schools in Cooper county were taught by Wm. Anderson, in 1817, near Concord church; by Andrew Reavis, in 1818, about one and three-quarters of a mile east of Boonville, and three-quarters of a mile east of the present residence of Wm. Gibson; by James Donaldson, in the south-eastern part of the county; by Judge L. C. Stephens at "Old Nebo" church; by Dr. William Moore in Palestine township, near the present residence of Jenus White, and by Rollins, near Big Lick, in Saline township.

These schools were all held in log school-houses, some without any floor but the earth, the remainder with puncheon floors, and no window-sash in the windows. The windows were made by cutting pieces out of the logs, which openings were closed with a plank at night, not so much as a protection against thieves, as to keep out the wild animals which prowled through the forest. Teachers, in those days, seemed to have learned well the maxim, that to spare the rod, was to spoil the child, for the most trivial offence against the iron rule of the "pedagogue," was visited with a severe thrashing, large and small scholars, alike, coming in for their share of the "dressings." So that the sound of the switch was often heard, as the teacher urged some tardy loiterer along the flowery path of knowledge. The teachers had many difficulties in teaching the scholars, for, from the very first of his life, the youthful settler was taught that self-reliance and independence, which works well, when taught to those of mature years, but which is liable to make the young rebel against any restraint, and which, at that time, tended to interfere seriously with the rule of the schools and the advancement of the scholars.

On the fourth day of July, 1820, the first celebration within the county of Cooper, of the anniversary of the Declaration of the National Indedependence, took place at Boonville, which then consisted of but a few houses. For some time notice had been circulated among the settlers, all over this portion of the State, and, on the morning of that day, great crowds gathered "from near and from far," to take part in this, to them, great day of thanksgiving, for, at that time in the nation's history, the Declaration of Independence and individual right meant something besides empty words.

The oration of the day was delivered by Benjamin F. Hickox, father of our honored townsman, Truman V. Hickox.

The feast, of which all were *specially* invited to partake, was spread on the grass and ground north and northeast of the court house. Such was the crowd present, that the table spread for them, reached from the vacant lot north of the court house, to the large mound still standing in the front yard of Mr. Jesse Homan. James Bruffee, a blacksmith, then living in Boonville, made a large wrought iron cannon, with which they fired the salutes in honor of the day.

The festivities continued through the day and the following night. After the speaking and the reading of the Declaration of Independence had been concluded, the people separated into groups, the young ones to dance and to play different games, and the old ones to watch the pleasant sports of the children, and to talk over the current gossip of the day, for it was very seldom that they ever met in a large crowd. This day is still remembered with pleasure by the old settlers, for many of them, on that day, met for the last time their friends who lived at a distance, and who soon became separated from them, and died without ever seeing them again.

During the year 1821, John V. Sharp, a soldier who had served in the Revolutionary war, and who was living in Cooper county, became paralyzed and as helpless as a child. He soon, not having any means of his own, became a charge upon the county. The cost to the County Court was two dollars per day for his board and attention to him, besides bills for medical attention.

After having endeavored in vain to raise sufficient funds to take care of him, the County Court, in the year 1822, petitioned the General Assembly of this State to defray the expenses of his support, stating, in the petition, that *the whole revenue of the county was not sufficient for his maintainance.* This may sound strange to persons living in a county in which thousands of dollars are levied to defray its expense. But the whole revenue of the county for 1822, as shown by the settlement of the collector, was only $718, and the support of Mr. Sharp, at two dollars per day, cost $730 per year, besides the cost for medical attention, which left the county, at the end of the year 1822, in debt, without counting in any of the other expenses of the county.

The petition not having been granted by the General Assembly, the court levied, for his support, during all the years from 1823 to 1828, a special tax of fifty per cent. of the State revenue tax, being an amount equal to the whole of the general county tax; and in 1828, ten per cent. of the State revenue tax was levied for the same purpose. He must have died sometime during that year, as no farther levy for his support appears upon the records of the county, thus relieving the county of a burdensome tax. If these facts were not matters of record, they would seem too incredible to be believed.

HISTORY OF COOPER COUNTY.

CHAPTER VII.

History of all the Newspapers that have been issued in Cooper County.

THE first newspaper, in Cooper county, was established at Boonville, about the year 1834, and was called the *Boonville Herald*. It was owned by James O. Middleton, and edited by Benj. E. Ferry, who was afterwards County Clerk of Cooper county. In the year 1838, Robert Brent bought one-half interest in the paper from Jas. Middleton, and on the 8th day of April in that year, they changed the name of the paper to that of *The Western Emigrant*. On the 7th day of March, 1839, C. W. Todd purchased Brent's interest in the paper, and the paper was edited about one year, by Messrs. Middleton and Todd. On the 30th day of April, 1840, C. W. Todd purchased Middleton's interest in the paper and changed its name to that of the *Boonville Observer;* C. W. Todd continued as sole proprietor of the paper, until the 3rd day of February, 1842, when he sold one-half interest in it to T. J. Boggs. On the 29th day of March, 1843, F. M. Caldwell and J. S. Collins purchased the paper from Todd & Boggs; they continued to edit it in partnership only until June 7th, 1843, when F. M. Caldwell purchased the interest of Collins, and became sole proprietor. Caldwell soon sold one-half interest in the paper to Allen Hammond, and it was edited under the firm name of Caldwell & Hammond, until the 9th day of June, 1846, when Caldwell sold out his interest to Allen Hammond, and returned to Virginia, on account of the feeble health of his wife. Hammond continued to edit it alone, until Nov. 7th, 1850, when F. M. Caldwell returned from Virginia and again purchased a half interest in the paper. They continued to edit it in partnership for several years, when they sold the paper to Augustine W. Simpson, who remained publisher of it, until it ceased publication in 1861, on account of the excitement incident to the war. In politics this paper was Whig, until the year 1854, when the Whig party ceased to exist; it then became Democratic, and remained so until it ceased publication.

The next newspaper established was the *Missouri Register*, published by William T. Yeoman. The first number of it appeared in July, 1839. It was the first Democratic paper published in western Missouri and was established mainly to aid in the campaign of 1840. On the 22d day of April, 1841, Yeoman sold one-half interest in the paper to Edgar A. Robinson, and the paper continued to be published by Yeoman and Robinson until the 9th day of August, 1843, when Ira Van Nortwick purchased it from them. It was afterwards successively owned by Quisenberry, Price, Ward & Chilton, the last named of whom continued to publish it until the great temperance excitement broke out in 1853. The paper had previous to this time, been taken up almost exclusively by political discussions, but it was then purchased by a man named Bowie, who filled its columns exclusively with discussions in regard to the great question of Temperance, which was then agitating the public mind. Bowie soon sold out the paper to Allen Hammond, and soon after this, the paper ceased publication, for want of patronage.

During the heat of the campaign of 1840, the editors of the *Missouri Register*, Messrs. Ward & Chilton, started a weekly campaign sheet, which advocated the claims of

Van Buren for President, as soon as the campaign was over, and Van Buren defeated, the paper ceased publication.

On the 31st day of December, 1850, Messrs. Caldwell & Hammond, proprietors of the *Boonville Observer* commenced the publication of a sheet called the *Tri-Weekly Observer*, which was printed three times a week. But it did not continue long, as it was forced, for lack of patronage, to cease publication March 8th, 1851.

The next paper was the *Boonville Patriot*, which was established by a gentleman by the name of Gill, in the year 1856. It was afterwards sold to F. W. Caldwell, who continued to publish it until the year 1861, when the materials, presses, &c., belonging to the office, were seized by Gen. Worthington, in command of some federal forces at Jefferson City, and taken by him to the latter place.

Soon afterwards, F. M. Caldwell went to Jefferson City, and with the assistance of some of the most influential federals, succeeded in gaining possession of the materials belonging to this office which Gen. Worthington had seized, and brought them back to Boonville. Immediately upon his return, Messrs. Caldwell and Stahl commenced the publication of the *Boonville Advertiser*, the first number of which appeared on the 15th day of June, 1862. After publishing it for some time, they sold out to Messrs. Drury and Selby, who published the paper for a year or two, when Messrs. F. M. Caldwell & Co. again got possession of it, and have continued proprietors of it to the present time. The editors of this paper, during this period, have been J. G. Pangborn, H. A. Hutchison, George W. Frame, Geo. W. Ferrel and Chas. E. Hasbrook; the last named, is editor at the present time. In politics, this paper is now and always has been democratic.

On the 25th day of October, 1875, the proprietors of the *Boonville Advertiser*, commenced the publication of a daily edition of the same, under the name of the *Boonville Daily Advertiser*. It is still published, and seems to have met with very good success.

The *Boonville Eagle*, a weekly paper, was established in September, 1865, by Milo Blair. On the 28th day of September, 1875, he took Chas. H. Allen into partnership with him, and the paper is still published by Messrs. Milo Blair & Co. In politics it has always been Republican.

The *Wachter Am Missouri*, a paper published in the German language, was established in 1867, by L. Joachimi. It was purchased in 1874 by F. W. Ludwig, who changed its name to *The Central Missourier*. F. W. Ludwig is the present proprietor. In politics it is Republican.

HISTORY OF COOPER COUNTY.

CHAPTER VIII.

The "Fantastic Company," and the Killing of J. L. Forsythe.

FROM the organization of the government of the State, until the year 1847, there existed a militia law, requiring all able-bodied male citizens, between the ages of eighteen and forty-five years, to organize into companies and to muster on certain days. They had, during the year, at different times, a company, a battallion, and a general muster. A company muster was the drilling of the members of one company; a battallion muster consisted in drilling the companies of one-half of a county; and a general muster was a meeting of all the companies of a county.

Muster day was, for a long time after the commencement of the custom, a gala day for the citizens, and was looked forward to with considerable interest, especially by the different officers who appeared in full military dress, captains and lieutenants, with long red feathers stuck in the fore part of their hats, and epaulettes upon their shoulders. The field officers mounted on their fine steeds, with continental cocked hats, epaulettes upon their shoulders, and fine cloth coats, ornamented with gold fringe, rode around among the men and gave orders, making themselves the "observed of all observers." Also the vendors of whisky, ginger cakes, apples and cider, took no small interest in the anticipated muster day, for on that day, every person being excited, bought more or less of these things. Always on muster days, after the muster was over, the rival bruisers of a neighborhood tried their strength upon one another, thus furnishing a great deal of amusement for those who attended. The little folks were also happy in the anticipation, if not in the enjoyment of being presented with a ginger cake and an apple upon that day.

But after a lapse of time these musters became tiresome to a portion of the citizens, as they were obliged to lose so much of their valuable time in order to attend them, or were compelled to pay a fine of one dollar for each failure to attend on muster day; besides they could see no real use in continuing the organization as there seemed no prospect soon of the State requiring any troops, as all was peaceful and quiet within its borders. Also, at the elections for officers, many of them were chosen on account of their personal popularity, instead of their qualifications to fill the office for which they were elected. Musters, therefore, after their novelty had worn off, became very unpopular, the citizens believing them to be an unnecessary burden upon them.

Therefore, sometime before the Battallion muster, which was to take place at Boonville, during the year 1842, a company, the existence of which was known only to its members, was formed at that place, among the members of which were some of the best citizens of the city. This company was styled the "Fantastic Company," on account of the queer costumes, arms, &c., of its members, they being dressed in all manner of outlandish costumes, carrying every conceivable kind of a weapon, from a broom-stick to a gun, and mounted upon horses, mules and jacks. The company was intended as a burlesque upon the militia, and to have some fun at their expense.

The regiment of State Militia, which was to be mustered at the above mentioned time, was commanded by Col. Jesse J. Turley and Major J. Logan Forsythe, and was composed of all of the companies in the north half of the county. On the morning of the muster day, Col. Turley formed his regiment in front of the court house. After they were organized and ready for muster and drill, the Fantastic Company, which was commanded by John Babbitt, each member dressed in his peculiar costume and carrying his strange weapon, marched up into full view of Col. Turley's command, and commenced preparations to drill. Col. Turley, feeling indignant that his proceedings should be interrupted by such a "mob," and believing that it was intended as an insult, ordered his command to surround the Fantastic Company.

There was a high fence on the eastern side of the vacant lot on which they were mustering, and Col. Turley's company surrounded the "Fantastic Company" by approaching on High street, on the alley between Fifth and Sixth streets, and on Sixth street, thus hemming them in on the vacant lot. The latter being closely pressed, retreated back across the fence, and then commenced a fight by throwing brickbats. The fight immediately became general and promiscuous, and resulted in serious damage to the several members of the State militia. Col. J. J. Turley was struck on the side by a stone, and two or three of his ribs broken. Major J. Logan Forsythe was struck by a brickbat in the face, just below his right eye, and died the next day of his wounds. The members of the Fantastic Company then dispersed and scattered in every direction.

The death of Major Forsythe caused great excitement throughout the county, and great indignation to be felt against the citizens of Boonville. So much so, that a petition was immediately circulated, asking, that the "county seat of Cooper county be removed from Boonville," to a more central point of the county. So great was the excitement, that some persons living within three miles of Boonville signed this petition. But the county seat, after a severe struggle before the County Court, was retained at Boonville.

The death of Major Forsythe was greatly regretted by all parties, for he was an excellent citizen and a very popular officer. It produced an ill-feeling throughout the county which lasted for many years. After the fight was over, the militia went through with their usual exercises, under the command of the subordinate officers, as Col. Turley and Major Forsythe were unable, on account of their wounds, to drill them.

POLITICAL HISTORY OF COOPER COUNTY.

CHAPTER IX.

First Election Held in Cooper County, List of Men who Voted at, and Result of it.—Result of Elections Held in May and August, 1820, and August, 1822.—Result of Elections Held in 1824, 1825, 1826, and 1828.—Change of Political Aspect of Cooper County in 1840.—State Whig Convention Held at Rocheport, in 1840.—Organization of the Know Nothing Party.—Members of the Different State Conventions from Cooper.—Politics Not Entirely Considered at Elections for First Thirty Years, &c., &c.

The first election after Cooper county was organized, was held on the second day of August, 1819, to elect a delegate to Congress, from the territory of Missouri. John Scott and Samuel Hammond were the candidates. John Scott had 117 votes, and Samuel Hammond 21 votes, making total vote of county, 138.

The townships which voted at said election were, Arrow Rock, Miami, Tabeaux and Lamine, which included the town of Boonville; but the votes cast in Tabeaux township were thrown out, because the poll book of said township did not state for whom the votes were cast, and this poll book was not put on file with the others. Therefore, the only votes counted were those cast in the other three townships.

Robert P. Clark, County Clerk, called to his aid James Bruffee and Benjamin F. Hickox, two Justices of the Peace, to assist him in counting the votes. As some of the readers may have some curiosity to know the names of those who voted at this first election, we give them as follows:

ARROW ROCK TOWNSHIP.

William Jobe,	Baker Martin,	Jesse Voves,
William Hays,	William White,	John Chapman,
Simon Odle,	Jacob Catoon,	William Cooper,
Phavess Clevenger,	Samuel Clevenger,	William Jobe,
Jack Clevenger,	James Wilhite,	James Anderson,
	John Ingram, vote rejected.	

Judges of Election were, James Anderson, William Cooper and William Jobe; and Clerks, John Ingram and James Wilhite.

MIAMI TOWNSHIP.

Andy Russell,	Christopher Martin,	William Warden,
Daniel McDowell,	Henry Estus,	William Gladin,
John D. Thomas,	William Estes,	John Evans,
William Shaw,	Charles English,	Jesse Gilliam.
Joel Nowlin,	Henry Hide,	

The Judges of Election were, John D. Thomas, John Evans and Jesse Gilliam; and Clerks, Charles English and William Gladin.

LAMINE TOWNSHIP.

Jonn H. Moore,	Robert Boyd,	Joseph Cathey,
Joseph Smith,	Robert Wallace,	George Cathey, Jr.,
Frederick Conor,	Dedrick Ewes,	Levi Odeneal,
William Gibson,	Samuel Smith,	John Cathey,
Humphrey Gibson,	Jordan O'Bryan,	Gabriel Tittsworth,
Stephen Cole, Jr.,	Abraham Jobe,	Stephen Cole, Sr.,
Muke Box,	Lewis Letney,	Charles B. Mitchell,
Jacob Eller,	Ephraiam Marsh,	James Long,
William H. Curtis,	Eli N. Henry,	George Houx,
William Moore,	James Reid,	Fleming F. Mitchell,
James Turner, Jr.,	James Hill,	John McClure,
Robert P. Clark,	David Ward,	David Trotter,
Joseph Dillard,	Samuel Peters,	Mathias Houx.
John J. Clark,	Littleton Seat,	William Chambers,
John Hiburn,	James Scott,	David McGee,
David Burress, Jr.,	Drury Wallace,	Thomas Rogers,

HISTORY OF COOPER COUNTY.

James McCarty, Sr.,
William Dillard,
Lawrence C. Stephens,
William D. Wilson,
Nicholas M. Fain,
Frederick Houx,
Jacob Thomas, Jr.,
William Fraser,
Nicholas Houx,
Anderson Demesters,
Peyton Hurt,
Zepheniah Bell,
Job Self,
William Bartlett,
Jacob McFarland,
Andrew A. Reavis,
William Savage,
James McCarty, Jr.,
Luke Williams,
Frederick Thomas,
John Roberts,
Geo. Cathey, Sr.,
Asa Morgan,
William George, Sr.,
David Fine,
George Fennile,
James Snodgrass,
Joseph Byler,
Frederick Shirley,
Joseph Westbrook,
John Grover,
Edward Carter,
Abraham Shelly,
Wm. Burk,
Wm. Snodgrass,
Peter Carpenter,
Thomas Butcher,
David McFarland,
Alexander Brown,
Jesse F. Roiston,
Nicholas McCarty,
John Swearingen,
George Potter,
John Potter,
David Burress, Sr.,
Joseph Scott,
Mansfield Hatfield,
John Ross,
Wm. Deakins,
John Nunn,
Wm. H. Anderson,
James Bruffee,
Eli Roberts,
Charles Force,
John Miller,
Larkin Dewitt,
Peter Stephens,
Joseph M. Bernard,
Samuel D. Reavis,
James A. Reavis,
Wm. Warden,
Samuel Snodgrass,
Delany Bowlin,
Jacob Thomas, Sr.,
Wm. Bowlin,
Ephraim Ellison
Benj. F. Hickox,
William McFarland,
George Crawford,
William Ross,
John Savage,

John Green, vote rejected,
Thomas Brown, vote rejected,
Hiram Musich, vote rejected.
William Mitchell, vote rejected.

The Judges of Election were, James Bruffee, Benjamin F. Hickox and William McFarland; and Clerks, George Crawford and William Ross.

It will be observed, that the first vote cast within the present limits of Cooper county, was cast by John H. Moore, who died many years ago; and the fourth vote by William Gibson, who is the only one who voted at that election who is still alive, that is, so far as is known to the authors. Yet this may be a mistake, as many of them, years ago, moved from this county, and have not been heard from since then, although they may still be alive. That election took place fifty-seven years ago, therefore, a man would have to be, at the present day, seventy-eight years of age to have cast a legal vote then. The wives of but two of them are still living, viz: Mrs. L. C. Stephens and Mrs. Frederick Houx.

The next election, for Delegates to the State Convention to frame a Constitution for the State of Missouri, was held on the 1st, 2nd, and 3d days of May, 1820. The following was the result in this county, viz:

Robert P. Clark,	For Delegate, had	557	Votes.
Robert Wallace,	" " "	395	"
William Lillard,	" " "	400	"
Charles Woods,	" " "	295	"
Richard W. Cummins,	" " "	359	"
Robert Johnson,	" " "	106	"
Robert Fristoe,	" " "	97	"
Henry Rennick,	" " "	91	"
George Sibley,	" " "	45	"
Peyton Nowlin,	" " "	31	"
Julius Emmons,	" " "	2	"
William Ross,	" " "	11	"

Robert P. Clark, William Lillard, and Robert Wallace, as shown by the vote, were elected. The townships in which this election was held, were as follows:

Arrow Rock Township,	which cast	120	Votes.
Lamine	"	" "	408	"
Tabeaux	"	" "	150	"
Moreau	"	" "	101	"
Miami	"	" "	40	"

Total vote of Cooper County   819

At the time of this election, Cooper county was bounded on the east and south by the Osage river, on the west by the Indian Territory, and on the north by the Missouri river. Lamine Township then, included about all within the present limits of Cooper county, and some territory not now included in its limits.

The next election was held on the 28th day of August, 1820, to elect a member of Congress, and State and County officers. The following townships voted at this election:

Arrow Rock Township, which cast 57 Votes.
Lamine   "   "   "   503   "
Jefferson   "   "   "   110   "
Osage   "   "   "   78   "
Miami   "   "   "   28   "
Moreau   "   "   "   71   "
Tabeaux   "   "   "   125   "

Total vote of Cooper County, 972

The following shows the result of this election:

For Congress,   John Scott   received   762 Votes.
For Governor,   Alex. McNair   "   766   "
For Governor,   Wm. Clark   "   196   "
For Lieut. Governor, Nathaniel Cook   "   573   "
For Lieut. Governor, Wm. H. Ashley   "   295   "
For Representative, James Edgar   "   139   "
        "   Thos. Rogers   "   549   "   (elected.)
        "   Wm. McFarland   "   425   "
        "   Thos. Smiley   "   528   "   (elected.)
        "   Abram Jobe   "   5   "
        "   John Dickson   "   158   "
        "   Abel Owens   "   310   "
        "   Sam. D. Reavis   "   157   "
        "   David Jones   "   380   "
        "   William Lillard   "   532   "   (elected.)
        "   Jason Harrison   "   94   "
        "   John Corum   "   30   "
        "   John D. Thomas   "   121   "
        "   William Wier   "   8   "
For Sheriff,   Wm. H. Curtis   "   549   "   (elected.)
        "   Wm. H. Moore   "   102   "
        "   Jas. Alexander   "   134   "
        "   B. W. Levens   "   45   "
        "   Wm. Kelly   "   67   "
        "   John Briscoe   "   59   "
For Coroner,   Bryant Sanders   "   332   "   (elected)
        "   J. C. Rochester   "   132   "
        "   Edward Bradley   "   165   "

Of the above list of candidates all have gone to their long homes, not one being left alive. And of the 503 voters, then voting in Lamine Township, which included all of the present territory of Cooper county, there are only four known to be alive, viz:

William Gibson, Samuel Cole, Henry Corum, and Lewis Edger, all still living within the limits of this county.

The result of the election which took place in the year 1822, was as follows:

For Congress,	John Scott received	316	Votes.		
"	Alex. Stewart	"	132	"	
"	J. B C. Lucas	"	72	"	
For Representative,	Benj. F. Hickox	"	364	"	(elected.)
"	Jordan O'Bryan	"	380	"	(elected.)
"	Austin K. Longan	"	229	"	(elected.)
"	Jas. McFarland	"	211	"	
"	Thos. Rogers	"	119	"	
"	William Ross	"	73	"	
"	Sam. D. Reavis	"	65	"	
"	Wm. Bryant	"	44	"	
For Sheriff,	Sylvester Hall	"	328	"	(elected.)
"	David P. Mahan	"	174	"	
For Coroner,	Thomas Riggs	"	174	"	

William Poor was the first Constable elected for Lamine Township, that officer having been, prior to that time, appointed by the courts.

It will be observed that the vote was much smaller in 1822 than it had been in 1820. This was caused by the territory of the county being much diminished, by the formation of Cole and Saline counties from it.

ELECTIONS IN 1824.

Cooper county voted for Henry Clay for president, in 1824. Only four poll books of this election could be found, which show that Henry Clay had 136 votes, and Andrew Jackson 53 votes. It was done as a debt of gratitude to

Clay, for his great services as a member of Congress, in the struggle of the State of Missouri, for admission into the Union.

She was admitted under certain conditions, viz:

"That the 4th clause of the 26th section of the 3d article of the Constitution of the State, shall never be construed to authorize the passage of any law, and no law shall be passed in conformity thereto, by which any citizen of the United States shall be excluded from the enjoyment of any of the privileges and immunities of citizens, to which such citizens are entitled under the Constitution of the United States."

The Legislature of Missouri assented to the conditions on the twenty-sixth day of June, 1821, and by proclamation of the President, James Monroe, the State was admitted on the tenth day of August, 1821.

The Constitution of the State of Missouri was adopted on the nineteenth day of July, 1820, without submitting it to the people. David Barton was president of the Convention. He died at the house of William Gibson, about one mile east of the City of Boonville, on the —— day of September, 1837, and was buried in the Walnut Grove Cemetery, at Boonville.

The question of the admission of Missouri into the Union, created great excitement in Congress, and all over the United States. The main point of difference, between the opposing factions, being the slavery question, which gave rise to what was called "The Missouri Compromise."

The following is the result of the election held in August, 1824:

For Congress,	John Scott received 507 Votes.	
" "	G. F. Strother "	81 "
" "	Robt. Wash "	5 "
For Governor,	Frederick Bates received 249 votes.	
" "	Wm. H. Ashley "	34 "

For Lieut. Governor,	Benjamin F. Reavis received 501 votes.	
" " "	Nath'l. Cook " 38 "	
" " "	Wm. C. Carr " 9 "	
" " "	James Evans " 3 "	
For State Senator,	George Crawford received 513 votes.	
" " "	James Miller " 78 "	
" " "	James McCampbell " 24 "	
For Representative,	Benj. F. Hickox received 473 votes. (elected)	
" "	Geo. W. Weight " 404 " (elected.)	
" "	Jordan O'Bryan " 333 "	
" "	Jos. Billingsley " 289 "	
For Sheriff,	Marcus Williams " 389 " (elected.)	
" "	J. H. Hutchison " 222 "	
For Coroner,	Hugh Allison " 204 "	
Constable Boonville Twp.,	Wm. R. Paine " 87 "	
" " "	Wm. C. Porter " 80 "	
" " "	Hugh Allison " 23 "	
" " "	Owen Ruble " 14 "	
" " "	Wm. W. Adams " 4 "	

1825.

On the eighth day of December, 1825, there was held a special election for Governor, to fill the vacancy caused by the death of Frederick Bates. David Todd, John Miller, Wm. C. Carr and Rufus Easton were the candidates. David Todd received a large majority in Cooper county.

1826.

At the election on the first Monday in August, 1826, John Scott and Edward Bates were candidates for Congress. Scott had a majority of one hundred and twenty-four in the county.

Michael Dunn, Jordan O'Bryan, James L. Collins and John H. Hutchison were candidates for Representatives. Michael Dunn and Jordan O'Bryan were elected. W. H. Anderson and David P. Mahan were candidates for Sheriff. Anderson was elected by fifty-three majority; and Hugh Allison was elected Coroner.

1828.

This was the first election in which party lines were closely drawn, for before that, men had voted for the man whom they considered best qualified; and not because he belonged to any party. The poll books of the presidential election could not be found, but the August election for Representative in Congress and county officers, having the same principles at issue, will show pretty clearly how the Presidential election went. There were two tickets, viz: Adams and Jackson, and the tickets on which the men were, who were elected is marked opposite their names.

The following is the result of the August election:

For Congress,	Edward Bates (Adams)	received	258 votes.
" "	Spencer Pettis (Jackson,)	"	492 "
For Governor,	John Miller (Jackson,)	"	662 "
For Lieut. Governor,	Samuel Perry (Adams,)	"	201 "
" " "	Daniel Durklin (Jackson)	"	381 "
" " "	Alex. Stuart	"	7 "
" " "	Alex. Buckner	"	87 "
" " "	Felix Leatt	"	42 "
For State Senator,	Jordan O'Bryan (Adams)	"	292 "
" " "	John Miller (Jackson,)	"	455 "
For Representative,	Archie Kavanaugh "	"	499 "
" "	David Jones "	"	508 "
" "	Michael Dunn (Adams,)	"	240 "
"	Geo. W. Weight, "	"	263 "
For Sheriff	David P. Mahan "	"	326 "
" "	Jos. S. Anderson (Jackson,) "		435 "
For Coroner,	Hugh Allison	"	122 "

At the election in November, 1828, the county voted for Jackson over Adams, by a majority of about two hundred and thirty votes; and also in 1832, Jackson was re-elected, and received a large majority in this county.

The county also gave a small majority to Martin Van-Buren, in 1836. The county remained Democratic until 1840, when the Whigs made a clean sweep, electing their full ticket. Reuben A. Ewing, a Whig, was elected State

Senator, over David Jones, Democrat; and John G. Miller, Jordan O'Bryan and Lawrence C. Stephens, Whigs, over John Miller, B. F. Hickox and Henry Crowther, Democrats, by an average majority of about seventy-five votes. There was great excitement during this election, and politics ran very high. The Whigs held public meetings in regular order on each succeeding Saturday in each township, until the full rounds were made. They had a band of music engaged for the occasion, flags and banners, with mottoes inscribed thereon; also with songs appropriate for the occasion, and eloquent speakers, the prominent among which were John G. Miller, Jordan O'Bryan, John C. Richardson, Robert C. Harrison, and others.

The Democrats did not make much display, but condemned the same as humbuggery, and trying to win votes by exciting the people. They held their meetings and had frequent public speakings without any display or show. Their candidates for the legislature were John Miller, Benjamin F. Hickox, and Henry Crowther.

A State convention for Harrison and Tyler, was held at Rocheport in June, 1840. It lasted three days, and seven steamboats were chartered by the delegates for the occasion, each of which had its band of music, two cannons, *a log cabin* and hard cider, and made a fine display of flags and banners with mottoes inscribed thereon. The most distinguished Whigs of the State were there, and many noted speakers from other States, among whom was the son of Daniel Webster.

Their line of march was the grandest display ever witnessed in Missouri. They had in the procession long canoes on wheels, and in them some of those who were engaged in the battle of Tippecanoe, in the act of paddling the canoes as they marched along. Every delegation had a large flag or banner, and many smaller ones with mottoes appropriate to the occasion.

The cause of this extraordinary campaign was, that times were and had been very hard for several years past, and as people are prone to lay their ills and misfortunes to the charge of somebody or party other than themselves, they then charged that Martin Van Buren and the Democratic party were the authors of their misfortunes.

The cry was reform, a national bank with a branch in every State, and a protective tariff. The result was that Harrison and Tyler were elected by a large majority. Harrison died within one month after his inauguration, and John Tyler became president. Several national bank charters were passed by Congress, but the president vetoed them all. Times continued hard until the Mexican war; from that time till 1857 they gradually improved, and from 1861 to 1873, times were good and money plenty. But since 1873, history has repeated itself, times have been very hard, and money of any kind hard to get and hard to keep. 'Tis a repitition of the old saying, "money close, but not close enough to get hold of."

The county remained Whig as long as the party lasted. The last candidate on the Whig ticket was General Scott, who was defeated by Franklin Pierce.

The campaign of 1844 was very lively, with not so much display and show on the part of the Whigs as in 1840. For President, Henry Clay was the nominee of the Whig party, and James K. Polk of the Democratic party. Clay in 1844, Taylor in 1848, and Scott in 1852 received a majority of the votes cast in this county. Taylor was elected in 1848, but he died in about one year after his inauguration, and Millard Fillmore, Vice-president, became the President, and history will certainly give him the credit of making an excellent chief magistrate.

About 1854, the American or Know-Nothing party sprang nto existence. This party was short-lived, being first defeated at a State election in Virginia, and many members deserted it, as rats would a sinking ship. Many old line Whigs joined the Democratic party, and the Democrats, who were quite numerous in the Know-Nothing party, returned to their first love, and some aspiring ones denied that they had *"ever been there."*

It is said that one prominent office holder who resided in Howard county, who was noted for having joined every party that ever sprang into existence, while on a visit to a "Know-Nothing" lodge, at Boonville, made a speech, shed tears, and said, "that he had found the right party at last," but was the first man in this part of the State to desert that party when it commenced to go to pieces.

A large majority of the "old line Whigs" formed an opposition party, and voted for Millard Fillmore for President, in 1856. At that time there were three candidates for President in the field, viz: James Buchanan, Democrat, Millard Fillmore, American, and John C. Fremont, Republican. There was no ticket in Cooper county for Fremont. Millard Fillmore carried Cooper county over James Buchanan by about eight votes, so nearly even were the two parties.

At the next Presidential election in 1860, the candidates were Stephen A. Douglass, Union Democrat, James C. Breckenridge, Southern Democrat, Abraham Lincoln, Republican, John Bell, Union. Douglass carried Cooper county by a small majority, Bell running him close. Breckenridge had but a small vote, and Lincoln but twenty votes. The names of those who voted for Lincoln were afterwards published in the newspapers as an item of curiosity.

Abraham Lincoln, Republican, and Geo. B. McClellan, Democrat, were the candidates for President in 1864. Lincoln carried Cooper county by a large majority. No great interest was taken in this election in this county. There was no restriction as to voters at that time, but many Democrats did not vote, and the Republicans, generally, turned out in full force. The Republicans carried the county at every election till 1872; the restrictions and the "test oath" having been almost unanimously abolished in 1870 by a vote of the people. The Democrats have been ever since in the majority in the county, their majority being about eight hundred.

There was a State Convention called in 1845 for the purpose of framing a new constitution, and Dr. F. W. G. Thomas was elected a delegate from this county. In 1846, the convention submitted the constitution which they had framed to the people of the State, and it was voted down by a large majority.

In 1861, a convention was called to consider the relations of this State to the United States, and to take such action in regard to the existing troubles, the late war of the Union having then commenced, as they should deem best for the interests of the State. The candidates for delegates to the State Convention were, William Douglass and Benjamin Tompkins, of Cooper county; Charles Drake, of Moniteau county, and J. P. Ross and William Tutt, of Morgan county; these three counties then comprising the 28th Senatorial district. William Douglass, Charles Drake, and J. P. Ross were elected. The history of the action of this convention is so well known, and having been incorporated in other general histories, has been so widely circulated that it is unnecessary to repeat it here.

Another convention was called in 1864. Two delegates were allowed to each Senatorial district. Harvey Bunce, of Cooper county, and Joel F. Humes, of Moniteau county, were elected delegates for the 28th Senatorial district. The delegates met at St. Louis, and on the 11th day of January,

1865, declared "that slavery or involuntary servitude shall no longer exist in Missouri." They framed a new constitution which has always been known as the "Drake constitution," submitted the same to the voters of the State, and it was adopted by a small majority.

It is a well-known fact that, from 1853 to 1860, party spirit did not prevail in elections, except as to State, Congressional, and Legislative candidates. In the elections in 1853 and in 1859, for the election of Judges and Clerks, and other officers, party was scarcely mentioned. Every candidate had to stand upon his own merits; and that was generally the case as to county officers from the organization of this county to the election in 1860. It is true, local questions would sometimes interfere and govern the votes of some, yet they seldom nominated party candidates for county officers, partizanship being confined almost exclusively to the nomination of National and State tickets.

At a Whig convention, in 1840, at "Old Palestine," after nominating candidates for the Legislature, it was proposed to make a nomination for Sheriff. After considerable debate, this proposition was voted down, for the reason that the office was not considered a political one. This statement may sound strange to some, considering the way nominations and elections are governed at the present day, but it is nevertheless true. And, in proof of this, the records show, that while the Democrats were in power, John H. Hutchison was twice elected Sheriff, James Hill, Sheriff, once, John Crawford, Assessor for several years, and Robert P. Clark, Circuit Clerk; all of these men were uncompromising Whigs. And while the Whigs were in power, Isaac Lionberger and B. E. Ferry were each elected Sheriff two terms, making eight years; B. E. Ferry was, also, twice elected County Clerk, Robert Turner, Assessor, and William Shields, a member of the State Legislature; and all of these men were strong Democrats. It is true, the citizens would vote for the candidate of their own party, if they deemed his qualifications for filling the office equal to those of his opponent; and some, though the number was small, always "stuck to" the nominee of their own party when opposite partisans were running.

Great interest was generally taken in elections. There was much more interest in and excitement over elections before than after the war. But, previous to the war, elections did not partake of that bitter personal feeling, which has characterized them since the war. Those in opposition could be political enemies and personal friends. Men were not, then, as now, proscribed for their political opinions. But, the people of this section of the country are proud to say, that, animosities, which were naturally engendered during the war, are gradually dying away, and, if left undisturbed for a few years, will only be things of the past, and have no real existence, except upon the pages of history.

WAR HISTORY OF COOPER COUNTY.
CHAPTER X.

Indian Scare on Flat Creek, in Pettis County, in the Year 1832, and the Part the Citizens of Cooper County took in Same.—Mormon War, in the year 1838, and Companies Raised in Cooper County, at Call of Governor, to Assist in the Same.—Company Raised in Cooper County to Take Part in the Mexican War of 1846, and the Actions of Same, Names of Officers, Privates, &c.

Sometime during the year 1832, a report became circulated that the Indians had broken out, and were attacking the settlers living within the present limits of Pettis county, then part of Cooper and Saline counties. The report that they were slaying men, women and children as they went, spread like "wild fire," and men rushed towards that part of the county to aid in the defense of the homes of their neighbors. The place of rendezvous for those who went from Cooper county, was "Wooley's Mill," on the Petite Saline Creek, where they organized by electing their officers. After they had organized they marched to the supposed seat of war; and on their arrival they found that no Indians had been there, and that it had been entirely a false alarm. These valiant soldiers then returned to their homes, and for a long time it was impossible to find any one who would acknowledge that he had been on that expedition.

The origin of this report was as follows: Some men, for their own amusement, dressed themselves and painted their faces, so as to resemble Indians, went to a corn field where some men were at work plowing, and, giving the Indian yell, shot off their guns, pointed in the direction of the settlers. They, supposing that the disguised men were hostile Indians endeavoring to slay them, took to their heels and spread the alarm, which, like a tale of scandal, traveled from neighborhood to neighborhood, gathering new items of horror as it went from lip to lip.

This originated several anecdotes, among which is the following: A wealthy farmer of Cooper county catching the alarm, *buried his bacon* to save it from the blood-thirsty savages; then going to a field in which a large number of his negroes were at work, waved his hand and hallowed at the top of his voice, "Put out! Put out! The Indians will be upon you! The Indians will be upon you!" The Africans taking the alarm, stampeded and scattered in every direction, as though the savages with their tomahawks and scalping-knives were already close upon their heels, when in reality there was not, at that time, an Indian within one hundred miles of the place.

THE MORMON WAR.

The Mormon war took place in the year 1838. The Mormons when they first arrived in Missouri, located in Jackson county, and the citizens not looking with favor on their customs, and being incensed at the many crimes which they committed under the guise of their religious views, soon drove them from that place and they located in Caldwell county, Mo.

The citizens of that part of the State being determined to drive them entirely from the State, but not having sufficient force to accomplish the desired end, called upon the Governor to send them troops sufficient to expel these false teachers. Gov. Lilburn W. Boggs issued a call for 7,000 volunteers to assist in driving the Mormons from the territory over which he had control.

In response to this call three companies were raised in Cooper county. One, called the "Boonville Guards," composed entirely of citizens of Boonville; this, under the existing laws of the State, was a standing company, and equipped at the expense of the State government. The second, a volunteer company raised at Boonville, composed of citizens of Boonville and the surrounding neighborhood. Of this company, Jessie J. Turley was Captain, Marcus Williams, Jr., First Lieutenant, and J. Logan Forsythe, Second Lieutenant. The third was raised at Palestine, the officers of which are not known. Of the forces raised in Cooper county, Joel E. Woodward was Brigadier General, Joseph Megguire, Inspector General, and Benjamin E. Ferry, Aid de Camp to General Henry W. Crowther.

These companies marched twice towards the Mormon settlement and the seat of war. The first time they marched as far as Jonesborough, Saline county, where the commanders, supposing from reports which reached them that there were sufficient troops already at the scene of war to conquer the Mormons, ordered them to return. They were shortly afterwards again ordered to the seat of war, and marched to Lexington, where they crossed the Missouri river. They then advanced about two miles into the prairie, and there camped for two days. The Mormon troops having in the meantime surrendered to Gen. John B. Clark, Sr., these companies returned home without having the pleasure of meeting the enemy or having the opportunity of testing their valor. On their arrival at Boonville these troops were disbanded.

The Mormons during this short war were commanded by Gen. Weite, an old British officer, who fought against Gen. Jackson in the battle of New Orleans.

The Mormons after the conclusion of this war left the State and located at Nauvoo, Illinois, where they remained for several years. Having had a difficulty with the authorities of the State of Illinois, and their prophet and leader, Joseph Smith, having been assassinated, they again "pulled up stakes" and emigrated to the shores of the

"Great Salt Lake," where they have ever since remained, believing and feeling that they are a persecuted people.

The prisoners taken and retained in jail as the leaders of the Mormons were Joseph Smith, Lyman Weite, Hiram Smith, Sydna Regdon, Roberts, Higby, and two others. These men were first imprisoned in the jail at Richmond, Ray county, and were afterwards removed to the jail at Liberty, Clay county, where they broke jail, escaped pursuit, and were never tried.

THE MEXICAN WAR.

In the month of May, 1846, a call was made for one company from Cooper county to join troops in Mexico, and assist in subduing that people. On the 21st day of that month the following bulletin extra appeared, and of which the following is a verbatim copy:

"THURSDAY, MAY 21st, 1846.

VOLUNTEERS.—A proper spirit seems to animate the citizens of our county and especially the young men.

The call for one company from the Fifth Division has been promptly responded to. Forty-three volunteers were raised by Gen. Ferry on Monday in Boonville, and on Tuesday at Palestine, under the direction of Gen.'s Ferry and Megguire, the number was increased to sixty-one. They then elected their officers, and the following gentlemen were chosen:

Joseph L. Stephens, Captain, without opposition, who delivered to the volunteers on that occasion a spirited and handsome address.

1st. Lieutenant—Newton Williams.
2d. Lieutenant—H. C. Levens.
1st. Sergeant—John D. Stephens.
2nd. Sergeant—William T. Cole.
3rd. Sergeant—Richard Norris.
4th. Sergeant—James S. Hughes.

HISTORY OF COOPER COUNTY. 91

1st. Corporal—Tipton Prior.
2nd. Corporal—A. B. Cole.
3rd. Corporal—Wesley Amick.
4th. Corporal—A. G. Baber.

The company, thus organized, assembled in Boonville on Wednesday, where they were exercised in military duty by their accomplished and gallant young Captain.

The following is a list of the privates, from which it will be seen a few more have been added:

Thomas Bacon,	Edward S. D. Miller,	W. B. Rubey,
Sam'l D. Burnett,	John Whitley,	W. H. Stephens,
Jacob Duvall,	Benj. P. Ford,	John M. Kelly,
Charles Salsman,	Phillip Summers,	George Mock,
Ewing E. Woolery,	George W. Campbell,	Samuel Elliott,
Heli Cook,	Samuel R. Lemons,	Alpheus D. Hickerson,
Joel Coffee,	John R. Johnson,	Edmond Eubank,
Joel Epperson,	Thompson Seivers,	Henderson C. Martin,
Jesse Epperson,	Charles F. Kine,	Spague White,
Hiram Epperson,	Jesse Nelson,	Wm. Woolsey,
John McDowell,	John Colbert,	Martin Allison,
J. R. P. Wilcoxson,	Robt. Rhea,	Henry Francis,
T. T. Bowler,	Edmond G. Cook,	Robt. H. Bowles,
William Sullans,	John B. Bruce,	Justinian McFarland,
Horatio Bruce,	Jas. P. Lewis,	Nathaniel T. Ford,
William J. Jeffreys,	Benj. C. Lampton,	James H. Jones,
James M. Jeffreys,	Oliver G. Ford,	James C. Ross,
Hiram Burnam,	U. E. Rubey,	Richard Hulett.

They departed to-day (Thursday) on the steamer L. F. Linn, for St. Louis, where they will be armed and equipped, and immediately transported to the army of Occupation on the Rio Grande. Our best wishes attend them. May victory ever perch upon their banners, and may they all return home to their friends full of honors, with the proud reflection that they have served their country faithfully."

When the steamer Louis F. Linn, Eaton, Captain, Jewell, Clerk, arrived at Boonville, on her downward trip, the company formed in line on the upper deck and many friends passed along the line, bidding farewell and shaking each volunteer by the hand. The landing was crowded with people. The boat soon started, with cheers from the multitude, and waving of handkerchiefs by the ladies.

INCIDENTS OF THE VOYAGE.

Our steamer laid up for the first night at Nashville, which is about fifteen miles below Rockport. The members of the company were all jolly fellows, and jest and laugh made the time pass pleasantly and quickly. The most of them had never been from home, and longed, with the anxiety of children to see new countries, and to take part in other than every day affairs of their lives.

Lieutenant Levens being on watch the latter part of the night after they had left Boonville, heard a terrible splash in the water, and on inquiring for the cause discovered that one of his men had fallen overboard. The deck-hands rescued him, and soon afterwards another of the company followed the example of his comrade, and was rescued by the same men. The Lieutenant becoming alarmed for the safety of the men of the company, waked up the Captain, informed him of what had happened, and told him that if he did not take measures to prevent it he might have his company considerably diminished before they reached St. Louis, if the men continued to fall overboard as rapidly as they had commenced. The Captain was greatly surprised at such unexpected accidents, and placed out a strong guard, which prevented any more occurrences of the kind. The trouble was that some of the men before leaving Boonville had imbibed rather freely, and having never been on board of a boat before, imagined they were on land and walked off without being aware of their changed circumstances.

They arrived at St. Louis without further accident, and were quartered at the Court House without any blankets to cover them, or any place except the naked benches on which to sleep. Most of the company expecting to draw their clothing and blankets at Jefferson Barracks, had nothing but the shirt and pants which they had worn from home.

Captain Stephens company was mustered into service by Gen. Robert Campbell. Gen. Taylor having gained an important victory over the Mexicans, and it being thought that he would be able to conquer his enemies without any further reinforcements, Capt. Stephen's company were ordered back, and directed to report to Adjutant General Parsons at Jefferson City, whither they hastened on the same boat, expecting orders from him to join Donaphan's expedition to New Mexico; General Parsons informed the Captain that he had no requisition for Cooper county, but to hold his company in readiness to march when called on. The members of the company were very much disappointed at being thus summarily dismissed to their homes, and felt very indignant at what they considered such shabby treatment; and though the company was ready and willing during the whole of the war, to go to the field of battle on the shortest notice, they were not called on. Some of the members of the company were so determined to go, that they joined other companies of General Donaphan's command. The company, although they were gone from home only a short time, had a rough introduction to military life, having been forced to live on "hard tack" on their trip to St. Louis and return, without bedding of any kind, and many of them without a change of clothes. Mrs. Andrews, an estimable lady of St. Louis, treated the company to as many pies as they could eat, for which they will always feel grateful to her.

But very few of the company had ever seen St. Louis or any other city, and it was a pleasing and wonderful sight to these men, who had during all their lives, been accustomed only to the quiet scenes of their every day life. The company, as it passed through the streets, seemed from the numbers who stopped to gaze at them to attract as much attention as a fantastic company on account of their queer costumes, arms and manners. As they expected to draw their uniform on their arrival at the "Great City," and as they expected to throw their citizen's suits away, they were not particular what they wore when they started from home. Most of them being dressed in back woods style, without uniform or arms, made a rather ludicrous appearance to "city folks." But the men cared little for that, and some of the "city gents" were made to measure their lengths upon the pavement for their uncalled for remarks in regard to the personal appearance and manners of the strangers.

Some of the company while in St. Louis had a row with some merchants on Water street for insulting one of the men. After some little quarreling, the merchants threatened to have them arrested and confined in the calaboose; but they were told if that threat was executed, they would level the calaboose, and if that was not sufficient to show their power they would level the whole city, and that they had sufficient men to accomplish that undertaking. So the merchants becoming alarmed, did not attempt to have the threat executed, and the difficulty was finally arranged without any serious consequences. On their return up the Missouri river on the same boat on which they had gone down to St. Louis, a fine dressed "gentleman" unthoughtedly made the remark, that "these soldiers were a rough set." The officers of Capt. Stephen's and Capt. Reid's companies demanded that he should be put ashore, and at the next landing he was made to "walk the plank," amidst shouts and cheers from the crowd; they thus gave him an opportunity of traveling on the next boat, where perhaps, he might meet with passengers more congeniel to his nature, and where he would not be forced to associate with those whom he considered beneath him in the social scale.

After this they proceeded without further incident to Boonville, where they were met by crowds of their friends and acquaintances, who, with loud cheers, welcomed them home. Soon after they arrived, the company was disbanded by the captain, with orders to be ready to assemble and march to the seat of war on very short notice. From that time to the close of the war the members of the company were prepared at all times to march to the front, whenever their services should be required, but they were never ordered forward to take part in the great struggle which had then been transferred to the enemy's country.

This is the only part the citizens of Cooper county took in the war of 1846, and though they did not partake directly in the struggle, they showed their readiness to do so, by organizing and keeping in readiness to march a company composed of some of the best citizens.

WAR HISTORY OF COOPER COUNTY.

CHAPTER XI.

The late "War of the Rebellion" in Cooper County.—Battle below Boonville.—Movements of the "Home Guards" in Cooper County.—Defeat of Captain Parks by Wm. Anderson.—Shelby's Raid into Cooper County, and his Engagements with the Federal Troops.—Price's Raid into Cooper County, and the Battles Fought near Boonville.—Bitter Partisan Feeling Engendered During the War, &c.

We would like to pass the history of this war, and leave it to be recorded by future historians, when the passions and bitter feelings engendered shall have passed away and been forgotten; but it is certain that it is not wise for the recorder of events to omit to tell the simple truth for fear that it may grate harshly upon the ear of some one. He must, impartially, write the facts as they occurred, without showing favor to either side. It is not intended here to give a detailed account of all that transpired during the unhappy conflict of the late war; but the following pages only profess to give, without any comment, some of the main facts as they occurred:

Cooper county suffered a great deal during the late war. Her territory was nearly all the time occupied either by one party or the other, and her citizens were called upon to contribute to the support of first one side and then the other. The first of the actions which took place within Cooper county, and indeed the second engagement of the war, was the

BATTLE BELOW BOONVILLE.

Gov. Jackson and Gen. Price, on the 11th day of June, 1861, left Jefferson City, where the Legislature was in session, sought an interview with Gens. Lyon and Blair, and made propositions for a compromise, on the basis of neutrality, &c. The two last mentioned Generals refused to make any compromise whatever, but claimed the "unrestricted right to move and station the troops of the United States throughout the State, whenever and wherever that might, in the opinion of the officers, be necessary, either for the protection of loyal citizens of the federal government, or for the repelling of an invasion."

Gov. Jackson and Gen. Price, after this unsuccessful endeavor to bring about peace, returned to Jefferson City, and the governor issued a proclamation, calling into the active service of the State, 50,000 men. Gen. Lyon, a few days afterwards issued a counter proclamation, in justification of his course in refusing to compromise with Gov. Jackson and Gen. Price.

Gen. Lyon then moved his troops to Jefferson City, and on his arrival at that place, he found that Gov. Jackson had moved his forces fifty miles above, to Boonville, cutting the telegraph lines, and destroying the bridges on the railway as he proceeded. Gen. Lyon, leaving Col. Boemstein in command of a small force at the capitol, on the afternoon of the 16th day of June, 1861, embarked his forces on three steamers, and ascending the Missouri river, they arrived at Rocheport about six o'clock on the following morning. There he ascertained that the State troops, under General Marmaduke, Price at that time being sick, were in full force a few miles below Boonville, and that resistance might be expected from them, should he attempt to reach Boonville by that road. Leaving this place and taking the steam ferry boat, Paul Wilcox with them, Gen. Lyon's command ascended the river, to the island, eight miles below Boonville, which they reached at about seven o'clock, A. M., and on the southern shore of which they disembarked.

No enemy being in sight, and the scouts reporting no signs of any, the troops at once marched up the Missouri river towards Boonville, and followed the road about a mile and a half, to the place where it ascends the bluffs, from the river bottom. At this place several shots from Gen. Lyon's scouts announced the driving in of Col. Marmaduke's pickets. Gen. Lyon then advanced for nearly a mile, and found Gen. Marmaduke well posted at the brow of the ascent. Capt. Totten opened the engagement by throwing a few nine pound bombshells into the entrenchments of the State troops, while the infantry commenced a heavy volley of musketry, which was well replied to, the balls flying thick and fast among the ranks of the troops and wounded several on both sides.

The State troops, under the command of Col. Marmaduke, were posted in a lane running from the Rocheport road in the direction of the river, and west of the residence of Wm. M. Adams, on the north-east corner of the junction of the two roads. During the fight, a couple of bombs were thrown through the east wall of Mr. Adams' house, causing the inmates to retreat to the cellar for protection. A heavy fire from Col. Shaefer's German infantry, Gen. Lyon's company of regulars, and part of Col. Blair's regiment, which were stationed on the left of the road, compelled the troops of Col. Marmaduke to retreat.

His force then clambered over the fence into a field of wheat, and again formed in line just on the brow of the hill. They then advanced some twenty steps to meet the federal troops, and for a short time the artillery of Capt. Totten was worked with great rapidity. Just at this time the State troops opened a galling fire from a grove just on the left of the federal center, and from a shed from beyond and still further to the left.

What had been before this a skirmish, now assumed the

magnitude of a battle, which continued only about one half of an hour. The State troops finding the federals too strong and too well armed and drilled to be successfully opposed by raw recruits, most of whom had never been under fire, and having no artillery with which to return the fire from Gen. Lyon's batteries, abandoned the fight and retreated. Captains Cole and Miller took possession of "Camp Bacon," where the State troops for two days had been encamped.

Gen. Lyon continued his march towards Boonville. He was met on the hill near the residence of T. W. Nelson, by James H. O'Bryan, acting mayor of Boonville, Judge G. W. Miller and other prominent citizens, who formally surrendered the town to him, and he immediately marched into and took possession of it.

Col. Marmaduke commanded the State troops on this occasion, Gen. Price was in ill health, and on the day on which the battle occurred he left Boonville on a steamboat for Lexington. Governor Jackson was on the battle-ground in the forenoon, but left Boonville on the Georgetown road about eleven o'clock of that day. In this engagement two of Lyon's men were killed and nine wounded. Among the State troops three were killed and several wounded, but the number of these is unknown.

Kelly's was the only well organized and well drilled company under the command of Col. Marmaduke, and it did not participate in the battle. It was said that General Price was opposed to making a stand against Gen. Lyon at that time, as all of his troops, except Kelly's company, were raw recruits, and very poorly armed and drilled, having rallied at Boonville during the preceding three days. There was considerable controversy among the officers and men, whether considering the circumstances a stand or retreat should be made; but some of the most enthusiastic, whose counsel prevailed, said, that they had come to fight, and they intended to do so There were several prisoners taken by Gen. Lyon, but they were afterwards released on parole.

The next day after the battle Gen. Lyon issued a proclamation offering full pardon to all who would lay down their arms, return to their homes, and relinquish their hostility to the United States government; and persons who did this were assured that they would not be molested for past occurrences. Many who had taken part in the battle, availed themselves of the opportunity offered by Gen. Lyon, and some of them never took up arms again during the war.

Gen. Lyon remained at Boonville for several weeks, during which time he purchased a large outfit of wagons, horses and mules, paying fair prices for them, no pressing or forced sales being made; he also captured every steamboat that passed down the river. On the third day of July, having received reinforcements of an Iowa regiment, he took his departure for the south-west, his objective point being Springfield. A short time before, Gen. Blair left for Washington, to take his seat in Congress, he having been elected a representative from St. Louis.

This being the first battle of the rebellion which was fought on land, the taking of Fort Sumpter having occurred only a short time before, produced great excitement throughout the United States, and Gen. Blair, on his way to Washington, was met by great crowds of his friends, and lionized, feasted and toasted, as the "hero of the hour."

Gen. Lyon, before he left Boonville, organized two companies of home guards, composed entirely of Germans, commanded by Major Joseph A. Eppstein, and threw up strong fortifications at the "Old Fair Grounds." When he moved to Springfield, he left Maj. Cully, who was shortly afterwards succeeded by Col. John D. Stephenson, in command at the fortifications.

Dr. Quarles was among the killed of the State troops. His body was found in the wheat field late in the evening after the battle, he having been severely wounded in the thigh, and not being discovered, he had bled to death. Young McCutchen was also wounded in the thigh, and was properly cared for, though all their efforts could not save him, and he died in a few days after the battle. The death of these two gentlemen, so young, so promising and kind-hearted, cast a gloom over the entire community, and their loss was universally regretted by all parties. The other gentleman killed, who was from Pettis county, was shot in the head, and his name is not recollected.

Gen. Parsons, with the artillery belonging to the State troops, arrived too late to engage in the battle. He came in on the Boonville and Tipton road, via Wilkins' bridge, and halted at the top of the hill, south of Boonville, near Dr. Wm. H. Trigg's present residence, where, learning the result of the battle, that Col. Marmaduke had been defeated and was retreating, took the road leading from Boonville to Prairie Lick, in a south-west direction, and soon formed a junction with Gov. Jackson's State troops.

Gen. Lyon, two days after the battle of Boonville, sent a detachment of his force south-west, by way of Syracuse, as far as Florence, Morgan county, in pursuit of Gov. Jackson. But finding that the State troops had moved still farther south, the command returned to Boonville without meeting any of Jackson's command.

MOVEMENTS OF THE HOME GUARDS IN COOPER COUNTY.

Gen. Nathaniel Lyon, on the twentieth day of June, 1861, organized and mustered into service a company of German "Home Guards," consisting of 135 men. Of this company

Joseph A. Eppstein was elected captain, Emil Haas, 1st lieutenant; Ernest Roeschel, 2nd lieutenant, and John A. Hain, orderly sergeant. This company was, on the fourth day of August, ordered to Jefferson City for the purpose of aiding in the protection of the capitol. They, together with Col. Brown's 7th Missouri regiment, were, a short time afterwards, ordered to Otterville. They went by rail to Syracuse, and marched on foot the balance of the way to Otterville, which they immediately occupied.

A large number of southern men living in the vicinity had organized a company, and under the command of Capt. Alexander, James B. Harris, and others, were camped near by. These two commands, not, for some reason wishing to attack each other, made the following compromise which had been suggested by the southern commarders, and after some parley, accepted by Col. Brown. It was agreed, that if the federal troops would withdraw from Otterville, Capt. Alexander would disband his forces, and Col. Brown ordered his command back to Jefferson City.

Afterwards, the home guards, with part of Col. Worthington's command, were ordered to Boonville. They ascended the Missouri river in a steamboat, and arrived at Boonville very early on the morning of the day following their start from Jefferson City. The morning was very fogy, so that the boat could hardly be seen from the shore. It passed Boonville under cover of the darkness and the fog, and landed at Haas' brewery, situa.ed about one-half of a mile west of the city. Here the "home guards" disembarked, and from thence marched around and surrounded the town before the citizens were aware of their presence. Col. Worthington, with the men of his command, dropped down on the steamboat to the landing at the foot of Main street, and marched up into the town. He then took a number of prominent citizens prisoners, and confiscated the contents of two tin stores and one shoe store, the owners of which were charged with selling goods to the Confederates; he also took possession of the *Advertiser* printing establishment, then owned by Messrs. Caldwell & Stahl, and had the presses, type, &c., boxed up and shipped to Jefferson City. This was all done under the orders of Col. U. S. Grant, now president of the United States, who was then in command at Jefferson City. The "home guards," together with Col. Worthington's command, on the afternoon of the same day, taking with them the prisoners and the property which they had confiscated. The prisoners were afterwards released, and returned home; but most of the property, except that belonging to the printing establishment, was never again seen by its owners.

On the twenty-eighth day of August, in the same year, the "home guards" were ordered to reinforce Col. Mulligan at Lexington, Missouri. Two days before, the 12th Illinois regiment of cavalry had been ordered to the same place, and had started. When Col. Eppstein, the commander of the "home guards" arrived at Tipton, he heard that a part of the 12th Illinois cavalry were at Boonville, and concluded to go there also, and reported to headquarters, that if they had any orders for him, to forward them to him at that place.

Col. Eppstein was ordered by Gen. Jeff. C. Davis, then stationed at Jefferson City, to remain at Boonville, and occupy the breastworks, which he did.

On the first day of September, 1861, the troops around Boonville formed themselves into a battalion, consisting of two and one-half companies; companies "A" and "B," infantry, and one-half of a company of cavalry. The officers of the battalion were Joseph A. Eppstein, Major; Emil Haas, Surgeon, and John A. Hayne, Adjutant; of company "A" infantry, were John B. Keiser, captain; John

Reatherd, 1st Lieutenant, and Charles Kock, 2nd Lieutenant; of company "B" infantry, were Charles Beihle, captain; Joseph Weber, 1st Lieutenant; John Fessler, 2nd Lieutenant. The half company of cavalry was commanded by Peter Ostermeyer.

About four days afterwards, this battalion received information that they would be attacked by the confederates from several surrounding counties. Col. Eppstein immediately arrested a number of the most prominent southern men in Boonville, viz: H. N. Ells, Rev. Painter, Wm. E. Burr and J. W. Draffen, and held them as hostages, hoping thereby to prevent the contemplated attack. But about six o'clock on the morning of the 13th day of September, 1861, while Eppstein's command was at breakfast, the pickets having all come in, the breastworks were attacked by a force of about eight hundred men under the command of Col. Brown, of Saline county. The fortifications were attacked on the west, southwest and southeast sides. The first attack was from the southwest, the next through Lilly's field on the south-east, and finally extended around to the west side. At the first the firing was very rapid from the southwest and southeast, and soon afterwards from the west side of the fortifications, the balls falling thick on every side. Col. Brown led the attack on the southeast, and made two charges upon the breastworks, but was compelled to fall back each time under the heavy fire from the intrenchments. In the second attack Col. Brown was mortally wounded, and fell within fifty feet of the breastworks; a short time afterwards, his brother, Capt. Brown, was also mortally wounded, and fell about ten feet behind him. The Browns were both brave men, and fought with desperation, and with utter disregard of their own safety. After the two Browns had fallen mortally wounded, and Major Poindexter been left in command of the confederates, Mr. Burr, who was one of the prisoners at the breastworks, having become satisfied that the intrenchments could not be taken, asked, and was granted permission to visit the confederates, under a flag of truce, in order to see what arrangements could be made so as to bring about a cessation of hostilities. The two commanders finally agreed upon an armistice for six days, Major Poindexter's troops to be withdrawn from the breastworks and city.

The home guards numbered about one hundred and forty effective men. Their loss was two killed and seven wounded. The names of the killed were John A. Hayne, adjutant, and Kimball, a private. The number of Colonel Brown's command who were killed and wounded is not known. Col. and Capt. Brown, were, after the battle, taken to hospital at Boonville. The Colonel died of his wounds the same evening; the Captain lingered until the next day, when he too died. Their bodies were taken to Saline county for burial.

At the commencement of the battle, messengers were dispatched by three different routes, viz: by way of Tipton, Jefferson City road, and down the river in a skiff, asking for reinforcements. Of these messengers, none reached Jefferson City except Joseph Read and Joseph Reavis, who went down the river. Those who went by the way of Tipton and the Jefferson City road, were captured by Col. Brown's men while they were on the way.

On the 14th, at ten o'clock, P. M., the force at Boonville was reinforced by the 5th Iowa regiment, under the command of Col. Worthington, which came up the river on a steamboat. After the armistice had expired, Major Poindexter drew off his men, and marched up the river to join Gen. Price at Lexington.

In November, 1861, a scouting party of three men, belonging to the "home guards," started out to gain information in regard to a band of bushwhackers, who were thought to have their headquarters somewhere in Clark's Fork township, in this county. While approaching the house of William George, in said township, they were fired upon from the house, and one of their number killed. The scouts then retreated to Tipton, and having obtained reinforcements, returned and burnt William George's house.

On the 16th day of September, 1861, Col. Eppstein's battalion was commanded by Col. Worthington to take possession of and guard the bridge across the Lamine river on the road from Boonville to Arrow Rock. Before their arrival at the bridge, they heard the firing of several minute guns behind them, which were intended to warn the State troops of the approach of Col. Eppstein's men. They reached the bridge in the night, and were fired upon from the opposite side of the river by the State troops, who seemed to have taken possession of the bridge. Col. Eppstein returned the fire, and mortally wounded a young man named Herndon, who lived in Lamine township, in this county. He was taken to the house of Mr. Wm. Higgerson, where he soon afterwards expired. The State troops soon retreated and left Col. Eppstein's troops in possession of the bridge, where they remained until the 19th day of September, when they were ordered to return to Boonville.

Soon afterwards, Col. Worthington ordered Col. Eppstein to take his command with him and burn this same bridge, it having been reported that Gen. Price's army was marching towards Boonville from that direction, and would probably cross the Lamine at that point. Col. Eppstein endeavored to dissuade him from his purpose, by telling him that this would only delay Price a single day, as he could cross a short distance above; but Col. Worthington replied that it must be done, as he deemed it to be a military necessity. So the bridge was burned in accordance with his order. Yet this proved to be a false alarm, as Price was not on his way to Boonville, and did not attempt to march in that direction.

Under a special law of Congress, passed on account of a general dissatisfaction among the "home guards" all over the State, Col. Eppstein's battalion was reorganized, and became a part of the Missouri State militia. Six companies were raised and organized at Boonville, and to these were added two companies from St. Louis, thus forming the 13th regiment of the Missouri State militia cavalry. The company of infantry which was commanded by Capt. Charles Beihle, joined the 1st Missouri State militia infantry. Afterwards, the 13th regiment was consolidated with four companies of the 12th regiment, and Skofield's "Bazars," and from that time formed the 5th regiment, the old 5th having previously been disbanded.

The officers of this regiment were, Albert Seigel, Col., Joseph A. Eppstein, Lieut. Col., John B. Kaiser, Major, and John Fetzer, Surgeon. This regiment after being first thoroughly organized and fully drilled and equipped, was ordered to Waynesville, in the Rolla district, where they remained and from whence they mostly operated during the war. Part of this regiment was under the command of Col. Brown, during his pursuit of Shelby, when in October, 1863, he made his raid through the State in the direction of Boonville.

PRICE'S RAID.

Six companies of the 5th regiment, under the command of Col. Eppstein, composed a portion of the forces of Gen. Sanborn during his operations against Gen. Price in his raid through Missouri in the fall of 1864. Gen. Sanborn at first supposing that Gen. Price would march in the direction of Rolla, concentrated his forces at that place, but finding that Gen. Price was making for Jefferson City, he moved his command to the latter place; on the way, marching nearly parallel with the confederates, for while he was crossing the Osage river at Castle Rock, General Price was crossing the same stream eight miles below. Col. Eppstein's command had a slight skirmish with the confederate advance guard, between the Osage and the Moreau Creek, but he succeeded in reaching Jefferson City first.

Gen. Sanborn had concentrated at that place, 3,000 infantry and 4,000 cavalry, most of them regulars, and all of them well-armed and drilled. Gen. Price's army numbered about 20,000 men, yet there were thousands of them who had no arms, and had never seen anything like a battle. Neither had his troops been organized and placed under commanders, as many of them had flocked to his standard as he marched through the State, and as he was continually on the march, he had no opportunity to effect organization in the ranks at this time, though shortly afterwards he had them under perfect control.

Price only made a slight attack on Jefferson City with a small portion of his forces, then withdrew without a general battle, and marched across the country in the direction of Boonville. Gen. Sanborn, as soon as he learned the true state of affairs, started his cavalry in pursuit of the confederates. The cavalry had skirmishes with the confederate rear guard, which was commanded by Gen. Fagan, at Stringtown, Russelville and California, on the 10th day of October, 1864. During these skirmishes, three of Colonel Eppstein's men were killed and thirteen wounded. The loss of the confederates is unknown. Price camped, on the night of the 10th, on the Moniteau Creek, just within the limits of Cooper county, and on the next day marched to Boonville.

The federals moved west and camped on the upper Tipton road, about eleven miles south of Boonville, at Crenshaw's farm. On the 12th of October, Col. Graveley, with about four hundred mounted men of Sanborn's command, advanced by way of the upper Tipton road to within about one-half of a mile of Boonville, to test the strength, and if possible, to find out the contemplated movements of Gen. Price's command. At what is known as the Vollrath Place, about one-half of a mile south of Boonville, Col. Graveley came upon some confederate companies in camp, and some lively fighting ensued, but finding the confederates too strong for them, the federals retreated to the main army.

On the 12th, Col. Eppstein, with about three hundred and fifty men of his command, moved towards Boonville, and camped at Bohannon's farm, about seven miles south of Boonville. Early on the morning of the 13th, he was ordered to advance as far as he could in the direction of Boonville, and reconnoitre Gen. Price's position. Immediately upon receiving this order, he commenced his march with the above mentioned number of men and two mountain howitzers, and on arriving at Wilkin's bridge, across the Petite Saline creek, his command was fired upon by a band of about four hundred men under the command of General Fagan, who were guarding the bridge. Col. Eppstein returned the fire, and ordered four mounted companies to dismount and deploy as skirmishers. After some little skirmishing, along the banks of the creek, Gen. Fagan leisurely retreated towards Boonville. After going north about one half of a mile, to where a lane crosses the main road south of Mrs. McCarty's house, Col. Eppstein, who was in pursuit, found that Gen. Fagan had barricaded the road with trees, &c. Here Miller's and Murphy's companies had a close fight with the confederates, even using swords and bayonets. These two companies were surrounded at one time and ordered by the confederates to surrender; but the other two companies of Col. Eppstein's command coming up to their aid, Gen. Fagan again fell back. At this place two of the federals were wounded, but none hurt upon the other side.

Gen. Fagan next made a stand at Anderson's branch, and here they had a more severe battle. Three of the federals were killed and seven wounded. The killed were, Fred. Hoecher, a man named Jones, and the name of the other is not known. The loss of the confederates, as was afterwards learned, was considerable.

Gen. Fagan by this time had brought up four pieces of artillery, and commenced shelling the woods along Anderson's branch in which Col. Eppstein was stationed. The federals then received orders to fall back, and retreated to California, Moniteau county, and there to obtain supplies. They soon afterwards returned to Crenshaw's farm, and there halted and took dinner. There Gen. Sanborn learned that Price had left Boonville, so marching west he camped for the night at New Nebo church. The next morning he continued his march in the direction of Georgetown.

In August, 1864, Capt. Parks, with two companies, of which Franklin Swap was 1st Lieutenant and Provost Marshall, being a part of the Iowa cavalry, had command at of the post at Boonville. Finding but little to do on this side of the river, they crossed over into Howard county, in search of "Anderson's bushwhackers," passed through New Franklin, and took the road east leading to Rocheport. Although warned by the citizens of his danger, as Anderson was known to be in full force in the neighborhood, Capt. Parks marched on.

When about one mile east of New Franklin, his company was suddenly attacked by Anderson's men, and cut into two parts, seven of them being killed by the first fire. The greater part of the command retreated to a house in the Missouri river bottom, and kept Anderson at bay by firing through the cracks of the house. Capt. Parks, at the outset, became separated from his men, and retreated towards Fayette until he met Major Leonard's command, which happened to be marching in that direction. With this he returned to the relief of his company, and Anderson having learned of his approach, drew off his men and retired.

The part of Capt. Parks' company which had been besieged in the house, finding that Anderson had drawn off his men, mounted horses, came back to Old Franklin in the night, and crossed the river in safety, although several men were missing. This part of the company knew nothing of Capt. Parks until the next day, when he made his appearance. They then recrossed the river, and having recovered the bodies of their companions who had been killed, buried them in one grave at the city cemetery in the southwest part of Boonville.

In the winter of 1862 and 1863, Col. Pope was the commander of several companies of home militia, with headquarters at the fair grounds at Boonville. They disbanded in 1863, and Col. D. W. Wear formed a battalion, and was commander of the post at Boonville. The battalion did considerable scouting, the details of which are not sufficiently known to be given.

Lieut. Col. Reavis, while under Col. Pope, learning that some confederate recruiting forces had crossed the river, making their way in a southern direction, he immediately started in pursuit, and overtook them while in camp in the brush, near Thomas Tucker's house, about two miles east of Bunceton, in Cooper county. He fired upon them, killing two men and wounding one. The recruits then separated, and made their way out of the country by different routes. The names of the confederates who were killed, were Joshua Lampton and Jones, from Boone county. They were buried at the "Vine" or "Concord" church. The wounded man, after recovering, was paroled by Col. Pope, and returned to his home in Boone county.

SHELBY'S RAID.

Gen. Joseph Shelby, of the confederate army, made a raid into Cooper county during the month of October, 1863. He passed through Otterville on the night of the 9th of said month, and burned the Pacific railroad bridge near that town. On the night of the 10th he camped near Bell Air, in a pasture belonging to Mr. Nathaniel Leonard, and on the next day he marched to Boonville. His movements becoming known in Boonville the night before, a meeting of the citizens was called by Mayor McDearmon. After some delay, the conclusion was reached, that the only alternative was to surrender the city to Gen. Shelby. Citizens were sent out to meet him, who returned without being able to gain any information as to his whereabouts, and conveyed the impression that he would not pay his compliments to the city during this expedition.

Therefore his arrival at Boonville on the 11th day of October was quite a surprise to the citizens. Several of the citizens had crossed the river into Howard county the night before, having concluded that discretion was the better part of valor, that their presence in Boonville would accomplish no good, and that there would be more safety in making themselves scarce.

Just as Gen. Shelby marched into Boonville from the south, Major Leonard, with about two hundred and fifty federal troops, appeared on the north side of the river, and commenced crossing his men. The first boat load had almost reached the Boonville shore, when some one called to those in the boat that the town was full of confederates, and that they had better retreat. The pilots immediately turned the boat around and made for the Howard shore. At this time some of Shelby's men appeared and commenced firing upon the boat with muskets. But the boat having gotten out of reach of this fire, the confederates brought up some artillery and opened fire upon the boat, two shots striking it before it reached the shore. As soon as Maj. Leonard landed his forces, the artillery was turned upon them, and they were soon forced to retire beyond the reach of the shells.

At the same time, Col. Crittenden, with about one hundred men, was seen steaming up the river in a boat, but on learning the situation of affairs at Boonville, he dropped back down the river, and landed a short distance below, in Howard county.

Gen. Shelby remained in Boonville the balance of the afternoon of that day, and encamped for the night west of the city on the Georgetown road. He came here to obtain supplies, such as clothing and provisions, which they found in great abundance, and which they took, wherever found. M. J. Werthumer, and Messrs. Lamy & McFadden were the greatest sufferers, each losing about $4,000 in clothing. The confederate troops did not molest any person during their stay, not a single man was killed or wounded, and they were very polite and gentlemanly to every person.

While the confederates were in Boonville, the federals, under Gen. Brown, were close behind them, and on the 11th day of October, were within eight miles of Boonville, on the Bell Air road. On that day Gen. Brown moved a portion of his troops west to the junction of the Sulphur Springs and the Boonville and Georgetown roads, which is about seven miles southwest of Boonville. But during the night he marched his command back again to the Bell Air road, and camped near Bellingsville. The next morning after Gen. Shelby had left, the federals passed through

Boonville in pursuit, their advance just behind the confederate rear guard. Two of Gen. Shelby's men who had stopped at Mr. Labbo's house, about one and one-half miles west of Boonville to get their breakfast, were killed by some federal scouts as they appeared at the front door, in order to make their escape.

A running fight was kept up at intervals, all along the route from Boonville to Marshall. The fight became pretty spirited between the Sulphur Springs and Dug Ford; and at Dug Ford two federals were killed and fell from their horses into the water. During this long running fight there was quite a number killed on each side, but the number is not known.

At Marshall, a lively battle took place, in which a number were killed and wounded on both sides. But General Shelby succeeded in escaping from his pursuers with the loss of only a small portion of the stores which he had obtained at Boonville.

This raid, of course, produced great excitement, and in the heat of passion, considerable censure was heaped upon the commanding officer, whether justly or unjustly, is left the reader to determine. Gen. Shelby succeeded in getting back to his lines without any great loss, but whether his entire anticipations in regard to obtaining supplies and reinforcements were fully realized, is not known. Major Leonard and Col. Crittenden crossed their commands over the river to Boonville about ten o'clock on the morning of the 12th, and after stopping for dinner, they started in the direction of Marshall. Boonville, then, was once more clear of troops, and the citizens had time to gather together provisions to feed the next lot of hungry soldiers who happened to land there, whether they were federals or confederates. Thus ended the famous "Shelby's Raid," as far as Cooper county was concerned.

PRICE'S RAID INTO COOPER COUNTY.

The federal troops, in the fall of 1864, having all abandoned Boonville, three companies of "home guards" were organized for the protection of the city against what were known as the "bushwhackers." One company was commanded by Capt. Horace Shoemaker, another by Capt. Harrison Thompson, and the third by —————. The two last mentioned companies were composed of men belonging to both parties, who had joined these companies with the understanding that they would only be required to protect the city against "bushwhackers and plunderers," and would not be compelled, against their wills, to fight against the regular southern troops.

Although there were frequent alarms, the "bushwhackers" never attacked Boonville, but often during the war made raids through the county, in which many citizens were killed. They always took anything they wished, no matter in whose hands it was found. There were also bands of robbers moving continually through the county, who cared nothing for either party, and who robbed and killed without discrimination or regard to party. During the year 1864, many good citizens belonging to each side, were shot down, first by one party and then by another, and many citizens abandoned their homes, seeking places of more security. The details of these murders and robberies are too disgraceful and sickening to enumerate in this brief history.

On the 11th day of October, 1864, scouts brought information that a large hostile force was approaching Boonville. These three companies being under the impression that these were "Anderson's bushwhackers," immediately erected a strong barricade across Fifth street, at the Thespian Hall, in Boonville. They were strengthened in the belief that these were "bushwhackers," from the fact that they had received a dispatch that afternoon from Mexico, Missouri, stating that Gen. Price had been repulsed at Jefferson City, and was retreating by way of Tipton.

So these companies of home guards expecting no quarter from Anderson's men, prepared to sell their lives as dearly as they could, thinking anyway that it would be certain death to fall into the hands of "Bill Anderson." Soon afterwards, Shelby's command entered the town with a dash, killing a German scout near Mrs. Muir's residence, about one mile east of Boonville. The "home guards" fired one round at the advance guard of Shelby's command as they advanced along Vine street near the Baptist church, but their fire injured no one.

But learning that this was but the advance guard of Gen. Price's large army, and that resistance would be useless, the home guards surrendered as prisoners of war. These prisoners were quartered at the court house and closely guarded, but the commissioned officers were paroled. Gen. Shelby, with his command, entered about sundown on the above mentioned day. Gen. Price and his staff made their headquarters at the city hotel, on Morgan street. On Tuesday, the 13th day of October, the prisoners were marched in front of the city hall, ranged in line, and Gen. Price made them a speech, and gave orders for their parole, on the condition, that if they were ever found with arms against the south, they would be shot.

Price had about 20,000 men, many of them late Missouri recruits, without arms. Some of his command were well armed and drilled, but the greater part were very poorly armed. Their general conduct towards the citizens during their stay in Boonville, was good.

On the night of the 13th, while Capt. Shoemaker, who was on parole, was going from Capt. John Porter's house to his residence, on the corner of Central avenue and

Sixth streets, he was captured by some men, who were afterwards discovered to be Anderson's men, taken to the fair grounds, killed, and his body thrown into the river. Two men, named Neef and Boller, were killed near their homes, about four miles west of Boonville; also a negro man who was concealed in a cornshock on the farm of J. M. Nelson, situated two miles west of Boonville. These were all the persons killed in this part of the country, who were not slain in battle, whose names are now recollected.

Thousands of volunteers in Missouri flocked to the standard of Gen. Price, believing that he would be able to hold the State. The rear guard of Gen. Price's army, and the advance guard of Gen. Sanborn's command, skirmished, at intervals, from Jefferson City to Boonville. Gen. Sanborn's command consisted of about 4,000 mounted men. The infantry command, under Gen. A. J. Smith, was also in pursuit, but never came within fighting distance of the confederates.

There was considerable skirmishing and some hard fighting, south and southeast of Boonville, during Price's three day's sojourn at that place, in which a number were killed and wounded on both sides. The Arkansas militia, under the command of Gen. Fagan, who were left to protect the rear of Gen. Price's army, were the greatest sufferers among the confederates.

A dash was made upon Gen. Price's out-posts, by a few companies of federals, who came so near Boonville, that the firing could be heard, and the smoke of the battle seen from the city. Gen. Price's artillery was brought into requisition, and soon compelled the federals to retire. The greater part of Price's regulars was then called out, and a general charge having been made all along the line, the federal army fell back on the road leading from Jefferson City to Georgetown, via Bell Air, and following that road, camped about four miles west of Bell Air, near the farm of A. J. Read.

Price's army left Boonville during the night of the 14th day of October, having remained there three days. His army took all the horses in the northern part, and the federal troops in the southern part of the county. Both parties foraged upon the people of the county for the support of their respective armies, and left the county pretty destitute, especially of horses, hardly a good one being left. This was virtually the end of the war, as far as Cooper county was concerned, no more battles being fought in it between organized armies.

The partisan warfare in Cooper county became pretty bloody during the summer and fall of 1864. The details of these occurrences, the writers must be excused from recording, leaving the task to some future historian, although they believe that they could give the particulars without partiality or prejudice, but others might not so consider them.

HISTORY OF COOPER COUNTY.

CHAPTER XII.

Character, Manners and Customs of the Early Settlers of Cooper County.

THE people in the early history of Cooper county, were industrious, hardy and honest; a better class of people never emigrated to any country. What they lacked in education, they made up in hard, common sense. Crime was very rare. They were social, clever and honest. Selfish or dishonest persons were not countenanced in society. There were then only two classes of people: The honest and industrious, and the dishonest and lazy. Persons who did not work for a living, were looked upon with suspicion, and always shunned by the better class. The neighbors were always ready to assist one another when needed. They assisted each other in house-raisings, log-rolling, (not political,) shuckings and reapings, with the sickle. No person thought of performing such work without calling in his neighbors to help him, and frequently, at the same time, the women would be called in and have a quilting. After the work was completed, all would engage in a lively dance, consisting mostly of Virginia reels.

At that time, people cared very little about accumulating wealth. Their families devoted a portion of their time to social and innocent amusements. They were very jocular, very fond of getting and making jokes on one another, and as to slander, they rarely resorted to it; if they did, they would soon have had no friends or neighbors, and would have been shunned by the good people as vipers.

If two men had a quarrel, they would meet and fight it out, then make friends and take a drink, thus quickly and easily settling their difficulty. Most persons kept whisky at their homes, and used it with moderation at public gatherings. Drunkenness was very rare, and was so very disgraceful, that few persons would venture to get drunk a second time.

The slaves were universally well treated, being considered almost as one of the owner's family, the only difference being, that they ate their meals from the kitchen and lived apart from the family. They were allowed to have their own parties and gatherings the same as the whites, and in all things enjoyed life about as much as their owners.

At the time of the organization of the county, the people had great respect for old age, or persons older than themselves, even greater than they have at present, and listened to, and often profited by their advice and counsel. The maxim then was, "Old men for counsel, and young men for war." If an aged person was imposed upon, insulted, injured or assaulted by a young man, there was always some person who was ready to rise up and assist in defending him.

Children had great respect, love and reverence for their parents; and obedience to their slightest commands was considered the first thing that should be taught them. There was, at that time, a much more strict government over children than there is at present. They were taught habits of industry and economy, and were under the complete control of their parents until they became of age, and seldom left their parents until that time. It was then disgraceful not to follow some useful and honest employment, and children were raised with that idea in view, and given to understand that the citizens had no use for a lazy, trifling man.

COURTSHIPS AND WEDDINGS.

Under the old customs governing courtships, and the settlers were pretty strict about matters of this kind, when a young man had "serious intentions" on the subject of marriage, his first action was to ask the privilege of setting up during the night, with the object of his affections, to whisper love into her ear. When this took place, it was generally supposed that the young man meant business. When house room was very scarce, the two young folks, after permission had been granted, as above, often sat up in the same room in which the parents of the young lady slept, such being the necessities of the times.

The people, at that time, universally traveled on horseback, and the gentleman who had been granted the privilege of the company of a young lady, rode with her to church, parties and elsewhere, and during these journeys she was under the young man's charge until they returned home. This custom still prevails, to some extent, but the practice of sitting up all night with a lady has been long since abolished in this county.

The weddings generally took place at one o'clock, P. M., at the residence of the bride's father. After which, dinner was served, and then the dancing and the playing games, such as "Old Sister Phebe," "Come my love and go with me," commenced, and were generally continued until late in the night. After breakfast, on the following morning, the company would form into double file on horse-back, the bride and groom in advance, the bride on the left and the groom on the right side. Immediately following them came their attendants, then the parents, brothers, sisters, and last of all, the other ladies and gentlemen who were invited guests. In this order they proceeded to the "infare" dinner at the residence of the father of the groom. After dinner, playing and dancing would commence, and continue as at the wedding. Thus showing that they considered weddings as one of the few things which being worth doing at all, was worth doing well.

HOUSEKEEPING.

Young men at that time did not generally venture to marry without having a home to which he could take his young wife. Unlike the young married men of this fast age, he would build and furnish his house in accordance with his means. The young couples would live plainly and economically, and thereby increase in wealth by degrees. They were proud of what they had, because it was their own, what they had obtained by industry and economy, and for which they were not in debt. When by this course of life they had amassed sufficient means, they would build a better and more stylish house, stock their farm better, and purchase more improved farming implements. To be plain and use a common phrase, they would "take things as they could stand them," and never attempt to reach beyond their height. They did not commence at the top of the ladder to ascend, but at the foot, from whence there was some chance to improve their condition.

These were the old fashioned ways, that were good then, are none the less good now because of their age, and should never have been abolished. In the present customs and fashions, people are truly and surely taking a step backwards, which generally leads those, who practice them, to almost certain distress, and, in most cases, to financial ruin. This is the cause of many of the crimes committed in high life, among the "Upper Ten," as they are *erroneously* called.

A young married couple in our present high and fashionable life, are not content to live in such homes, have such furniture, and clothe themselves as their means will permit. But they must commence with a fine, costly house, elegantly furnished, with a fine piano and other finery in proportion; but they shortly find themselves at the foot of the ladder, too proud to beg and too lazy to work. What then is the result? Some resort to stealing, robbery, arson or murder, and are sent to the penitentiary or the gallows. While others, in desperation, seek refuge in death, and commit suicide rather than reform. There is no doubt that this fast living produces more crimes, murders and suicides than any other single cause.

Young married people who are much too poor to afford it, yet for the sake of being fashionable, take an expensive bridal tour instead of saving the money which they spend in that way to enable them to commence housekeeping. Such things as these will do for the wealthy, but it is manifest, that the poor cannot afford to "put on such airs." 'Tis an old adage, but nevertheless a true one, that it is "hard for an empty sack to stand upright," and if you continue taking out of the meal tub without putting into it, you must soon come to the bottom.

We would, therefore, earnestly endeavor to impress upon the minds of our young readers, the necessity of following our advice before financial ruin overtakes them, and of commencing at the foot of the ladder, and slowly and carefully ascending, as this is the only safe road to fortune and respectability. It is true, for human nature is a strange compound of good and evil, that many of their old time friends will pass them by unnoticed, but they must have the moral courage to disregard such persons, and to persevere in the course which they have mapped out. They will soon have cause to be thankful that such pretended friends, for they are no other, have withdrawn from their society, for they are only parasites, which live by taking from others the life-blood which sustains them.

The solid, sensible, wealthy people will never cast you off for using economy and living within your means, but will give you credit for your financial ability, and your wise and judicious actions will secure their confidence and respect, and they will be only too proud of your society.

PARTIES.

The women, in old times, had "quiltings" and "cotton pickings," and when the work was completed, the young men of the neighborhood would come in. They then engaged, until late at night, in a jovial dance and the old fashioned plays. Corn-shuckings, log-rollings, house-raisings and reapings took place at their proper seasons People living in a new country are more dependent upon one another than the inhabitants of an old country, and this caused them to be more accommodating and unselfish than they are at the present time.

Corn-shuckings were lively times with the colored men, who would amuse themselves, during their work, by singing "corn songs." They would frequently separate the corn into two piles, and dividing the company into two parties, each party would choose a captain, and have an exciting race. The party which first completed the shucking of their pile, would claim the privilege of carrying the owner around the house on their shoulders, and place him at the head of the supper table.

At all of these frolics they usually had whisky to enliven the occasion, and some of the men would occasionally get quite lively, but very little drunkenness ever occurred. Many married people would engage in the dances, and seem to enjoy themselves as much as the single ones. They had colored musicians who most of the time played upon the violin, making music which was quick and lively.

Christmas was duly celebrated, the whole week being occupied in such sports as hunting, dancing and playing, at parties given in the neighborhood. The colored people, Christmas week, being a holiday to them, turned themselves loose, and enjoyed themselves as much as their owners.

The people at that day, as at the present, had their fashions. They were different, it is true, but the fashionable class, especially in the towns, adhered as closely to them as they do at the present time. Although pictures and descriptions of the old fashions appear queer and almost laughable to the people of the present day, yet we have often been assured that they were more comfortable and pleasant in every respect than those which curse the country now.

HISTORY OF COOPER COUNTY

CHAPTER XIII.

Different Towns in Cooper County, and Description of Each.

BOONVILLE.

BOONVILLE, the county seat of Cooper county, is located on the south bank of the Missouri river, about 230 miles west of St. Louis by water, and 187 miles by rail. It is surrounded by a beautiful and fertile country, inhabited by an intelligent, enterprising and thrifty population, and it has a very good local trade. It is celebrated for its educational advantages, its healthy location and its "vine clad hills." It has a large and commodious public school building and grounds, costing about $40,000, where the public school has been in successful operation for the last ten years. Also a good colored school, taught in a separate building. It has two male and two female schools where the higher branches of education are taught with commendable success. There are, besides, a good Catholic school and several other select schools for smaller children. Here children can obtain a good edncation and moral training without the expense of going away from home.

The Missouri, Kansas & Texas railway crosses the river here, on the great iron bridge, putting the city in direct communication with the lakes at Chicago, and the Gulf of Mexico at Galveston, Texas. And the Osage Valley & Southern Kansas railroad connects Boonville with the Missouri Pacific railroad at Tipton.

This town was laid off by Asa Morgan and Charles Lucus, and the plat filed on the first day of August, 1817.

It was surveyed by William Ross. The first lots were sold in 1819. A donation of fifty acres was made by Morgan and Lucus to Cooper county, was accepted by the commissioners, and the county seat located thereon. The first donation lots were sold in 1821.

THE EARLY HISTORY OF BOONVILLE.

Mrs. Hannah Cole, mother of Capt. Samuel Cole, made the first settlement on a part of the land on which Boonville is located, in the year 1810, and took a pre-emption, which she sold to Bird Lockhart and Henry Carroll, January 25th, 1819, for a trifle. The first settler in the old limits of Boonville was Gilliard Roupe, who built his residence on the lot now owned and occupied by Capt. James Thompson, on the south side of Spring street, near the cement factory. (This information was obtained from Samuel Cole, William Gibson and Judge McFarland.) The stream in the western portion of the "old town" was called from his name, "Roupe's Branch." The next was a ferry house, built by Roupe, at the mouth of the above branch, where he had a ferry landing. The first ferry was kept by the widow Cole's boys. There were several houses built on the flat below the branch, extending south as far as the corner of Morgan and Second streets, before the town was located.

A Frenchman named Reubadeaux kept the first store in Boonville, in a cabin built of poles. Shortly afterwards a man named Nolin kept a grocery on the flat, at the mouth of the branch; Mrs. Reavis and William Bartlett kept boarding houses in the same locality; and Thomas Rogers built a house on the corner of High and Second streets, and used it as a residence, hotel and store.

This part of the town was mostly built in 1816 and 1817.

From the best evidence that can be had from old citizens, the first houses built after the town was laid off, were two brick houses still standing on Morgan street, one east of the jail, and the other east of and near the Central National bank, built by Asa Morgan. Some other old houses, now standing, are Dr. Triggs, on Morgan street, and a log house on the north side of High street, on the corner of Seventh street, occupied by a colored woman by the name of Carter; also a brick house on High street, northeast of court house, built by Hon. R. P. Clark, and now owned by Joseph and William Williams.

The next merchants after Reubedeaux, were Jacob Wyan and Archie Kavanaugh, who had a store and residence, north of the court house square. The other early merchants were McKenzie, Bonsfield, Col. Thornton, Mrs. Dobbins, Thomas M. Campbell, and Judge C. H. Smith. The next hotel was built by Justinian Williams, afterwards sold to John Dade. It is still standing, and used as a hotel, Mr. Secongost being the present proprietor. There was also a hotel on the lot north of the jail, now occupied by the residence of C. W. Sombart.

Among the earlier lawyers were, Peyton R. Hayden, Wm. S. Brickey, John B. Clark and Littleberry Hendricks. Robert P. Clark was the first post master. He was also Circuit and County Clerk, County Treasurer, School Commissioner and Executor, Administrator and Guardian of a number of estates; and last, but not least, a delegate to the Barton Convention, in 1820. All these offices he held at the same time, which the records will show, and they would not much more than support himself and family at that time.

Divine service was held then in private and school houses, having no churches. The first church built was the Methodist, about 1831; then the Presbyterian, both of them still standing. The first school house was a brick house, built near the residence of Dr. M. McCoy; and there was a populous graveyard near the same place. The remains of most of the dead were removed to other cemeteries. The early school teachers were Judge Abiel Leonard, Wm. H. Moore, Dr. Edward Lawton, and others. The ministers were Luke Williams, a Baptist; Justinian Williams, a Methodist; and Chamberlain, a Presbyterian.

James Bruffy was the first blacksmith. He made a cannon of wrought iron for the celebration of the 4th day of July, 1820, which was held in front of the present residence of Jesse Homan, on an old Indian mound still standing in his front yard. Mr. and Mrs. Jesse Homan were present at the time, and from them we have received the full particulars of the celebration, but there is not room enough to insert at this place. They also gave the details of a fight on Christmas day 1819, between the young men of Old Franklin and the Boonville boys. The former crossed the river on the ice for the express purpose as they termed it, "of cleaning out Boonville." The fight was a bloody one and lasted a long time. The old men of Boonville had to come to the rescue of their young men, and the contest for some time remained in doubt; but at last Boonville had to give way to superior numbers, there being but few inhabitants here then. There was no one killed or mortally wounded. But where is old Franklin now? Then the metropolis of Western Missouri. The seat of commerce, wealth, fashion and power, swept away by the turbulent waters of the Missouri river. The only house left is now owned by Mr. Wm. Smith, built in the suburbs of that once populous city. If the present generation were to go over there now, there would be nobody left to tell of the her former greatness and grandeur. The most of them have left this world of trouble, strife and turmoil, and gone, it is hoped, to a brighter and better world beyond the vale. Alas, time will tell. It waits for no man. Peace to their ashes. But their heroes will live in history and in grateful remembrance as long as time shall last.

The early physicians of Boonville were George C. Hart, N. Hutchison, Parks, McCutchen, Gale, Martyn, and others.

Some of the fashions worn by the gentlemen, were high stiff coat collars, padded with buckram, reaching half way up the back of the head, and five or six cravats covering the neck, and tall stove pipe hats, wide at the top tapering downwards. And the ladies wore large leghorn, and long sun bonnets, projecting about ten inches in front of their faces, so that you could not see a lady's face without placing yourself immediately in front of her, securely protecting their delicate faces from sunburn, and large tortoise shell combs, making a semi-circle on the back part of the head. They wore very long hair of their own growth, generally reaching half way down from the head to the ground. From five to six yards of calico were sufficient for a dress.

In the winter of 1818, while Dr. Hutchison and Mrs. Kelly (then Miss Lawless) were crossing from Old Franklin to Boonville on foot, when half way across, the ice broke and they both fell in. Another young gentleman close by helped her out, and the Doctor got out himself. Their condition was so perilous that the occurrence still lives in the memory of Mrs. Kelly, the only witness now living to what might have ended seriously.

MODERN HISTORY OF BOONVILLE.

Before the Missouri Pacific railroad was built, Boonville commanded the wholesale trade, and was the principal shipping point of Southwest Missouri, and Northern Arkansas—and Boonville is now no doubt, the best point for the location of manufactories in the West, having an abundance of timber suited for making furniture, farming implements, and all kinds of machinery, and also bountiful supplies of coal and cement rock of the best quality in the vicinity.

Boonville has a very large furniture factory, not now in operation, sufficient for the employment of fifty hands; also two furniture stores, and a cement factory. It has three potteries making large quantities of stone and earthenware. One of them has been in successful operation for many years. It has a large and extensive tobacco factory, manufacturing the very best chewing and smoking tobacco. These wares and tobacco are sold by wholesale, extending their trade over the west, half way across the continent, and down south into Arkansas and Texas. A woolen factory with an extensive trade; a glass factory, a machine shop, two gun smith shops, three flour mills, a foundry, not now in operation, several shoe shops, and stores, two cigar stores, five clothing stores, three tin stores, two jewelery stores, four drug stores, three breweries, ten dram shops, two dry goods stores, a large number of grocery and staple dry goods stores, four bakeries, six confectioneries, two restaurants, four notion stores, large number of bonnet and dress makers, one marble yard, three lumber yards, six carpenter shops, four brick yards, four wagon and two carriage shops, four plow manufactories, one agricultural store, about ten blacksmith shops, two abstract of titles, one saw mill, two banks, one National and one State. An excellent steam ferry across the Missouri river at Boonville. About twenty school teachers, about six music teachers, ten physicians, fifteen lawyers, eleven ministers of the gospel. The United States land office for this district of Missouri is located here. The public buildings are the court house, Thespian hall, City hall, a Masonic and Odd Fellows hall, county jail, city calaboose and workhouse. The Thespian hall is one of the largest and most substantial public buildings west of St. Louis. It has eleven churches: Methodist South, Presbyterian, Baptist, German Methodist, Catholic, Lutheran, Episcopal, Methodist colored, and two Baptist colored. The grape is cultivated very extensively. It has about seven wine gardens. Boonville is noted for its graded and macadamized streets, its extensive paved sidewalks, its orchards, gardens, shade trees and beautiful front yards, decorated with flowers and evergreens, and last, but not least, its substantial buildings and its solid wealth. It has never had a mushroom growth, but has slowly and steadily increased in population and wealth, and has never taken a step backwards. She has lavished her money for internal and local improvement, and has always promptly paid her honest debts even before they became due.

Her bonds are now at a premium and her debt is only $69,000, which was contracted in honesty and good faith, and will be promptly and fully paid. Rate of taxation in 1875 was only $1.20 on the $100.

Boonville has at least four citizens, each of whom could pay the whole debt of the City and have plenty left to maintain their families.

But if in the course of human events our city should go down amidst the general crash of financial ruin, we will bury her decently without a stain of dishonor on her children; and if they should inherit no fortune from us, we shall leave them a better inheritance which money cannot purchase—honor and integrity. And if we must, we will go down with our colors flying and these words emblazened thereon.

MANUFACTORIES.

Before closing the history of Boonville, we deem it our duty to say something to her people on the subject of manufactories. We frequently hear our citizens wonder why Boonville does not increase more in population and wealth, being the most beautiful and healthy city in the State, or perhaps in the West. And it has the M. H. & T. railway extending from the lakes in the North, to the gulf in the South, and the branch road connecting Boonville with the Missouri Pacific at Tipton; and the Missouri river which will always give cheap transportation to and from Boonville. Then she has coal, timber, and cement rock in the immediate neighborhood of the best quality in great abundance, and an inexhaustible supply of water from the Missouri river, and two small streams on each side of the city. Then, why does not Boonville improve? We answer that it is for the want of manufactories. That before railroads were constructed in our State, Boonville was a great commercial point. Every depot is now a commercial point. You can no longer depend upon commerce to build up this or any other city. The secret now in building a town is to *create* something for laboring men to do that will pay both the employer and employee. You will thereby have a population, and prosperity in proportion thereto. You must establish and maintain in your city manufactories. That is the only hope for the prosperity of this city or any other. The day is past for building cities by commerce alone. If Boonville had work for 20,000 people, she would have them here in one month, and the whole community would prosper. And bear in mind that it is labor that makes the town and country. But you will answer how are we to do this? Have we not tried and failed more than once? We know that is true, but *try again*, keep trying, and you will succeed. Don't give up the ship as long as a plank is left. If others succeed why not you? You must start right, and have men of experience, energy and honesty at the head of affairs. The trouble is that you are waiting for capitalists to come and build up your town. Let us tell you that you will wait forever. You must first put *your own* shoulders to the wheel. How can you expect strangers to invest their capital in something that you are afraid of yourselves. Providence is always on the side of those having pluck and energy enough to help themselves.

These remarks will apply to Otterville, Bunceton, Pilot Grove and other towns. If they will follow this advice and Boonville lies still, they will soon find themselves ahead of her. We have tried old fogyism long enough to be fully satisfied with it. Now let us try something else, and if a stranger comes among us to locate, let us take him by the hand and welcome him in his new home, and he will write back to his old home telling his friends what a fine country and clever people he has found, and they will also be induced to cast their lots among us.

OTTERVILLE

Otterville is located on the Missouri Pacific railroad, in the southwestern part of the county. It has an abundance of timber and water, and would be a good location for manufactories. It was incorporated in 1857. It has a good public school building, in successsful operation for ten years; also a good select female school, in a good brick building, belonging to Mrs. A. M. Drennan, proprietress; four churches, a Masonic and Odd Fellows hall, two colored churches, and about fourteen stores. The houses in the business portion of the town are substantial brick structures; its population is about 800. Lead abounds in large quantities in the vicinity. It is the largest and most important town in the county except Boonville. It is surrounded by a rich and fertile ccuntry, and an industrious, thrifty and wealthy population. [See chapter xv.]

BUNCETON.

Bunceton is located on the Osage Valley & Southern Kansas railroad, fourteen miles south of Boonville. It has one church, a Masonic hall, an excellent flour mill, about six stores, two shoe shops, one tailor shop, two drug stores, three physicians and one lawyer. It is surrounded by excellent timber, good coal mines, and cement rock near. It was located in 1869, and has a population of about four hundred. It also has an excellent high school, taught by Prof. Cully, with commendable success.

PILOT GROVE.

Pilot Grove is situated on the Missouri, Kansas & Texas railway, about twelve miles southwest of Boonville, and was located in 1873. It has a rapid growth, and bids fair to make a very important town. It has one church and Odd Fellows hall. It has about six stores, two blacksmith shops, one wagon shop, one drug store. It is located in a thickly populated country. The soil is excellent and the people prosperous. It has a good flour mill near by. Its population is about 250.

PLEASANT GREEN is located on the Missouri, Kansas & Texas railway, about eighteen miles from Boonville; has two stores and one drug store. It is in a good timbered country; has one church and school house convenient to the town, and is an important shipping point.

NEW PALESTINE is situated on the Osage Valley & Southern Kansas railroad, about twelve miles south of Boonville. It has one store and one blacksmith shop, and about one hundred inhabitants.

BELLINGSVILLE is a station on the Boonville branch, about six miles south of Boonville, and has one store. It is in a heavily timbered country, and has an abundance of excellent cement rock.

BELL AIR, two and one-half miles west of New Palestine, has one store, a school house and church, a blacksmith shop and post office, and is located in one of the most wealthy and educated portions of the county.

CLARK'S FORK postoffice is situated nine miles southeast of Boonville, and has one elegant mill and one store, surrounded by a good wheat country.

CLEAR CREEK postoffice, sixteen miles southwest of Boonville, has one store, two churches and two school houses.

CONNER'S MILL postoffice, eight miles east of Boonville, is situated in a good wheat growing country.

GOOCHE'S MILL postoffice, twelve miles east of Boonville, has one store and one blacksmith shop. It is celebrated for its salt lick near by, and mostly called Big Lick, which is the place James Cole and James Davis killed two Indians in 1812.

HARRISTON, a station and postoffice on M. K. & T. R. R., fifteen miles southwest of Boonville, was located by Dr. N. W. Harris in 1873; has two stores and one blacksmith shop. It is in a very fertile and beautiful prairie country, and is an important shipping point.

LAMINE postoffice, fourteen miles west of Boonville, has two stores, and is surrounded by a very fertile country settled 64 years ago.

LONE ELM postoffice has one store and a blacksmith shop. It is located in very fertile prairie land, and the people are in a very prosperous condition.

OVERTON, situated eleven miles east of Boonville, has a post office, several stores and a blacksmith shop. It is situated on the Missouri river opposite Rocheport. It has a ferry across the Missouri river. It is an important shipping point, surrounded by heavily timbered land, soil very rich. Wheat of the very best quality is successfully raised on the hills South of the town.

PRAIRIE HOMES postoffice, eighteen miles southeast of Boonville, has one store and two schools—one public, and one a private boarding school, kept by Prof. Slaughter. It is also surrounded by a very fine wheat country. Prof.

Slaughter is one of the most successful teachers in the county.

VERMONT, a station and postoffice on the Osage Valley & Southern Kansas railroad, three miles south of Bunceton, and seventeen miles south of Boonville, has one store and one blacksmith shop. It is located on high prairie, which is not surpassed in fertility and beauty by any portion of the county.

CLIFTON, a station and postoffice on the Missouri, Kansas & Texas railway, is located near the Pettis county line, surrounded by a timber and prairie country, has one store and blacksmith shop. It is an important shipping point.

PISGAH is located in the southeast part of Cooper county, about seventeen miles from Boonville. It is the oldest town in the county except Boonville; located about 1830. The Hon. David Jones being the first settler. It has two churches, the Christian and Baptist. It has two or three stores and blacksmith shops, two physicians and one lawyer. It has heavy timber on the south, and beautiful and fertile prairies on the north. It and its vicinity has long been noted for the intelligence and refinement of its inhabitants, and its early, moral and religious training. There, in early days, at the Pisgah church, the gospel was preached by such good old Christians, as the Revs. John B. Longden, Kemp, Scott, and others, who have long since been gathered to their fathers, but their words of wisdom and religious influence are not lost. It is there where Richard D. Bonsfield, an English gentleman, one of the oldest and most successful merchants in Central Missouri, resided, having followed that business in Old Franklin, Boonville and Pisgah, in a very early day. He has long since retired on a princely fortune, honored and respected by all who know him

OLD PALESTINE.

Old Palestine was laid off by Michael Son in the year

1833. It was located about one mile west of New Palestine, and twelve miles southwest of Boonville. It was for many years the voting precinct of Palestine Township, and always voted the Whig ticket.

Michael Son built the first house in Old Palestine, and in it kept what was then called a "grocery." Judge John Briscoe and his son Wm. M., built the second house which was used as a storehouse. Michael Son, Isaac Lionberger, Ward and Parsons, Dr. Samuel J. Tutt and T. P. and Jas. Bell were the earliest merchants of this town. At this place James Taliaferro had a saddle shop, and Jacob Schutler, Taylor, Hammer and some others had blacksmith shops. Alexander Evans, Judge J. Hazell, and Sebrom, who were mechanics, were among the very early settlers. J. Lawrence Stephens, R. J. Parrish and Chas. F. Moore were among the last merchants. Old Palestine was indeed, for many years a good business place.

At this place in the early history of the county, the political conventions and meetings of the county were frequently held; also justice's court, and company, regimental, general and drill musters. The sporting classes of the community had at different times during the year horse and foot races.

The citizens at that day were very lively, gave much of their time to enjoyment and had their jokes and their fun. They were generally accustomed to meet at Old Palestine on Saturday, and after their week's work was completed, and had a good time generally. They would sometimes settle disputes by going in on their "muscle," and after the fight had been finished, the two contestants would make friends.

Two of the best fighters of the neighborhood, were "Bill" Hedrick and Joseph Wrench. They "locked horns" at last. "Bill" was a large, tall, rawboned man, and Wrench was low and heavy set. Wrench got the better of the fight, which was terrible while it lasted. The best citizens of the neighborhood were in sympathy with Wrench, for he was a very quiet, peaceable man, and would fight only in self-defense; but Hedrick was inclined to be overbearing in his conduct towards others, in other respects, a jolly, clever fellow.

One day while Hedrick was sitting on his horse in Old Palestine, a number of those with whom he had fought, clubbed together and gathered around him with the intention of giving him a good thrashing, and became quite noisy in their threatenings against him. He remained quiet until they had somewhat subsided, when he remarked: "Gentlemen, are you going to whip me?" "Yes, we are," they answered. "Well," said he, "if that is the case, I'll not remain to see it; so I bid you good bye!" He then put spurs to his horse, pulled off his hat, waved it in defiance, and galloped away.

Another anecdote: A. and B. were about to fight. A. was making for B., and B. was backing all the time, keeping out of striking distance, yet appearing greatly excited. At this time his friends came up, and said, "Go it, B., pitch into him, B., and we will back you!" B then remarked, "I'm not afraid of any man, if I am, —— me." This caused a general laugh from the crowd, and broke up the fight.

A drill muster which lasted for three days took place at Old Palestine some time during the year 1841. On the first day, one of the officers imbibed pretty freely, and commenced cutting up and quarreling with some of the citizens. Some of those who had gathered to see the muster, concluded that he would be a good subject out of whom to have some fun. So they organized a mock court, making Dr. William Moore, judge, and another one of the citizens, constable.

The officer, who by this time had become pretty tight, was arrested by the pretended constable, with what appeared to be a regular writ, on a charge of attempting to kill some of the citizens. He thinking all this a *terrible reality*, engaged one of the bystanders to defend him, and tremblingly asked his lawyer if he thought he could save him. The attorney replied, that it was a hard case, and that he feared that nothing could save him, as the evidence against him was so strong, although he promised to use his best efforts in his defense.

The "Prosecuting Attorney" commenced the testimony for the State, and the "Judge" asked the first witness if he thought the accused had any intention of killing any person, and casually remarked: "If that was the case, *he would have him hung before night*. This remark caused the prisoner to turn pale, and tremble with fear. After the taking of the testimony was concluded, the attorney for the State made his speech, asking in it, that the prisoner be hung without delay, as they had clearly proved that he was guilty as charged. While the defendant's attorney was speaking, strongly pleading for his client's life, some one, under the guise of friendship, whispered to the prisoner, that the only way to save his life, was to jump out of the back window and make for the woods. He accordingly, while, as he supposed, the attention of the audience was directed towards his attorney, jumped out of the window, mounted his horse which happened to be standing near by, and galloped away as fast as his horse could go, with the crowd shouting after him. Along the road, on his way home, he was seen passing several houses under whip.

Although he was afterwards told that all that had passed was intended as a joke, it had so much the appearance of reality that he could not be persuaded that it was a joke, and never returned to that part of the country again.

Another anecdote will suffice for Old Palestine. There came to this place a fast young man from some of the Eastern States, whom we will call "Curtis W." One day he had a fight at that place with another young man; got the better of him, and then said: "Gentlemen, I have fought over fourteen States, and this is the first man I ever whipped." Many other like occurrences which took place at this famous old town might be related, but no more space can be spared from the general history for that purpose.

Old Palestine was laid off on a high, beautiful prairie, almost surrounded by timber, and its location is considered very healthy. D. E. Putnam, Alexander Evans, Darius Day, Daniel Hickerson, Lovel Patterson, and two other families are all that are left in this once populous village, D. E. Putnam being the mayor, and Daniel Hickerson city clerk.

HISTORY OF COOPER COUNTY

CHAPTER XIV.

Early History of the Different Townships in Cooper County, which could not be included in the General History of the County.

BLACK WATER TOWNSHIP.

This township is a peninsular, being almost entirely surrounded by the Lamine and Blackwater rivers. The soil is rich and exceedingly productive. The bottom land is low and swampy, and the ridge land fertile and susceptible of early cultivation. In the bottom, corn and timothy are grown in large quantities; on the ridge land, corn, wheat, oats, tobacco, potatoes, and all kinds of garden vegetables are produced in great abundance. The different kinds of wood are ash, beach, black oak, black walnut, cherry, cottonwood, elm, maple, hickory, redbud, sugar tree, white oak, and white walnut.

The minerals which are found in this township, are iron, which appears in large deposits, and lead which crops out on every hillside.

There are, in this township, six salt and a great number of fresh water springs. Salt was successfully manufactured at these springs as early as 1808, and from that time till 1836 the manufacture of it was carried on pretty extensively by Heath, Bailey, Christie, Allison and others. There are four public schools for white, and one for colored children, supported by the inhabitants of this township.

There are two churches in this township; one a Cumberland Presbyterian church, established in 1850; and the other a Baptist church, established in 1853

There is at this time no store or mill in the township, although both are much needed by the citizens. There are two warehouses, from which the surplus productions of the township are shipped.

There is one physician, Dr. Thomas E. Staples, and three ministers of the gospel, viz: N. T. Allison, Jr., Baptist, Robert Crockett, Cumberland Presbyterian, and C. Q. Shouse, Christian.

William Christie and John G. Heath temporarily settled in this township in 1808, but only remained long enough to manufacture a small quantity of salt, when they returned down the river. James Broch, the first permanent settler, arrived in 1816; Enoch Hambrich came in 1817; David Shellcraw, in 1818, and planted an acre of cotton which yielded very well. George Chapman, the father of Mrs. Caleb Jones, in 1818; Nathaniel T. Allison, Sr., in 1831; Fleming Marshall and Robert Clark, in 1832; Nathaniel Bridgewater, in 1835, and Edmund M. Cobb and Larkin T. Dix, in 1838.

The above information was obtained from N. T. Allison, Sr., and his son, the Rev. N. T. Allison, Jr., for which we are grateful.

BOONVILLE TOWNSHIP.

As an extensive history of the City of Boonville has already been given, it is exceedingly difficult to give a separate history of the township without a repetition of something which has appeared in the history of the city. The first settlers of the township were Stephen and Hannah Cole, who settled there in the year 1810.

The settlers who arrived previous to the year 1815, were Giliad Rupe, Muke Box, Delany Bowlin, William Savage, James Savage, John Savage, and Walter Burress; and in 1815, Umphrey and William Gibson.

Those who settled in this township between the years

1815 and 1820, were William McFarland, John S. and Jesse McFarland, George, Samuel and Alexander McFarland, William Mitchell, James Bruffee, Robert P. Clark, Joseph and William Dillard, Littleberry Hendricks, Wm. Bartlett, Jesse Ashcraft, Russell Edgar, John M. Bartlett, Abram Gibson, Thomas Twentyman, James Dillard, Jacob Newman, William Potter, Frederick Houx, William Poston, George Potter, Benj. L. Clark, John J. Clark, Kyra Dunn, K. McKenzie, Marcus Williams, James, Robert and Alexander Givens, Jacob Chism, John B. Lucus, Charles B. Mitchell, Nicholas McCarty, Lewis Edgar, John B. Seat, Jacob McFarland, James McCarty, William Ross, Abiel Leonard, Joseph W. Bernard, James McFarland, Ephraim Ellison, John Roberts, Thomas Mitchell, Reuben George, Fleming G. Mitchell, Jesse Thomas, Asa Morgan, Peter B. Harris, James Chambers, Benj. F. Hickox, William H. Curtis, William W. Adams, John D. Thomas, William Lillard, James H. Anderson, Peyton R. Hayden, John S. Brickey, Peyton Thomas, David Adams, Luke Williams, John Potter, Andrew Reavis, David Reavis, Jonathan Reavis, Jesse Homan, John H. Moore, Green B. Seat, W. D. Wilson, Thomas Rogers, Mrs. Mary Reavis, William Chambers, James Chambers and Justinian Williams.

There were, no doubt, many others not mentioned above, who resided in this township between the above years, but their names are unknown, and perhaps some few of those mentioned above resided in some other township. The above list was taken from the poll books of the township for 1820, and of course those who lived there at that time, but did not record their votes, are not included in the same.

From the best information that can be obtained, all the persons mentioned in the foregoing list of early settlers are dead, except William Gibson, John S. and Jesse McFarland, Lewis Edgar, Jonathan Reavis and Jessie Homan.

Mr. John Kelly and Mrs. Tibitha Kelly were there frequently between 1818 and 1820. They then resided in Old Franklin, but are now living in Boonville. Of the ladies now living who resided in Boonville township previous 1820, are Mrs. Jesse Homan, Mrs. Frederick Houx, Miss Mary Reavis, Mrs. B. F. Hickox, Mrs. Jennie Wadley and Mrs. Dikie Dallas, the two last mentioned being the sisters of Samuel Cole.

Wm. McFarland, the first Sheriff of Cooper county, was born in Buncome county, North Carolina, in the year 1778. He emigrated to St. Genevieve, now St. Francis county, Missouri, in 1811, and from thence to Cooper county, and on the 16th day of October, 1816, he settled on the north side of the Petite Saline Creek, where Joseph Byler now resides. He had two neighbors living on the south side of the creek whose names were John Glover and Warden. He had no other neighbors nearer than the immediate neighborhood of Boonville. He was in 1818 or 1819 a member of the Territorial Legislature from the southern district of Howard county, which included that part of the county lying south of the Missouri river. He was a farmer, a man of great energy, an affectionate husband and father and a good neighbor. He died in the year 1834.

Benjamin F. Hickox was born in the State of New York, and emigrated to this country at an early day. He was elected a member of the Legislature from Cooper county in 1822, 1824 and 1838, and County Court Justice from Sept. 24, 1844, to Nov. 2, 1846. He was also one of the Commissioners to superintend the building of the first court house at Boonville. He was a successful farmer, an affectionate husband and father, an honest, upright man, an excellent neighbor, and very charitable to the poor, never turning them away from his door without relieving their wants. He died about twenty years ago, beloved and respected by all who knew him.

Luke Williams, a Baptist preacher, was a farmer, and resided about five miles west of Boonville. He is celebrated as being the first preacher in Cooper county, having located there several years before the county was organized.

Justinian Williams was born in Bath county, Virginia, and while young emigrated to Kentucky and there married. He then moved to Howard county, Missouri, from thence to Cooper county, and settled at Boonville in the year 1818. In this year he located the first Methodist church in Cooper county. He was a cabinet maker by trade, and followed that business for several years, preaching and organizing churches at intervals. He was also the local preacher at Boonville for several years. In the year 1834 he built a steam boat called the "Far West," about two miles above the mouth of the Bonne Femme Creek, in Howard county, and was the commander of the same for some time. During that year he emigrated to Tennessee, where he died.

Marcus Williams, the first mayor of the City of Boonville, was born in Bath county, Virginia, and when young moved to Kentucky; from thence to Boonville, Cooper county, Missouri. He was a brick mason by trade, and manufactured the first bricks ever made in Cooper county, having opened a lime kiln in the western part of Boonville. At the "Vollrath" Place in 1840, he made the first stoneware ever manufactured in western Missouri. He emigrated to California at the time of the gold excitement in 1849, and settled at San Jose, where he died about the year 1860.

This township at the time of its first settlement was partly prairie, in the west and southwest, but after the lapse of many years, the prairie became timbered land. Great fears were entertained by the early settlers about the scarcity of timber, but it is believed that there is at the present time, more timber in the county than there was fifty years ago.

This was the first township of the county which was settled, and for many years few ventured outside, or at most, far from its boundaries. The early settlers believed that the prairie land was only suited for grazing and not fit for cultivation. In the year 1830, a few persons ventured to cultivate prairie land, and finding it so productive, many other farmers settled on the prairies, and at this time nearly all of the prairie land is under fence, and is covered with the most valuable farms in the county.

Persons in the early history of the township settled near the river, that affording the only means by which they could ship their surplus productions to market. But the building of railroads has revolutionized everything. Land near the river has become less valuable, and that on the prairies, which a few years ago was considered almost worthless, has now become more valuable. Timbered land is still preferred by many farmers, for the reason that it is much better for the growing of wheat, and equally as good, if not better, for other productions.

The soil of this township is very productive, and is especially excellent for growing fruit. It has also large quantities of coal of a good quality, which could be shipped at large profit.

CLARK'S FORK TOWNSHIP.

From the best information that can be obtained, John Glover was the first settler of this township, he having located there in the year 1813. He built a round log cabin on the south bank of the Petite Saline Creek, and cleared a few acres of ground near where Rankin's mill now stands, but nothing is known of his history.

The next settlers were Zepheniah Bell and John C. Rochester. The last named gentleman was the grandson of the founder of the City of Rochester, New York, who having lost a princely fortune by having to pay a large security debt, sought seclusion by emigrating to this country and the society of the people, who required nothing, save honesty and industry, to admit a person into their social circles. He married Miss Sally Kelly, a beautiful and accomplished lady, the daughter of James Kelly, who was an honored soldier of the Revolution. He was well educated, considering the times, and his occupation was that of a farmer. He died in the township many years ago. Mr. Bell was also a farmer, a good citizen, and an honest man. He has been dead many years.

Some of the other old citizens were Joshua H. Berry, William Read, William and Reuben George, Clayton Hurt, Samuel Carpenter, Edward, Andrew and Charles Robertson, James, Robert and John Johnston, Samuel, Robert and William Drinkwater, Gabriel Fitsworth, William Shipley, Acrey Hurt, Peter Carpenter, George Crawford, George W. Weight and Martin Jennings.

Geo. Crawford was the first Assessor of Cooper county, which office he filled for many years; he was also a member of the Legislature from this county. Judge George W. Weight was born in Dutchess county, New York, on the 22nd day of February, 1784. When quite young, having been, by the death of his parents, left alone in the world, he emigrated to West Virginia, and from thence to Ross county, Ohio, where he married Miss Elizabeth Williams. In 1820, he with his family moved to Howard county, Missouri. In 1822 he settled in Clark's Fork township, Cooper county, and lived there until his death, which occurred on the 29th day of January, 1857. He taught school in West Virginia, Ohio and Cooper county; he was a good violinist, and in his early days taught dancing school. He was Judge of the County Court and County

Surveyor of Cooper county for many years. He also represented the county in the State Legislature.

It will be observed that some of the old settlers mentioned above, really lived in that part of Clark's Fork township, which was lately annexed to Boonville township. The Petite Saline Creek was formerly the dividing line between the townships above mentioned, and but little information, as to the location of the old settlers, in respect to this dividing line could be obtained; therefore the writers in placing those above mentioned in this township, were compelled mainly to rely upon their own knowledge, which may, in some cases, prove to be inaccurate.

It may be safely stated, that the average farming land within this township is equally as productive as that of any other in the county. There is a little poor land in the township, and the farmers are generally prosperous. There is no town located within its limits.

CLEAR CREEK TOWNSHIP.

Among the early settlers of this township, were James Taylor, who had three sons, William, John and James. He emigrated from the State of Georgia to New Madrid, Missouri, where he witnessed the long series of earthquakes which occurred in 1811; from thence he moved to Cooper county, in the year 1817. He had a large plantation, raised and always had on hand large quantities of corn, upon which, when cribbed, he placed a certain price, and would not dispose of until he could get for it what he demanded. He was a very eccentric, plain, matter of fact kind of man, and was charitable to such as would work, but he had no patience with a lazy, trifling or profligate man. He was also a good judge of human nature.

At one time when corn was very scarce throughout the county, and very little could be had for love or money, two men came to Mr. Taylor's house asking to purchase some corn, of which he had a large quantity, on credit, as neither of them had any money with which to pay. One was very poorly dressed, with his pants torn off below his knees, and what there was remaining of them, patched all over. The other was almost elegantly dressed. Mr. Taylor sold the poorly dressed man, on credit, all the corn he wished. He told the other one that "he could get no corn there, unless he paid the money for it, and that if he had saved the money which he had squandered for his fine clothes, he would have had sufficient to pay cash for the corn.

He had a large number of negroes, and required them, during the day, to perform a great deal of work. Shovel plows were mostly used in his day, and the wooden mole board just coming into use. It is related, that the shovels of Mr. Taylor's plows had, at one time, worn off very blunt, and he was very averse to buying new ones. So that one negro man plowed once around a field before he discovered that he had lost the dull shovel to his plow, the plow running just as well without as with it. He was a leader in the Baptist church, and was a devoted member, a kind neighbor, and a strictly honest man.

Jordan O'Bryan, a son-in-law of James Taylor, was also one of the early settlers of this township. He was born in North Carolina, moved to Kentucky when young, and to Cooper county in 1817. As will be seen from the abstract, he was elected to the State Legislature in 1822, 1826, 1834 and 1840, eight years in all; in 1844 he was elected State Senator for four years. He was a fluent speaker, a man of no ordinary talents, and an uncompromising Whig. In about 1830 he removed to Saline township, where he remained until his death.

Charles R. Berry, the father of Finis E. Berry, Isaac Ellis and Hugh and Alexander Brown, are among the oldest citizens; others of a later date, were Herman Bailey,

William Ellis, Samuel Walker, A. S. Walker, H. R. Walker, Finis E. Berry, James and Samuel Mahan, the Rubeys, Jeremiah, William G., and Martin G. Phillips, Samuel Forbes, Ragan Berry, Hiram Dial, Samuel and Rice Hughes, and Willis Ellis.

Lamine river, the bottom lands of which are very fertile, forms the boundary line between this and Black Water townships. The greater part of the population are Germans, who have proved themselves to be a very industrious and thrifty people. They have mostly settled on the hills which the Americans thought too poor to cultivate, and have made them "blossom as the rose." They have succeeded in raising good crops, made good livings, and have been generally prosperous and happy. In the hills they cultivate the grape very successfully, and a large amount of wine is manufactured here every year. The Missouri, Kansas and Texas railroad runs about five miles through this township, furnishing the inhabitants transportation for their surplus productions.

KELLY TOWNSHIP.

This township, from the best information which can be obtained, was settled early in the spring of 1818. The first settlers were John Kelly, William Stephens, James D. Campbell, James Kelly, William J. Kelly, Caperton Kelly, William Jennings, Gen. Charles Woods, Philip E. Davis, Rice Challis, Hugh Morris, Jesse White, Hartley White, Jeptha Billingsley, Joshua Dellis, and William Swearingen.

James Kelly, who was one of the first settlers in this township, and the father of the other Kellys mentioned above, was a revolutionary soldier, and died in 1840 at an advanced age. John Kelly, Charles Woods, and James D. Campbell served as soldiers in the war of 1812. The Kellys came from Tennessee, and James D. Campbell from Kentucky.

William Jennings, who was the first preacher in the township, emigrated from Georgia to Cooper county in 1819. He had a large number of slaves, owned a large tract of land and was quite wealthy. He was for many years pastor of "Old Nebo" church, and was an honest man in his dealings with his neighbors.

James D. Campbell was an early Justice of the County Court and acted in the capacity of Justice of the Peace for many years. He was a prominent politician, always voting the Democratic ticket.

Gen. Charles Woods was for many years the leading Democrat in his neighborhood. He was a man of no ordinary ability, of pleasing address, and a liberal, high-toned gentleman. He died in 1874, at the advanced age of 78 years.

Joseph Reavis settled in this township in the year 1823. He, together with his sons, Lewis, William T., Jackson, and Johnston, for many years carried on the business of manufacturing wagons. They turned out excellent work, and their trade extended for many miles around; their wagons even being purchased by the Santa Fe traders.

Of the persons mentioned above, all are now numbered with the dead, except Johnston and William P. Reavis, and they were quite young when their father settled in the township.

There was no church within the limits of this township for many years, and the settlers attended the services at Pisgah and "Old Nebo."

The first school within this township of which there is any knowledge, was taught by Joseph S. Anderson, who came there about 1824. He was a young man with more than ordinary education, whose only earthly possessions were a horse, saddle and bridle, and a moderately good suit of clothes. A good school teacher being very much needed, he soon succeeded in making up a large school, and taught with great success until 1828, when he was elected sheriff of Cooper county. In 1830 he was re-elected sheriff, and in 1832, he was elected to the Legislature from Cooper county. Previous to his death, he became a large land holder and quite a wealthy man. His residence was on the hill north of Bunceton. The place at which he taught school was near the ground on which Hopewell church is located.

For many years afterwards a school was taught at the same place, by Mr. William Robertson, who was a very successful teacher. He has been for many years a very zealous minister of the Baptist church.

The first mill in this township was built by Robert McCulloch, the father of Judge Robert A McCulloch.

Rice Challis was a prominent Whig, and in respect to his politics stood almost alone in his neighborhood. He was a carpenter by trade, and resided near the present residence of Joseph Reavis. He died a short time ago.

The land of this township is at least three-fourths prairie, which is under fence and in a high state of cultivation. The soil is very productive, and the farmers are generally in good condition, many of them being very wealthy. The Pacific railroad lies a short distance south of the township, and the Osage Valley and Southern Kansas railroad runs eight miles directly through its center, affording the inhabitants easy facilities for the shipping of their productions.

Corn, grasses and oats are the principal productions, the farmers being principally engaged in raising stock, which affords them lucrative profits. It has, within its limits, several good public schools, which are taught from four to ten months in each year.

Kelly township always was and is now strongly Democratic, never having voted any other ticket from the time it was headed by Gen. Jackson to the present day. This township received its name from John Kelly, the first settler within its limits, and was formed from Moniteau and Palestine townships, in the year 1848.

LAMINE TOWNSHIP

was settled first in 1812, by a few pioneers. The very first settlers were David Jones, a revolutionary soldier, Thomas and James McMahan, Stephen, Samuel and Jesse Turley, Saunders Townsend and some others, who came soon afterwards.

Those who arrived later were John Cramer, Bradford Lawless, John M. David and William Reid, Hezekiah Harris, Elijah Taylor, John, Peter, Samuel and Joseph Fisher, William, Jesse and Moon, Rudolph Haupe, Isaac Hedrick, John Smelser, William McDaniel, Wyant Parm, Harmon Smelser, Samuel Larnd, Pethnel Foster, Julius Burton, Ezekiel Williams, and some others at present unknown.

In the year 1812 or 1813 there was a fort, called "Fort McMahan," built somewhere in this township, but the exact location could not be ascertained.

The soil of this township is excellent, and the inhabitants are in a prosperous condition. It is noted as one of the most wealthy townships in the county. It is bounded on the north by the Missouri river, on the east by the Lamine river, on the south by the Black Water river, and on the west by the Saline county line. It is noted for voting always almost unanimously in one way; it was anti-Democratic, until 1864, since which time it has been almost as strongly Democratic as it was Whig in days gone by.

Lead has been found and worked in paying quantities in this township. It has an abundance of timber of the very best quality, and a large quantity of lumber and cordwood is shipped every year by means of the Black Water and Lamine rivers. These streams abound with fish of very fine quality, and the Boonville market is principally supplied by them.

MONITEAU TOWNSHIP.

This township takes its name frome Moniteau Creek, which runs through the entire length of the township. Moniteau township has always, since its organization, voted the Democratic ticket.

It was first settled in 1818. It is uncertain who was the very first settler. But among the early settlers, were Thomas B. Smiley, Seth, Joseph, Waid and Stephen Howard, William Coal, James Stinson, Hawking Burress, David Burress, Charles Hickox, Samuel McFarland, Carrol George, James Snodgrass, Martin George, Mathew Burress, Jesse Martin, Alexander Woods, William Landers, Jesse Bowles, James Donelson, William A. Stillson, Samuel Snodgrass, James W. Maxey, Job Martin, James Jones, David Jones, Augustus K. Longan, Patrick Mahan, Valentine Martin, John Jones and John B. Longan.

Thomas B. Smiley was elected to the Legislature from Cooper county in 1820, with Thomas Rogers and William Lillard. He was a man of considerable information, a good historian, and possessed with more than ordinary education. He raised a large family of children, and died about the year 1836. He was honest and industrious, a strong friend to education, and an uncompromising Democrat.

David Jones settled at Pisgah at an early date, but the precise time is not known. Yet it was previous to the year 1820, as his vote was recorded in that year. He, with Archibald Kavanaugh, was elected to the State Legislature in 1828. He was re-elected Representative in 1830, 1832 and 1834; in 1836 he was elected State Senator for four years. He was defeated for this office by Reuben A.

Ewing in 1840; but in 1848 he was again elected to the State Senate, this making him a member of the General Assembly during a period of sixteen years. He was a Democrat, a prominent member of the Baptist church, a good citizen, and noted for his hospitality. He died about the year 1859, loved and respected by all who knew him.

Pisgah and Mount Pleasant churches were built by the Baptists at an early day, and were presided over by John B. Longan and Kemp Scott, who were both able preachers.

Augustus K. Longan moved to Cooper county in the year 1818, and was elected to the State Legislature in 1822. He was re-elected in 1844 and 1852, and served in that capacity for six years. He was the father of George Longan, the talented and distinguished minister of the Christian church.

The first school in this township as far as can be ascertained, was taught by James Donelson. He only professed to teach arithmetic as far as the "Double rule of Three."

The first mill was erected by a man named Howard, at what was afterwards known as "Old Round Hill." Judge C. H. Smith, and an Englishman named Summers, also kept a store at that place.

At a later day Patrick Mahan built a tread mill, which was a great improvement on the old style "Horse Mill." Mr. Richard D. Bonsfield kept a store at Pisgah at an early time. He first merchandised at Old Franklin, then at Boonville, and finally at Pisgah. He is still living at an advanced age.

HISTORY OF COOPER COUNTY.

CHAPTER XV.

Early History of the Different Townships, &c., Continued.

OTTERVILLE AND LEBANON TOWNSHIP.

The following history of the townships of Otterville and Lebanon was written by Mr. Thomas J. Starke, of Otterville, and was read by him on the 4th day of July, 1876, at a meeting of the citizens of that town. By his kindness, and at the request of many of the leading citizens of the above mentioned townships, the whole of the history, as read by Mr. Starke, is here inserted:

"At the solicitation of a few leading citizens of Otterville, the undersigned has prepared the following brief history of this place and vicinity since its first settlement up to the present time; embracing short biographical sketches of the lives and characters of some of the older citizens, together with facts and incidents of interest which have transpired in this county during the first period of its existence.

"It is not pretended by the author that the production possesses any peculiar merits of its own as affording information, other than of a strictly local character. Nor is it designed otherwise than for the entertainment and amusement of those who are more or less familiar with the history of the people, and incidents pertaining to this immediate neighborhood, and who, with many others of our inhabitants, of a later period, meet with us to-day, on this joyful and happy occasion—the one hundredth anniversary of the Independence of our common country.

"The writer does not lay claim to entire originality in the

production of these brief sketches, although he has been an eye witness to most of the occurrences presented, and personally acquainted with nearly all of the characters mentioned.

"He takes pleasure in acknowledging himself indebted to Messrs. Samuel Wear, George W. Smith, James H. Cline, John W. Parsons, Thomas C. Cranmer, and other old settlers who are here among us to-day, for much of the subject matter embraced in these pages of local history, and he refers to it for its authenticity.

"While it is apparent to all who may read this manuscript that this is only an obscure and insignificant village, situated in a remote corner of old Cooper, whose very existence is scarcely known beyond our own immediate neighborhood, yet to many of us who meet here to-day together, some of whom are descending the western slope of human life, *Otterville does possess* a name and a history, dear to us, though unknown and unnoticed by others.

"In presenting these sketches, it will perhaps be necessary to glance back at the first settlement of *New Lebanon*, six miles north of Otterville, as this neighborhood was peopled some time anterior to the settlements south and west of the Lamine.

"About the fall of 1819 and the spring of 1820, the following named persons moved to New Lebanon and into that neighborhood embracing a portion of the territory now known as Lebanon township, in Cooper county. This county then extended south to the Osage river, to wit:

"Rev. Finis Ewing, Rev. James L. Wear, John Wear, James H. Wear, who was the father of William G. Wear, of Warsaw, and Samuel Wear, now of Otterville; Alexander Sloan, Robert Kirkpatrick, Colin C. Stoneman, William Stone, Frederick Castell, Reuben A. Ewing, Jas. Berry, Thomas Rubey, Elizabeth Steele, sister of Alexander Sloan's wife, a man named Smiley, Rev. Laird Burns and his father John Burns, John Reed, Silas Thomas, Jas. Taylor, Hugh Wear, who was a brother of James L. and John Wear, James McFarland and Rev. William Kavanaugh.

"The Rev. Finis Ewing was a distinguished minister of the gospel, and one of the original founders of the Cumberland Presbyterian Church. He was from Kentucky; was ordained a minister in the year 1803, and in conjunction with Samuel McAdam and Samuel King, founded this church in 1810.

"The cause which gave rise to the establishment of this branch of the Presbyterian church was, that the mother church required her ministers to possess a classical education before ordination, which was by the new church not regarded as absolutely indispensable, though its ministers were required to cultivate a knowledge of the elementary branches of the English language.

"At this place these early pioneers pitched their tents, and soon began the erection of a rude building as a sanctuary, which, when completed, they called "New Lebanon," in contradistinction to the house in which they had sung and worshipped in the State from which they had formerly emigrated.

"It was built of hewed logs, and the settlers of this little colony united in the project, each furnishing his proportionate quota of the logs requisite to complete the building.

"These logs were double; that is each log was twenty-four feet in length, being joined in the middle of the house by means of an upright post, into which the ends were mortised, thus making the entire length of the church forty-eight feet, by thirty feet in width.

"This building served as a place of worship for many years, until about the time of the war, when the new and neat brick church of the present day, was erected on the site of the old one which was torn away.

"The members of this church constituted the prevailing religion of the neighborhood for many years; and most of the characters portrayed herein were connected with this denomination.

"The Rev. James L. Wear, was also for many years a Cumberland Presbyterian preacher. He was a good man, and lived close to New Lebanon, where Frank Asberry now lives. He died at the old mansion about 1868. He was a brother of John Wear, who first lived at New Lebanon at the place now owned by Mr. Majors; and afterwards at Otterville where Mr. Anson Hemenway now lives. The first school taught in Otterville, or in Otterville township, was taught by his son, known by the "sobriquet" of "Long George." They were originally from Kentucky, moved to Howard county in 1817, and afterwards to New Lebanon at the date above indicated.

"Samuel Wear, Sr., and James H. Wear were brothers, and came from Tennessee; the latter being the father of Wm. G., and Samuel Wear, Jr., as before stated, and lived at the place now occupied by William Walker. He was a successful farmer, and died in good circumstances.

"Samuel Wear, Sr., lived where Wesley Cook now lives, and sold a large farm there to Samuel Burke, late of this county.

"Alexander Sloan was from Kentucky, and settled the place now owned by Peter Spillers. He was the father of William Sloan, who died at Otterville several years ago, and also of the Rev. Robert Sloan, who was an eminent minister of the Cumberland Presbyterian church, and who married a daughter of the Rev. Finis Ewing.

"Robert Kirkpatrick was a Kentuckian, and lived near the New Lebanon graveyard. He died many years ago.

He was a Revolutionary soldier, and had a son named David, who was an able minister of the Cumberland church. David met his death by accident; he was thrown from a carriage, severely wounded, and afterwards died from the amputation of his leg.

"Colin C. Stoneman was from Kentucky, and lived at the old cabin still to be seen standing near Andrew Foster's place. He was a practitioner of medicine of the Thomsonian school, and died many years ago.

"William Stone was a Kentuckian, a plain old farmer, and lived on the farm now owned by the Rev. Minor Neale. He was a good man, and died at an advanced age.

"Rev. Frederick Casteel was a minister of the gospel of the Methodist church, and lived near the place now owned by Mrs. Abram Amick.

"Reuben A. Ewing, and his brother Irving Ewing, were Kentuckians, and lived east of Lebanon. The former was a successful farmer, a good man, and died at an advanced age, honored and respected.

"James Berry was also a Kentuckian, and one of the oldest settlers of this new colony. He lived where his son Finis E. Berry, now lives.

"Thomas Rubey was from Kentucky, and lived at Pleasant Green. Henry Small lived at the Vincent Walker place.

"Mr. Smiley was also a Kentuckian, and settled where Mr. Thomas Alexander now lives. Rev. Laird Burns was a Cumberland Presbyterian preacher, and lived where Mr. John P. Downs now lives, in what is known as the Ellis neighborhood.

"John Burns was his brother and lived close to New Lebanon. He was a soldier in the war with Great Britain, was present at the battle of New Orleans, and would often talk with pride about that great event; of the fearful roaring of the cannon, of the sharp whistling of the bullets, and the thrilling echoes of martial music, which stirred the hearts of the soldiers to deeds of valor, and enabled the brave army of General Jackson to achieve the glorious victory which ended the war with '*Old England.*'

"Rev. John Reid was also another minister of the Cumberland Presbyterian church, a Kentuckian; he first lived on Honey creek, and afterwards at so many different places, that for want of space in this brief sketch I dare not undertake to enumerate them. Suffice it to say, that he settled more new places in the neighborhood than any half dozen pioneers of the infant colony. He was a very eccentric character in his younger days, would fight at the "drop of a hat," and was never known to meet his match in a hand to hand combat. The writer of this sketch was intimately acquainted with him for many years, during the latter period of his life however, and can truly say he never knew a man of steadier habits, nor one more remarkable for strict rectitude of conduct, or exemplary piety. An anecdote is related of him and the Rev. Finis Ewing, which occurred in his younger days. It was told to me by Mr. Samuel Wear.

"Reid was driving a team for some man who was moving to this county with Mr. Ewing, who had ear bells on his six horse team. The young man liked the jingle of these bells so much that he begged Mr. Ewing to allow his teamster to divide with him, in order that he might share the music; but Mr. Ewing 'could not see it' and refused to make the division as requested. Whereupon Reed bought a number of old cow bells and hung one on each horse in his team, which soon had the effect of bringing the preacher to terms. He was so much annoyed with the discord produced by these coarse bells, that he soon proposed a compromise by giving Reid his sleigh bells, provided he would stop the cow bell part of the concert.

"Silas Thomas was another Kentuckian, and lived on Honey Creek, near where Lampton's saw mill stood a few years ago.

"James Taylor, better known as 'Old Corn Taylor,' lived in an old log cabin which may be still seen standing a short distance west of the Anthony Walker place. He was another remarkably eccentric character. He had a host of mules and negroes; always rode with a rope bridle, and raised more corn, and kept it longer than any half-dozen men in Cooper county. This he hoarded away in pens and cribs with as much care as though every ear had been a silver dollar, in anticipation of a famine, which, for many years he had predicted, but which, happily, never came, though the neighborhood was several times visited with great scarcity of that valuable commodity. Although he was miserly in this respect, yet during these times of scarcity, he would generally unlock his granaries, and, like Joseph of old, deal it out to his starving brethren, whether they were able to pay for it or not; that is, if he thought a man was industrious, he would furnish him with what corn he considered necessary; but tradition informs us that he invairiably refused the required boon to a man, who was found, on examination, to wear "patched breeches," especially if the patch happened to be in a particular locality, which indicated laziness.

"Hugh Wear was from Kentucky, and lived in the Ellis neighborhood. He was the father of the Rev. Wm. Bennett Wear, another Cumberland Presbyterian of considerable distinction. When his father, who was a Revolutionary soldier, enlisted, Hugh, although too young to enter the army, was permitted to accompany his father, and served, during the war, as a soldier, notwithstanding he was under the age prescribed for military duty. This was done to prevent his falling into the hands of the tories.

"Rev. William Kavanaugh was a Kentuckian, and another Cumberland Presbyterian minister of considerable note. It was said of him, that he could preach louder and longer than any of these old worthies.

"William Bryant was a Kentuckian, and was with Gen. Jackson at the battle of New Orleans. He first settled at New Lebanon, at the place which he afterwards sold to Finis Ewing; the old brick house where Mr. Kemp now lives. He then moved to the farm now occupied by Wm. B. Harlan.

"Samuel Miller was from Kentucky, and settled on the place now owned by Green Walker. He was a farmer, and afterwards moved to Cold Neck.

"There yet remains but one other man to notice who belonged to New Lebanon. He was a member of the numerous family of Smith, whose christian name I cannot now recall. He settled at a very early period on what is known as the Cedar Bluff, at a nice, cool, clear spring, not far from the place where Mrs. John Wilkerson now lives. Here he erected what was then called a 'band mill,' a species of old fashioned horse mill, so common in those days. It was connected with a small distillery at which he manufactured a kind of 'Aqua mirabilis,' with which the old folks in those days cheered the drooping spirits in times of great scarcity. But Mr. Smith never 'ran crooked.' He paid no license, and sold or gave away his delicious beverage without molestation from revenue agents, just as he deemed fit and convenient. Revenue stamps and revenue agents were unknown then, and good whisky (there was none bad then,) was not only considered harmless, but drinking hot toddies, eggnog and mint julips was regarded as a respectable, as well as a pleasant and innocent kind of amusement, and quite conducive to health.

I have thus briefly glanced at the early settlement in the vicinity of New Lebanon, and come now to treat of the colony which was planted south and west of the Lamine, and which was peopled at a subsequent period, known as Otterville township, and which will perhaps embrace a portion of the adjoining territory, included within the limits of Morgan and Pettis counties.

"Thomas Parsons was born in the State of Virginia in the year 1793; moved to Franklin, the county seat of Simpson county, Kentucky, about the year 1819, emigrated to this county in the fall of 1826, and settled at the place now owned by James H. Cline, northwest of Otterville. About the last of October of that year Parsons sold his pre-emption right to Absalom Cline, the father of James H. Cline. In 1826, at the time Mr. Parsons came to this neighhorhood, there were only three families living west of the Lamine in this vicinity. These were James G. Wilkerson, William Reed, and William Sloan.

"Mr. Parsons established the first hatter's shop south of Boonville, and was an excellent workman in that line. He was an honest, upright citizen, lived to a ripe old age, and was gathered to his fathers, honored and respected by all who knew him. At the time of his death, on the 7th day of September 1875, he was the oldest free mason in Cooper county, having belonged to that institution nearly three score years.

"William Reed mentioned above, was, perhaps, the first white man who settled in this neighborhood. He was a Tennesseean, and lived near the old camp ground, a little west of what was then known as the 'camp ground spring,' in the old field now owned by George W. Smith, a short distance southwest of the old graveyard. He was the grandfather of A. M. Reed, now of Otterville. He was remarkable for his strict integrity and exemplary piety.

"James G. Wilkerson was from Kentucky, and settled the farm now owned by George W. Smith, one mile west of Otterville. The old mansion stands, though almost in a complete state of dilapidation, to remind the passer by of the perishable character of all human labor. He sleeps with several other members of his once numerous family, on a gentle eminence a few yards south of the decayed and tottering tenement in which he spent many years of honest toil.

"William Sloan was the son of Alexander Sloan, mentioned in the notes pertaining to New Lebanon, was the last of the three mentioned above. He first settled the place where Charles E. Rice now lives, in 1826, but afterwards lived, until his death, at the place now owned by Joseph Minteer. He was always remarkable for his scrupulous honesty and piety.

"Elijah Hook was from Tennessee, and settled near where Henry Bender now lives, in 1827. He was a hunter and trapper, and obtained a subsistence for his family after the manner of Nimrod, his ancient predecessor, mentioned in the Bible as 'the mighty hunter.'

"James Brown was a Kentuckian, a farmer, a hard working man, and settled where T. C. Cranmer lives, in 1827. He also was a 'Nimrod,' and hunted with Daniel Boone.

"James Davis was a Tennesseean, and settled the place now known as the McCulloch farm, in 1827. He was an industrious farmer, and a great rail splitter.

"James Birney was a Kentuckian, and married the daughter of Alexander Sloan, of New Lebanon. He was a farmer, and a man of some note. He settled, in 1827, the farm where John Harlan now lives. He had a grandson, Alexander Birney, who was formerly a lawyer at Otterville.

"Frederick Shurley, the mightiest hunter in all the land round about Otterville, in 1827, settled the place now owned by his son Robert Shurley, southeast of Otterville. He was with General Jackson in the Creek war, and was present at the memorable battle of the Horse Shoe Bend, where the Indians, by the direction of their prophets, had made their last stand. He used to recount, with deep interest, the thrilling incidents connected with this muzzle to muzzle contest, in which over half a thousand red-skins were sent, by Jackson and Coffee, to their happy hunting grounds.

"Nathan Neal was a Kentuckian, and settled the old place near the Lamine, two miles north of Otterville, in 1827. He was an orderly, upright and industrious citizen.

"George Cranmer was born in the State of Delaware in 1801, moved to near Paris, Kentucky, while young, and to Boonville, Missouri, in the year 1828. He was a millwright and a very ingenious and skillful mechanic. He settled at Clifton in about 1832, and shortly afterwards he and James H. Glasgow, now living on the Petite Saline Creek, built what was known as Cranmer's, afterwards Corum's mill, precisely where the M. K. & T. railroad now crosses the Lamine. Cranmer named the place 'Clifton.' The principal mechanics who helped to build this mill were Ben Gilbert, Jim Kirkpatrick, Nat Garten, son-in-law of William Steele, Esq., a blacksmith named John Toole, Noah Graham and the renowned 'Bill' Rubey, known to almost all the old settlers south of the Missouri river. Cranmer lived first at the mill, and afterwards at what was long known as the John Caton place, where Thomas C. Cranmer was born in 1836. The old log cabin is still standing, as one of the very few old land marks yet visible, to remind us of the distant past. Cranmer died at Michigan Bluffs, California, in 1853.

"Another man will perhaps be remembered by some of our old citizens. He was crazy, and though harmless, used to wander about to the great terror of the children of those days. His name was John Hatwood.

"Clifton was once a place of memorable notoriety. In those early days it was not unfrequently called the 'Devil's Half Acre.' There was a grocery kept there, after the people began to manufacture poisoned whisky, which had the effect very often of producing little skirmishes among those who congregated there. It was not uncommon for those fracases to end in a bloody nose, a black eye, or a broken head. Happily, however, these broils were generally confined to a few notorious outlaws, whom the order-loving people would have rejoiced to know had met the fate of the cats of Kilkenny.

"There are many amusing incidents connected with the history of the place, but space forbids allusion to only one or two. A man by the name of Cox, who was a celebrated hunter and trapper in this neighborhood, was known as a dealer in tales, connected with his avocation, of a fabulous and munchausen character. There is a very high bluff just below the old mill; perhaps it is nearly five hundred feet high. During one of his numerous hunting excursions, Matthew met with a large bear, which, being slightly wounded, became terribly enraged, and attacked the hunter with his ugly grip before he had time to reload his rifle. This formidable contest between Bruin and Matthew occurred just on the verge of the fearful precipice above described, and every struggle brought them nearer and nearer, until they both took the awful leap, striking and bounding against the projecting crags every few feet, until they reached the bottom of the terrible abyss. You will now naturally say, "Farewell, Matthew!" but strange to relate, he escaped with a few slight scratches. The bear had, fortunately for Matthew, been on the under side every time they struck, till they reached the bottom, when he loosed his hold of the hunter and closed his eyes in death.

"Matthew Cox's tales were generally much like this, almost always terminating favorably to himself, and fatally to his adversaries. This anecdote gave the name of 'Matthew's Bluff,' well known to everybody in this neighborhood.

"Some time during the year 1832, the people of this neighborhood became terribly alarmed by the report that the Osage Indians were about to attack and massacre all the settlers in this vicinity. This report started first, by some means at old Luke William's on Cold Camp Creek. The people became almost wild with excitement. They left their plows in the fields, and fled precipitately in the direction of the other settlements towards Boonville. Some of them took refuge in a fort at Vincent Walker's, some at Sam Forbes', and others at Collin Stoneman's and Finis Ewing's. Hats and caps, shoes and stockings, pillows, baskets and bonnets might have been seen along the old military road to Boonville, lying scattered about in beautiful confusion all that day and the next, until the excitement had ceased. Fortunately the scare did not last long, as it was soon ascertained that the alarm was false, and that the Osage Indians had not only not contemplated a raid on the white settlements, but that they had actually become frightened themselves, and fled south of the Osage river. But the panic was complete and exceedingly frightful while it lasted. A fellow by the name of Mike Chism lived near the Bidstrup Place. Mike had a wife and two children. They were already preparing for flight. Mike's wife was on horseback and had one child in her lap and one behind her, and Mike was on foot.

"At this moment, a horseman came galloping up in great trepidation, and informed the little family that the Indians were coming by the thousands, and that they were already this side of Flat Creek. On receiving this intelligence, Mike, in great terror, said to his wife, *'My God! Sallie, I can't wait for you any longer,'* and suiting his actions to his words, he took to his scrapers in such hot haste that at the first frantic jump he made, he fell at full length, bleeding and trembling on the rocks. But the poor fellow did not take time to rise to his feet again. He scrambled off on 'all fours' into the brush like some wild animal, leaving his wife and children to take care of themselves as best they could. He evidently acted upon the principle, that 'It is better to be a live coward, than a dead hero.'

"Reuben B. Harris was from Kentucky. He was a country lawyer; had no education, but was a man of good natural ability. He settled the place where Montraville Ross now lives, on Flat Creek. He settled here in 1827. He was also a great hunter.

"Hugh Morrison was a Kentuckian. In 1827 he settled the place where the widow of Henderson Finley now lives.

"John Gabriel was also from Kentucky. Settled at Richland, at a place two and a half miles east of Florence. He moved there at a very early period in 1819 or 1820. He had a still house, made whisky and sold it to the Indians. He was a rough, miserly character, but honest in his dealings. He was murdered for his money, in his horse lot, on his own plantation. He was killed by a negro man belonging to Reuben B. Harris. The negro was condemned and hung at Boonville. Before his execution, this negro confessed that he had killed Gabriel, but declared that he had been employed to commit the murder by Gabriel's own son-in-law, a man named Abner Weaver. This villain escaped punishment for the reason that the negro's testimony was then, by the laws of the United States, excluded as inadmissible. Justice, however, overtook him at last.

His crime did not stop at the instigation of Gabriel's murder. He was afterwards found in possession of four stolen horses somewhere in Texas. In endeavoring to make his escape, he was shot from one of these horses, and thus ended his villainy.

"The first church erected in this neighborhood was built by the Cumberland Presbyterians. It was of logs, and stood near the old grave yard. It was built about the year 1835. Here, for many years, this denomination annually held the old fashioned camp-meetings, at which large numbers of the old citizens were wont to congregate, and here many of them would sometimes remain for days, and even weeks, on the ground in camps and tents, engaged in earnest devotion. But this order of things and this manner of worship have long since gone into disuse. Not a hawk's eye could now discern a single mourner's track, and every vestige of the old church and camp have vanished like the mist before the morning sun, and the primitive religious customs have been entirely abandoned.

"In the foregoing sketches I have briefly glanced at the lives and characters of most, in fact, nearly all of the older citizens who figured in the history of New Lebanon settlement, which then comprised our own township, and included the country between the Lamine and Flat Creek. Most of them belonged to a class of men which have passed away.

"It is not my purpose to make inviduous comparisons between them and those of the present day. It is but justice, however, to say, that with few exceptions, they were men of great moral worth, true and tried patriotism, and scrupulous integrity.

"I come now to take a brief survey of matters connected with a later date. The town of Otterville was first called Elkton. It was laid out by Gideon R. Thompson, in the year 1837. The first house built, stood where Judge

Butler's house now stands. The public square occupied the space of ground now lying between Butler's and Geo. W. Smith's, extending east to a line running north and south, near the place where Frank Arni's house formerly stood. William G. Wear entered the forty acres on which Elkton was built, in the year 1836, and sold it to Thompson in 1837. About that time Thompson built the first house as before stated, and he and George Wear built a storehouse directly east of Thompson's dwelling, and little George Wear built a dwelling house on the present site of Colburn's house. James Allcorn built on the north side of the square about the same time. 'Long' George Wear built the first house within the present limits of Otterville proper, where W. G. Wear's house now stands.

'The town of Otterville was regularly laid out by W. G. Wear in 1854, though several houses had been built previous to that time within its present limits.

"There was no postoffice at Otterville until about 1848. The mail for this neighborhood was supplied from Arator postoffice kept by General Hogan, where Van Tromp Chilton now lives. W. G. Wear was the first post master. He held the office until 1851, when the writer of these sketches was appointed, who held the office about ten years. The mail route was a special one from Arator, and was carried on horse back. W. R. Butler was the first contractor, and employed James H. Wear, son of W. G. Wear, to carry the mail twice a week. The mail carrier—then a small boy—now one of the leading merchants of St. Louis, made the trip twice a week, riding a small grey pony called 'Tom,' which had been bought of Tom Milam, who was then a well known character of the neighborhood. About the time the town was first established, several houses were built on or near the public square.

"Among these were the Masonic hall; the dwelling house

built by George W. Embree, north of the hall; one by Samuel Wear, now occupied by John D. Strain; one by Harrison Homan, in which he now lives; and about this time Robert M. Taylor built an addition to the 'Taylor House.' The brick storehouse known as the 'Cannon & Zollinger' storehouse, was not built until about the year 1856.

"The Masonic Lodge, called 'Pleasant Grove Lodge No. 142, A. F. & A. M.,' was established on the 15th day of July, A. D. 1854, A. L. 5854. The dispensation was granted by the M. W. G. M., of Missouri, L. S. Cornwell, on the 6th day of November, 1854. This dispensation was granted to the following named persons: Wm. E. Combs, Harrison Homan, S. H. Saunders, Wm. Devine, Tarleton T. Cox, Strawther O'Rourk, Moses B. Small, Aaron Hupp, Wm. A. Reed, Wm. R. Butler, Robt. M. Taylor and Geo. W. Embree. The charter was granted May 31st, 1855, and signed by L. S. Cornwell, G. M.; Oscar F. Potter, D. G. M.; J. W. Chenoweth, D. G. W.; Henry E. Van Odell, J. G. W. The first officers were as follows: S. H. Saunders, W. M.; Aaron Hupp, S. W.; H Homan, J. W.; R. M. Taylor, Treasurer; W. R. Butler, Secretary, George W. Embree, S. D.; Strother O'Rourk, J. W., and R. J. Buchanan, Tyler.

"The Odd Fellows Lodge was established in October, 1856, under the name of Otterville Lodge, No. 102, I. O. O. F.

"The first officers were as follows: W. G. Wear, Noble Grand; H. A. B. Johnston, Vice Grand; Samuel M. Homan, Secretary, and John S. Johnston, Treasurer.

"The present Cumberland Presbyterian church was built by Milton Starke, in the year 1857.

"The old Presbyterian church was built by John D. Strain, in 1866, and is now owned by the Baptists.

"The Methodist and Christian churches were built about the same time in the year 1872. The former was built by M. C. White, and the latter by T. C. Cranmer and T. M. Travillian. They are both neat brick buildings, and ornaments to our village.

"The public school building was erected in 1869, costing $6,000.

"The Pacific railroad was completed to Otterville from St. Louis in 1860, and this place for a short time became the terminus. Whilst the road remained here, and in fact for a long time previous, Otterville commanded quite a brisk trade, presented a very active and business like appearance, and indeed for a time it flourished like a "green bay tree." But it was not destined to enjoy this prosperity long. The railroad company soon pulled up stakes and transferred the terminus to the then insignificant village of Sedalia, which, at that time, being in its infancy, had scarcely been christened, but, though young, it soon rose like magic, from the bosom of the beautiful prairie, and in a few years Sedalia has become the county seat of one of the richest counties in the State, and a great railroad centre, while truth compels me to say that Otterville has sunk back into its original obscurity.

"The town of Otterville was incorporated by an act of the Legislature of Missouri, on the sixteenth day of February, 1857.

"About the year 1860, for a short period, a considerable wholesale business was done here. Among the wholesale establishments, were the following: W. G. Wear & Son, Cloney, Crawford & Co., from Jefferson City; Clark & Reed; Concannon; the Robert Brothers; Lohman & Co., &c., &c.

"About this time the 'Mansion House' was built by a man named Pork; the 'Embree House' by George W.

Embree and Chris Harlan. The latter was quite a large hotel near the depot, and was afterwards moved to Sedalia by George R. Smith, and about the same time several other houses were moved by different parties to that place. There was, after this time, a considerable business done in a retail way around the old public square. Among the most prominent merchants here, were W. G. Wear & Son, and Cannon & Zollinger, who carried on a large and profitable trade for many years.

"But having already extended these notes far beyond what I had at first anticipated, I am admonished to close them rather abruptly, lest they become wearisome. They were prepared at a very short notice, and might have been made much more interesting, had sufficient time been given the writer to arrange them with some regard to order.

"I hope that due allowance will be made by an appreciative public for this defect in this hastily-written memorandum.

"In conclusion, I will take occasion to say, that one hundred years ago, where we meet now to rejoice together, at the happy coming of our first *Centennial*, this part of Cooper county, nay, even Cooper county itself, was a howling wilderness. The hungry wolf and bear; the elk and the antelope; the wild deer and the buffalo, roamed about undisturbed, save by the feeble arrows of the red man.

"To-day, through the little village of Otterville, within a very few yards of this spot, a double band of iron, stretching from the Atlantic to the Pacific, connects San Francisco with the city of New York. Over these lines of metal rails ponderous trains are almost continually passing to and fro, freighted with innumerable articles of commerce; the rich merchandise of the east; the varied productions of the west;

the teas and silk of China; the silver of Arizona, and the gold of California.

"Let us, therefore, rejoice and be merry, for we have abundant reason for these manifestations of joy."

[Signed.]   THOMAS J. STARKE.

HISTORY OF COOPER COUNTY.

CHAPTER XVI.

Early history of the Different Townships, &c , Continued.

PALESTINE TOWNSHIP.

WILLIAM MOORE and Joseph Stephens were the first settlers of Palestine township. Wm. Moore emigrated from North Carolina, and settled about eight miles south of Boonville, in the timber close by a good spring, north of and adjoining the farm where Jenus White, Esq., now resides. His family consisted of Geo. W., Wm. H., James, Andrew, John, Thomas, Robert and Joseph H. Moore, and Margaret, Sallie and Mary Moore; seven sons and three daughters. Margaret married Judge Lawrence C. Stephens, in 1818. Sallie married Col. John H. Hutchison, and Mary married Harvey Bunce. Col. Hutchison was Sheriff of this county for four years, and Representative for two years. Judge Stephens was Representative for four years, and County Judge for one term, and Harvey Bunce was Sheriff for eight years, Representative for two years, and a member of the State Convention in 1865. There are only two of the Moore children now living, viz: Joseph H. Moore, and Margaret Stephens, widow of the late Judge L. C. Stephens.

Mrs. Margaret Stephens says that in the fall of 1816, after her father settled in this county, she went to Boonville, with her uncle, a Mr. McFarland. and on their arrival, she asked her uncle where Boonville was, thinking she was com ng to something of a town. Her uncle pointed to

Robadeaux's store, a round log cabin, with the bark on the logs, and said, "There's Boonville." They then alighted from their horses, and after making some purchases, they returned home. That store-house was *the only building which she then saw at Boonville.* It is also certain, from other good evidence, that the place on which Boonville now stands, was called "Boonville," before any town was built or located here.

Mrs. Stephens also tells of the first church she attended in the neighborhood, which was held at the house of one of the settlers. Luke Williams, the preacher, was dressed in a complete suit of buckskin, and a great many of his audience were dressed in the same style. She was so dissatisfied with the appearance of the state of things, in this backwoods county, that she cried during the whole of the services; but she soon became accustomed to the new order of things, and was well contented. At that meeting, grease from the bear meat, stored in the loft, above the congregation, dripped down and spoiled her nice Sunday shawl, which was a fine one, brought from North Carolina, and which could not be replaced in this backwoods country.

Joseph Stephens, Sen., was the next settler of what is now called Palestine township. He emigrated from Kentucky, and stopped one and one-half years, near Winchester, East Tennessee, in the fall of 1817; he, in company with several others, started for Cooper county, and landed at Boonville on the 15th day of November, 1817.

Before they arrived here, they had bought land in what is now Palestine township. They remained at the place called "Boonville," and were piloted to their new home by Maj. Stephen Cole. They crossed the Petite Saline Creek at the McFarland ford, at the place where Rankin's mill is now situated. The only persons at that time, living in that part of the county, were William and Jacob McFarland on the north, and John Glover on the south side of the creek. After crossing the creek they soon entered the Lone Elm prairie, and on the evening of the same day, they arrived at their new home where they camped for the night.

A hunter by the name of Landers, had made his camp in the bottom, near the present residence of Joseph Stephens, jr., and had an acre of growing corn and 15 hogs, which were purchased by Joseph Stephens, Sr. Mr. Landers then "pulled up stakes" and moved farther west. The next spring James D. Campbell settled on the hill, south of Bunceton, Peter Stephens, one half of a mile north of Old Palestine, and William Stephens and John Kelley three and one-half miles southeast of Joseph Stephens, near the Moniteau creek. These men were the sons and the sons-in-law of Joseph Stephens, Sen., and emigrated to Cooper county with him.

The next year, 1818, Samuel Peters settled about two miles north of Joseph Stephens, at a place now called Petersburg, on the Osage Valley and Southern Kansas railroad. He also had a large family of boys and girls; Samuel and Newton C. Peters were his sons. One of his daughters married Mr. McFarland, one James Hill, who was Sheriff of this county for eight years; one Harvey Harper; one Katie Peters, Thomas Patrick, and afterwards, Samuel Cole; and Sallie, the younger, James Gallagher.

When Samuel Peters raised his dwelling, he invited his neighbors to come and help him, stating that he would, on that occasion, kill a hog and have it for dinner. As this was the first hog ever butchered in this part of the State, and as very few of the settlers had ever tasted pork, it was no little inducement to them to be present and assist in disposing of such rare and delicious food, for the settlers, previous to that time, had subsisted entirely upon wild game. Always on such occasions they had a little "fire water" to give life to the occasion.

In the winter of 1818, Miss Rhoda, the daughter of Jos. Stephens, Sr., was married to Dr. B. W. Levens, the ceremony being performed by the Rev. Luke Williams. On the same evening Miss Elizabeth, the daughter of Samuel Peters, and James Hill were united in marriage by the same minister. The two last mentioned had been engaged for some time, yet did not expect to be married so soon. But Mr. Peters declared that if they intended to marry, they must do so that night or never. So the parson immediately went down to Mr. Peter's house, and in accordance with the statutes in such cases made and provided, pronounced them husband and wife.

Col. Andrew and Judge John Briscoe settled in the same township in 1818. They were both very prominent men, and prominent leaders in their respective parties, Andrew being a Whig, and John a Democrat.

Some of the other early settlers were Henry, Hiram, Heli and Harden Corum. Mr. Tevis, the father of Capt. Simeon Tevis, Thomas Collins, Jacob Summers, Michael, James and William Son, John and Joseph Cathey, James David, and John H. Hutchison, Nathaniel Leonard, John and Andrew Wallace, Henry Woolery, Holbert and Samuel Cole, James Bridges, James Simms, Russell Smallwood, Thomas Best, Greenberry Allison, Wm. C. Lowery, Anthony F. Read, and others not recollected. No better citizens than those mentioned above ever settled in any community.

Mr. Greenberry Allison dug the first cistern in the county, which proved to be a great success, and caused many of his neighbors to imitate his example, as they had, previous to that time, been compelled to depend for water upon springs and wells.

Palestine township, from the beginning, took the lead in education. The first schools were taught by Lawrence C. Stephens, Dr. William H. Moore, and a young man from Virginia by the name of William H. Moore, who was considered the best scholar in his day, in this part of the country. The teachers of a later day were Mr. Huff, Green White, Josiah Adams, now residing in California, Missouri, and Philip A. Tutt. The first grammar school was kept by a Mr. Rodgers, at the residence of John Wallace.

The first dancing school was opened in 1832, at the residence of B. W. Levens, about one-quarter of a mile east of the present site of Bunceton, by a gentleman named Gibson. He was a polished gentleman, and an excellent teacher, and was the first to introduce "cotillions," which were, until that time, unknown in this part of the country. Mr. Gibson at that time had two other schools; one at Boonville, and the other at Arrow Rock, and he taught, during the week, two days at each place.

The names of a few of the dancers who attended the school at B. W. Levens' residence who are at present remembered, are as follows: Newton C. Peters, David Hutchison, Andrew B. Moore, John M. Briscoe, Mr. Huff, Daniel Ogle, Thomas and Bonaparte Patrick, Thomas and Luther Smith, James Corum, Joseph S. Anderson, Green White, Andrew Collins, and Tobe Briscoe. Misses Margaret and Elizabeth Hutchison, daughters of James Hutchison; Elmira Ann and Sarah Ardell Hutchison, daughters of John H. Hutchison; Zerilda and Emarine Levens, Mary and Patsy Briscoe, Katie and Sallie Peters, Susan and Rhoda Campbell, Parthena Kelly, Julia Collins, Annie Best, and a Miss Ramsey.

Most of the persons mentioned above have been dead many years. Among the gentlemen, Mr. Huff was alive a few years ago, though he may be dead at this time, as he has not been heard from for some time. So far as is known none of the other gentlemen are alive. Of the ladies, Margaret, Elmira Ann and Sarah Ardell Hutchison, Margaret Stephens, Zerilda Levens, Patsy Briscoe, Katie and Sallie Peters, and Rhoda Campbell, are still alive—the others are all dead.

On the first day of January, 1845, Henry C. Levens was employed at Lone Elm, John D. Stephens in Palestine district, Joseph L. Stephens in the Harrison district, in the Bunceton neighborhood, and George H. Stephens in the Round Grove district, to teach the respective schools for three months. All these districts are now in school township 47, range 17. These teachers found that the people were not sufficiently aroused on the great importance of of giving their children a good education, and for some time had been studying to discover some plan by which to arouse the patrons of the school to a full knowledge of their responsibility.

They had found that the parents could not be forced to perceive the vast importance of education, by merely telling them of its benefits; but that in order to produce this change, inducements must be placed directly before both parents and pupils; something tangible, sufficiently inviting to arouse them from their lethargy. They thought that they must determine upon some plan to *create and keep up an excitement*, so as to induce the patrons to continue their schools for a longer period than three months, thereby benefitting both teachers and pupils.

They finally agreed upon the plan of offering a banner to the school, which, taking all of the classes into consideration, had made the most progress at the close of the school. The examination for the awarding of the banner was to take place at Old Palestine. On the first day Arithmetic, Geography and Grammar were to be examined, and on the second day the four schools were to have a joint exhihition consisting of speeches and dialogues.

The above named teachers, in accordance with an agreement among themselves on the opening day of their schools, placed the whole subject before the scholars, and gave them until the next day to decide whether they were willing to enter the contest or not; and the members of each school unanimously voted in favor of their teacher's proposition.

This produced a greater excitement than was contemplated or wished for by the teachers, so much so, that it was more difficult to control than to create. All classes of the people took a deep interest in the progress of the schools, and they received frequent visits from trustees, parents and others.

On the days of the examination at Old Palestine, the scholars of the different schools marched in double file to the place of examination, with music and banners, with appropriate mottoes, in advance. The girls of each school were dressed in the same colored dresses, and the boys wore badges of the same color as the dresses of the girls of the school to which they belonged. On each day there was a very large attendance to witness the examination and exhibition.

The excitement became so great that the teachers instructed the judges not to make any award, particularly, as the scholars of all four schools had acquitted themselves so well, that it would have been almost impossible to decide between them. After it had became known, that because of the general excellence of the schools, no award would be made, the excitement attending the contest soon quieted down. The examination and exhibition gave universal satisfaction, and although when the schools closed it was spring and the busiest time of the year, all four of the teachers were offered schools again at the same places.

After this, schools were well attended and supported in Palestine township, and has continued so even to the present day.

Although the object of these teachers was partly selfish, in that they wished to procure constant employment, they conferred innumberable blessings upon that and following generations, by creating among the settlers a desire to give their children every opportunity of acquiring a good education.

PRAIRIE HOME TOWNSHIP.

This is a small township lately organized and taken from the territories of Clark's Fork, Saline and Moniteau townships. It is mostly prairie, and the land is generally very fertile. The oldest settlers according to the best information that can be obtained, were James McClain, Lacy McClanahan, Adam McClanahan, Jacob Carpenter, Absalom McClanahan, Michael Hornbeck, Samuel Carpenter, Wm. H. McClanahan, Wm. G. McClanahan, and Jeremiah Smith.

It appears that these men were located in this township, previous to 1820, as their votes were recorded in that year. Some of them may not be confined to the limits of the township, but they were not far distant from the line.

The history of this township is so closely connected with that of the three townships mentioned above from which it was taken, that it will not be repeated at this place. For its history, the reader is referred to that of the three above named townships.

PILOT GROVE.—POSTOFFICE, TOWNSHIP AND TOWN.

The town of Pilot Grove is situated on the Missouri, Kansas & Texas Railway, about twelve miles southwest of Boonville. It was located in 1873. It has had a very rapid growth and bids fair to make a very important town. It is located in a thickly settled country. The soil of the surrounding country is excellent, and the inhabitants prosperous.

TOWNSHIP.

Among the earliest settlers of the township were Manty Hatfield, John Miller, the father of Judge George W. Miller, Samuel Roe, Sr., John McCutchen, the father of Judge John M. McCutchen, William Taylor, James Taylor, Jr., John, George, Nicholas and Mathias Houx.

This township in early times was celebrated for its camp meeting grounds, there being two within its limits; one held by the Presbyterians, and the other by the Methodists. These camp meetings which were held by each denomination once a year, were largely attended, many persons coming from great distances. Many camped on the grounds, entertaining "without money and without price" the people who attended, and were particularly hospitable to strangers from abroad.

For a more full history of this part of the county, the reader is referred to the following letters of Mr. William G. Pendleton, a young gentleman living in Pilot Grove township, viz:

PILOT GROVE, Mo., July 14, 1876.

Messrs. H. C. Levens, & N. M. Drake, Boonville.

Gentlemen.—A letter of late date, to Mr. E. H. Harris, has been placed in my hands by that gentleman, with the request that I respond to the same. This I shall proceed to do to the best of my ability, assuring you that the following information is at least authentic.

As you are probably already aware, Pilot Grove, as a postoffice and place of rendezvous, for the surrounding inhabitants, is one of the oldest in the county, and takes its name from an ancient grove of Hickory trees, located upon the high prairie in the immediate vicinity. In early days before well defined trails had been marked out, this grove served as a "pilot" to persons traveling from Boonville and Old Franklin to points in the southwest. The name "Pilot Grove" came thus to be applied to the postoffice established near by, and kept by Samuel Roe, Sr.

This gentleman, now the patriarch of our community, aged ninety years, continued to fill the position of post master until the close of the war of the Rebellion. 'Twas while he was acting in this capacity, and at his residence, where the neighbors had gathered upon a bright afternoon in the spring of 1874, awaiting the arrival of the mail, that the dreaded "Bill Anderson" suddenly appeared with his guerrilla troupe, and forming the trembling citizens in line, proceeded to divest them of their personal valuables.

Mr. Wm. Mayo, one of the citizens, refused to deliver up his elegant gold watch, and started to flee; passing the house he was joined by Mr. Thomas Brownfield, now of our community, and who had kept concealed. The guerrillas, of course, gave pursuit, and overtaking Mr. Mayo, who had became separated from Mr. Brownfield, they killed him by a pistol shot in the face.

One guerrilla had pursued Mr. Brownfield, who was endeavoring to reach a thicket of brush some rods distant. The guerrilla fired repeatedly upon Mr. Brownfield, wounding him in the hand, when, upon a near approach, Brownfield, who was armed, and a man of nerve, suddenly turned, and covering him with his revolver, compelled the guerrilla to retreat. This act doubtless saved his life, since it enabled him to reach the coveted thicket, from which concealment he defied his foes, who dared not penetrate the his retreat, and who, after surrounding the thicket, and being several times fired upon by the desperate man within, sought less dangerous fields of conquest.

After the war this postoffice several times changed hands, and was once removed several miles from its ancient locality, still, however, retaining its old name.

Upon the construction of the M. K. & T. railroad through our community, in 1873, a depot was located near the ancient site of Pilot Grove, upon the land of Samuel Roe, Sr. This gentleman's son and business agent, Mr. J. W. Roe, superintended the laying off of a town and disposal of lots, which were at once in demand. The place was christened "Pilot Grove," and from the alacrity with which tradesmen and mechanics moved in, was seen the appreciation the people had of the brief prospects of the future village. Thinking men clearly saw that Pilot Grove occupied a position which would insure to enterprising tradesmen and mechanics a permanent and profitable business.

The village is located on the M. K. & T. railroad, eleven miles southwest of Boonville, in the township of Pilot Grove, one of the best in the county. Its situation is elevated and very healthful, surrounded on every hand by a beautiful and fertile stretch of country, having an extensive prairie on the east and south, and timber on the north and west.

The timber in the immediate vicinity is young, though vigorous and of valuable varieties, such as black and white oak, walnut, hickory, elm, with a small percentage of ash, wild cherry, &c.

The farm products embrace the varieties of grains and grasses, as corn, wheat, oats, timothy, blue grass and clover, with the character of live stock, which such a combination of crops would suggest; especially large numbers of prime cattle and hogs are annually produced and marketed from this vicinity.

Good brick-clay is to be found adjacent to the town. The nearest worked mines are two coal mines; one three miles north, the other one mile south, and the Collin's lead mines eight miles north. Fine indications of lead in paying quantities are found several miles west.

The town of Pilot Grove has at present three dry goods and grocery stores, one well appointed drug store, three blacksmith and wagon maker shops, one gunsmith shop, one tin shop, one saddler shop, one shoe shop, one milinery establishment, and one barber shop, two agricultural depots and one lumber yard; there are also two public schools near this town.

Of dwelling houses there are twenty-three, with the usual number of out-buildings; one private and no public school, one church of the Methodist Episcopal South denomination, established many years ago. A Cumberland Presbyterian, a Baptist and a northern Methodist Episcopal church within convenient distance. A good flouring and saw mill one mile south.

The professional men living here are Dr. J. W. H. Ross, M. D., and Dr. Blevens, present pastor of the Methodist church. The number of inhabitants is computed at about 150; and it is believed that the books of the M. K. & T. freight office at this place, will show in the amount of freight shipped from and received at this point, more business done than at any other town in the county except Boonville. This town was surveyed in July 1873, by Surveyor W. W. Trent, of Boonville.

The town is accessible from all directions by good roads, and it is the outlet of all the produce of its surrounding territory, and also of a large district lying west and northwest which is attracted here by a good road, opened for them by the enterprise of our citizens.

* * * * * * * *

Your most obedient servant,

W. G. PENDLETON

PILOT GROVE, Mo., August 7th, 1876.

Messrs. H. C. Levens & N. M. Drake:

* * * * * * * *

Gentlemen.—The following narration of the killing during the late war, of citizens of our community, by lawless bands, upon either side is doubtless correct in the main, yet in view of the considerable lapse of time since the occurrence of these events, the fallibility of the human memory, and many other circumstances which would have their effect, it would not be strange should error exist in some of the minuter details.

Considered in order of time in which it occurred, I mention first the killing of Joseph Sifers, two miles north of Pilot Grove, which took place about the beginning of the war. He was a Union man, whose house was surrounded at night by unknown men, who demanded of him his fire arms. Purporting to have them hidden upon the outside of his dwelling, he went out intending to discover who they were; when, doubtless, under the belief that his life was in danger, he ran, endeavoring to reach a cornfield adjacent, but in the attempt was shot down by a sentinel of the party. It was never known who perpetrated this outrage.

In the summer of 1864, during a revival meeting in the southern Methodist Episcopal church at Pilot Grove, Capt. Todd, one day during the hour of service, surrounded the building with a company of about sixty savage looking "bushwhackers," who rudely entered the sacred house, stopped the services, and unceremoniously ejected the worshippers. After refreshing themselves with the eatables prepared for the occasion, and selecting such horses as they desired, from the many secured to the trees near by, they departed, taking with them two citizens, Peter Mitzell and Otho Zeller as hostages, as they called them, whose safety would depend upon the good conduct of the citizens, in not pursuing, intercepting or informing on them, there being, at that time, State Militia stationed at various places around.

These two unfortunate men were that night, barbarously butchered some miles east of here, near Lone Elm prairie, and their bodies found a day or two later. Zeller had belonged to the State Militia, which fact, to those who knew the character of the guerrillas, accounts for the reason of his killing. Mitzell was loyal, though a very quiet and inoffensive man; he had, a short time previous, met a squad of guerrillas, and mistaking them for militia, had, doubtless, indiscretely expressed his sentiments, for which offense, in a time when men were killed for opinion's sake, he paid the forfeit with his life.

The same party of bushwhackers, returning a day or two later, passed through the German settlement three miles west of here, and killed two citizens, John Diehl and —— Vollmer, who, it seems, unfortunately fell into the same error as Mitzell, of mistaking them for federal troops, a number of them being dressed in blue.

A Mr. Nichols was killed near Bell Air, in this county, during the same summer of 1864. This act was committed by a band of Hall's State militia. Mr. Nicholas was a Kentuckian, a conservative Union man, and very quiet and peaceable. The provocation of this crime, if any, was never known.

Thomas Cooper, of this vicinity, was arrested in the fall of 1864, in James Thompson's store, in Boonville, by militia, taken to a secluded spot near the fair grounds, and brutally murdered and his body mutilated. Cooper was a southern man, and known to his neighhors as quiet, tolerant and inoffensive.

These gentlemen are the only cases of which I can learn.

* * * * * * * *

Yours very truly,

W. G. PENDLETON.

SALINE TOWNSHIP.

Saline township was settled as early as 1812, by Joseph Jolly, who had only two children, John and William. He settled in the upper part of what has ever since been known as "Jolly's Bottom," and which received its name from him. He remained in this township until 1826, when he removed to the "Stephen's" neighborhood, in Palestine township. He there set out the first apple orchard in that part of the country, and erected a horse mill which would grind a bushel of corn an hour, and this was considered by the people of that day as a great achievement. He peddled apples, cider and ginger-cakes at all the musters and elections.

William Jolly was a gunsmith, a wheelwright, a blacksmith, a cooper, a miller, a distiller, a preacher, a doctor and a farmer. John Jolly kept a ferry across the Lamine river, on the lower ferry road, which is still known as "Jolly's Ferry." The next settlers of this township were William Lamm, James and John Turner, Joseph Pursley, Levin Cropper, Henry Levens, B. W. Levens, (the grandfather and father of Henry C. Levens, of Boonville,) Josiah Dickson, Charles Force, John Farris, Thomas Farris, Jesse Wood, David Fine, Joshua and Lacy McClanahan, George Dickson, Frederick and James F. Conner, John Calvert, Adam and Absalom McClanahan, Elverton Caldwell, Noding Caldwell, Joseph Westbrook, Alexander Woods, Robert Givens, Leonard Calvert, August McFall, Alexander R. Dickson, William Calvert, Jr., James Farris and Robert Dickson.

At what time these men settled here is not known to the present generation, but they certainly arrived between 1816 and 1820, for they all voted at Boonville at the August election in the latter year.

William Lamm settled in the bottom in 1816, and Henry and B. W. Levens and Levin Cropper came here in 1817 or 1818, as they voted in 1819, and the law required that a person should reside in the county one year before he could vote.

Henry Levens was born in Baltimore, Maryland, in 1774, married at Hagerstown, Maryland, and emigrated to Washington county, Pennsylvania, where all his children were born. He afterwards emigrated to Randolph county, Ill., and lived there about fifteen years. His wife being dead, and all his children of age, he emigrated with his son, to Cooper county. He died at his old home in Illinois, in 1838. He was a soldier during the whole of the Revolution, and received a pension for same till his death.

Big Lick church, belonging to the Baptist denomination, was built at a very early time, and is now, and has been for many years, in a flourishing condition. John B. Longdon was the first pastor of this church.

The first school in the township was taught by one Stillman, an eastern man, a place now occupied by the Higland schoolhouse.

The first school recollected by one of the writers, he being one of the pupils, and in his youth having lived in this township, was taught by a man named Rogers. He was a very fair scholar, for the times, and pleased his patrons with the advancement which was made by his scholars.

Just before Christmas in the year 1818, the boys of this school had determined to "turn the teacher out," and force him to treat the scholars, by taking him to the creek and ducking him. This proceeding, though showing little respect for the dignity of the teacher, generally had the desired effect. The fear of it, in this case, had the desired effect, for the teacher, hearing of the plans of the scholars, voluntarily gave them a week's holiday, and on New Year's day treated them to a *keg of whisky*. This, no doubt, will sound strange to most of our citizens at this day, but it is nevertheless true.

It must not be thought from this that that was a terribly demoralized community, for it certainly was not, but on the contrary, one of the most refined in the county. It was customary, at that time, to find whisky in every house, and a man who did not take his dram, was the exception and not the rule. But drunkenness was then considered very disgraceful, and on that account was rarely heard of. People then could drink without taking too much.

It is not to be understood, that even considering the customs of the settlers, at that time, the teacher was justified in treating his pupils to whisky, and the people for suffering it to be done. It was wrong then, and at the present day would not be tolerated in any community.

To the credit of the patrons and teachers of the schools of the past, it may here be said, that there is only one other instance known of a proceeding of this kind being allowed. It was considered at that day that it was not so much the *use* as the *abuse*, which made whisky so objectionable and demoralizing. If at that day, a young gentleman, the least bit intoxicated attempted to wait upon a respectable young lady, he was told that his company was not *absolutely required* at that house, and that the sooner he left the better it would be for all concerned. *How is it now?* Our readers live in the present, and are capable of passing judgment upon present customs.

There was a town called "Washington," laid off by B. W. Levens, about one mile below Overton, near the Missouri river, on the farm lately occupied by Timothy Chandler. Several lots were sold, houses built, and for a while considerable business done. But the site of the town has long since disappeared, and the spot on which it was located cannot be designated by any persons living. Indeed, but few in that locality are aware of the fact that such a town was ever located and inhabited.

Another town called "Houstonville," was laid off by B. W. Levens and John Ward at the ferry landing, opposite

Rocheport, and some lots were sold, but not much improved. The site of the town has long since disappeared under the encroaching waters of the Missouri river.

Another town, the name of which is now unknown, was located at the "cross roads," north of Conner's mill, near the late residence of Judge Jesse Ogden, but was soon abandoned.

Only two of the old pioneers are now living, viz: Wm. Lamm and James F. Conner.

Mr. Lamm was born in Roan county, North Carolina, twelve miles from Saulsberry, and is 81 years of age. His parents removed with him to Tennessee, in 1796, taking him with them. He came to and settled in Saline township in the fall of 1816, and has remained there ever since.

Mr. James F. Conner was a small boy when he, with his parents, settled in Saline township. He is the proprietor of the Conner's mill, situated on the Petite Saline Creek, about nine miles east of Boonville, which was erected by Charles Force, and until it was purchased by Mr. Conner, who changed it into a steam mill, it was run entirely by water power. This mill was built at a very early day, and has proved of great benefit to the inhabitants of this township, as it gave them a market at home for their surplus products.

This township is one of the best wheat districts in the county, probably not finer wheat being raised in the State. It also produces, with little cultivation, all other kinds of grain, fruits and garden vegetables.

This township, as well as the rest of the county, had its troubles in the late civil war. There were nine Union and three southern men killed within its borders. The southern men who were killed were, Benjamin Hill, William Henshaw and Radford Bass. These men were murdered at or near their homes, about the last of September, 1864, by a scouting party of Union soldiers, being a part of the command of Col. Hall, Missouri State militia. They were not belligerents, and the cause of their being slain is unknown.

The Union soldiers who were killed, were slain by "bushwhackers" from Howard and Boone counties, seven of them on the 7th day of October, 1864, and two of them on the 27th day of May, 1865. The following is a list of them: Henry Weber, Franz Haffenburg, Jacob Eder, David Huth, Bernhard Deitrick, Gerhardt Blank, Peter Diehl, Jacob Good, Sr., Jerry Good, Jr. There was also a "bushwhacker," whose name is unknown, killed on the 27th day of May, 1865.

This township has always been strongly Democratic in principle since the organization of the county, and still remains the same.

For this information the authors are under obligations to Dr. T. H. Winterbower and David Schilb.

HISTORY OF COOPER COUNTY.

CHAPTER XVII.

Biographies of some of the Old Citizens, which were not placed in the History of the Township in which they lived.

ROBERT P. CLARK, JOSEPH STEPHENS, SR., JOHN MILLER.

Robert P. Clark was born in Bedford county, Virginia, in the year 1791, and whilst yet a youth, emigrated with his father and family to Clark county, Kentucky. He was there placed as an apprentice in the clerk's office, with his uncle, David Bullock, and after serving the usual time and passing the customary examination, he was appointed to the clerkship of Estill county, Kentucky. He held this position until about the year 1816, when he resigned, and with his father and other members of the family, emigrated to Howard county, Missouri, where he arrived in the year 1817. The next year he moved to the present site of Boonville.

On the first day of March, 1819, he was appointed clerk of the Circuit Court of Cooper county, by Hon. David Todd, judge of said court. In May, 1820, he was elected a member of the "Missouri State Convention," which framed the first constitution for the State, and which was presided over by Hon. David Barton.

He held the offices of clerk of the Circuit and County Courts, and also postmaster of Boonville, from the formation of the county until the year 1835, when he resigned the office of postmaster. During this year the clerks of the different courts having become elective, he was a candidate for, and was elected to the office of clerk of the Circuit Court, which office he continued to hold until his death. He also held the offices of County Treasurer and Commissioner of School Lands until the year 1832.

He was called by the old settlers, on account of his intimate knowledge of the statute laws applying to the county, and of his being general adviser in matters of this nature, "The Father of the county."

He first with his family, resided in a log cabin, containing only *one room*, which stood southwest of the present residence of Capt. James Thompson, and was a very unpretending round log affair. In these more refined days it would seem impossible for a family like his, with the late Judge Abiel Leonard, Peyton R. Hayden, Charles French, and John S. Buckey, then constituting the bar of Boonville, as his boarders, to live in a house having only one room, but such were the necessities of the times, and every thing flourished.

He built a house on High street, on the lot where Adam Eckhard now resides, and moved there in the fall of 1820. In this house the first County Court was held, on the 8th day of January, 1821. He afterwards built a large two story brick house on the corner of High and Sixth streets, now owned by Joseph and William Williams. It is still standing, and was, at the time it was built, considered a very fine and elegant structure.

Joseph Stephens, Sr., was born in Wythe county, Virginia, in 1763, and was there married to Miss Rhoda Cole, the sister of Maj. Stephen Cole, and in 1801 emigrated to Wayne county, Kentucky, where he remained until the year 1815. In the last mentioned year he moved to Tennessee, and from thence, in November, 1817, to Cooper county, Missouri. The company of which he was a member, came overland in wagons, and crossed the Mississippi river above Alton, and the Missouri river at Boonville. He settled about fourteen miles southwest of Boonville, his house being located in the bottom, one-quarter of a mile north of the present site of Bunceton, a few yards west of the railroad leading from Boonville to Tipton. He and his family lived during the first winter in a half face camp. All his children came with him except Mary Weatherford, who remained in Kentucky. He was married twice. The names of the children of his first wife were William, Peter, Lawrence C., Joseph and James Madison—five sons, and Nancy, Nelly, Mary, Johanna, Frances, Rhoda and Zilpha—seven daughters; there were also three other children who died when infants, whose names are not known. Nancy married Thomas B. Smiley; Nelly, James D. Campbell; Mary, Archibald Weatherford; Johanna, John Kelly; Rhoda, B. W. Levens, and Zilpha, Pemberton Cason.

Joseph Stephens' first wife died in 1822, and in 1824 he married Miss Catherine Dickson; this union was blessed with four sons: John D., George D., Andrew J., and Thomas H. B., and five daughters: Margaret, Alpha, Harriet, Isabella and Lee Ann, making in all twenty-four children of which he was the father.

Of the children of Joseph Stephens who emigrated to Cooper county with him, Joseph, James M., Nelly and Zilpha are still alive. Joseph Stephens was the first settler in that part of the county. At the time of his settlement, his nearest neighbor being seven miles distant. He was a very prosperous farmer, and an excellent manager in business affairs, never went in debt, and advised his children to follow his example. He was economical and saving, and just in all his dealings with others. He was a generous, good neighbor, a man of good moral character, and of unquestioned veracity, and his word was considered as good as his bond or his oath.

He gave all his sons a tract of land, and his daughters a negro slave, and to each of his children he also gave a horse, saddle and bridle, a cow and calf, a sow and pigs, a flock of sheep, and a bed and bedding. He then warned them to take care of and add to this property, as it was all he ever intended to give them.

His precepts and example are not lost, but live in the hearts of his descendants and neighbors to this day.

He died in May, 1836, at the age of 73 years. He was always a strong Jackson man, and took considerable interest in politics, but never would become a candidate for or accept any office.

John Miller, the father of Judge George W. Miller, was born in South Carolina, and raised in McLanburg, North Carolina. When he was 20 years old, he moved to Knox county, Tennessee, where he married and resided for a few years. About the year 1805, he emigrated to Christian county, Kentucky; and in 1818, he came to Missouri, then a territory, and settled near Glasgow, in Howard county. He was elected from that county to the House of Representatives in 1822 and 1824. The other members of the Legislature from that county in 1822, were Alfred Bayse, the father of Judge George W. Miller's wife, Nicholas S. Burkhart, Ignatius P. Owings, and Stephen Trigg; and in 1824, Alfred Bayse, William J. Redd, William Ward, and Edward V. Warren. He always said that he would keep out of politics if he remained in Howard county, although it might keep him poor all his life.

He moved to Cooper county in the fall of the year 1825, and settled within the present limits of Pilot Grove township. In the previous spring he had sent his son, George W., accompanied by a hand, to make a crop at his future home, and as young George was an industrious boy, loving work so well that *he could lie down and sleep by it*, of course they must have succeeded well with their undertaking.

But history will show that Mr. Miller did not keep out of politics as he had intended, when he moved from Howard county, as he was elected to the State Senate in 1828, on the Jackson ticket, and re-elected to the same office in 1832, having served in that capacity for eight years. In 1836 he was selected to carry the returns of the presidential election of this State, for that year, to Washington City. In 1838 he was again elected to the House of Representatives. He was also appointed Indian agent at Omaha by president Polk.

The father of John Miller was of Scotch-Irish decent, and came from Ireland to this country a short time before the Revolution. He was a soldier in the war of the Revolution during the whole time it continued, until he was killed in the battle of Utau Springs. He belonged to a company of cavalry, and fell by the side of his friend and comrade in arms, Mr. Johnston, the great grandfather of James H. Johnston, the present Prosecuting Attorney of Cooper county, who gave the following account of his death: "As the battle was about being closed, Mr. Miller was heard to shout, 'They are fleeing,' and at that instant he was shot from his horse.

This happened about four months before the birth of John Miller, and about one month after his birth the Tories set fire to the house in which his widowed mother resided, and burned it to the ground. As it was then winter, and the weather very cold, Mrs. Miller became sick from the exposure, and died in a few days, leaving John and his three little brothers in destitute circumstances, and without any known relatives in the United States.

Mr. Johnson, who was with their father when he was killed, took charge of the little orphans, and, in due time, they were bound out, and raised separate from each other.

John Miller survived all his brothers, and died in this county at the advanced age of eighty-five years, honored and respected by his countrymen, with the consolation that the world had been bettered by his having lived in it. He was an earnest, zealous member of the Cumberland Presbyterian church. In politics he was always a Democrat.

Peyton R. Hayden was born in Bourbon county, Kentucky, on the 22d day of February, 1796, and came to Old Franklin, Howard county, Missouri, in 1817, and there married in December, 1819, Miss Maria Adams, daughter of the Hon. John Adams, sister of Judge Washington, and Mr. Andrew Adams, of Boonville, and the niece of Judge John Boyle, of Kentucky, and then settled with his family the same month in the village of Boonville, where he remained up to the time of his death, which took place on the 26th day of December, 1855. He was the first attorney admitted to the Boonville bar—in March, 1819. He first taught school in Howard county for twelve months, for a livelihood, being a poor young man who had cast his lot among strangers in what was then almost a wilderness, and there was not then sufficient practice to support one lawyer. He practiced law in all the courts in western Missouri, and in the State Supreme Court with Hamilton R. Gamble, Edward Bates, Charles R. French, Abiel Leonard, John F. Ryland and others, who afterwards became eminent. He was a leading and successful lawyer, having accummulated considerable property. He was noted for his zeal in advocating the cause of his client, and for his great energy and untiring industry. He was a man of affable manners, kind hearted and charitable, and always took undisguised pleasure to aid by counsel and advice, the efforts of the young members of the bar, struggling for practice. Judge Washington Adams and Emmett R. Hayden his son, were law students under his teaching who became eminent in their profession, both of whom are yet practicing law in Boonville.

His younger son, Henry C. Hayden, studied law under Judge Washington Adams, and practiced the same successfully in Calloway county, Missouri, until 1870, and then removed to Saint Louis and engaged in the practice in partnership with the Hon. John B. Henderson, until the 1st of August, 1873, when he died at Long Branch where he had gone to spend the summer with his family. Peyton R. Hayden was a Whig in politics, but never made a political speech nor was he ever an aspirant for office. He was a kind and indulgent father, a good neighbor and citizen, and died honored and respected by all who knew him. His funeral was attended and his memory honored by all the citizens.

HISTORY OF COOPER COUNTY

CHAPTER XVIII.

Celebration of July Fourth, 1876, at Boonville, and Synopsis of the Exercises which took place on that Day.—Poem of H. A. Hutchison, read at Boonville, July Fourth, 1876.

SINCE the "late war," Cooper county has gradually increased in population and wealth. The bitter feelings engendered during the war are slowly dying away; and it can with truth be said, that there is no county in the United States, where life, limb and property are better protected than in Cooper county. The people are generally intelligent, moral, hospitable, kind hearted and enterprising.

Perhaps there is no better climate in the west, east of the Rocky Mountains, than this part of Central Missouri, and it is not like other parts of the west, subject to severe storms.

As this history is intended to close on the one hundredth anniversary of our National Independence, it is only necessary, in conclusion, to give a description of how

THE 4TH DAY OF JULY, 1876,

was celebrated by the citizens of Cooper county, and a synopsis of the exercises which took place at Boonville on that day.

The celebration at Boonville commenced on the evening of the 3rd day of July, with the firing of cannons and a grand illumination of the principal streets, and a very long torch-light procession. Main street was in a perfect blaze of light, with gas jets, candles and lanterns, and every business house was decorated with flags and banners having appropriate mottoes; in fact, with hardly an exception, the people participated in the grand display.

The streets were crowded with people during the whole of the evening, and it was frequently remarked, "Where did so many people come from?" A great many attended from different parts of this and surrounding counties, Howard county being especially well represented in the procession. The procession was considered a great success, even beyond the most sanguine expectations of the committee of arrangements.

It could perhaps be here remarked, that the celebration at Boonville of the "nation's birthday," was not, in proportion to its population, excelled in any respect by that of any other city or town in the United States. The property holders and occupiers seemed to strive with one another as to whose premises should make the best appearance both in the illumination and the display of flags, lanterns, &c. The citizens were very quiet, and made no boast of what they intended to do, but when the signal was given for "lighting up," they astonished every body else, and even themselves. It will not be undertaken to give an adequate description of the display on this occasion, for it would have to be seen to be appreciated.

On the evening of the 3d, the procession was formed by Judge T. M. Rice, Chief Marshal, with Col. Robert McCulloch and Capt. George Meller, Assistant Marshals. In front was a large wagon, containing thirteen young ladies, who represented the thirteen original States of the Union. Then followed twelve men dressed in Continental uniform, who represented Washington, Jefferson, Lafayette, John Adams, Alexander Hamilton and others, among the most prominent men who took part in the Revolutionary struggle. Then came men bearing flags and torches, in all forming a procession more than one-half of a mile long. Twelve men on horseback dressed in Indian costume, rode several times pell-mell through the streets, yelling and giving the Indian warhoop. This was a ludicrous, attractive and prominent feature of the procession. Three bands of music marched at different places in the procession; the Boonville Silver Cornet, the Clark's Fork and the Pilot Grove bands. After the procession had marched and counter marched through the principal streets of the town, it halted at the Thespian hall, where the assembled multitude was entertained by an address prepared for the occasion, and delivered by Mr. Malcolm McMillan, of Boonville; and last, as the closing exercise of this the first day of the great celebration, the crowd witnessed several of the best tableaux ever seen in Boonville, the principal characters of which were the young ladies who represented the thirteen States. It was past eleven o'clock before the exercises of the evening were concluded, and the people dispersed to seek rest, to prepare for the duties and pleasures of the following day, for the greatest efforts had been expended to make that the "crowning glory" of the celebration.

The morning of the 4th was dark and gloomy; rain fell in torrents, and the heavy boom of the "artillery of heaven," drowned that of the "feeble sons of earth." But this day had been set aside by the people for enjoyment, and early crowds of people thronged the principal thoroughfares of the town, seeking the place where the closing exercises of the celebration were to take place. At 4 o'clock in the morning all the bells in the city were rung, and thirty-eight shots were fired by the cannon, one for each of the present States of the Union.

As the morning was very disagreeable, although the rain had ceased falling about eight o'clock, the procession was not formed until about 11 o'clock, when it proceeded to

Lilly's Grove, about one-half of a mile east of Boonville, there to listen to the reading of the Declaration of Independence, and to the speeches and addresses prepared for the occasion.

After an appropriate prayer by Rev. —— Curtis, of the Episcopal church at Boonville, the Declaration of Independence was read by Prof. J. P. Metzger. He was followed by Col. H. A. Hutchison, who read an excellent and appropriate poem written expressly for the occasion, and which will be found in full at the close of this chapter.

Col. William Preston Johnson, of Virginia, was then introduced and delivered a most eloquent speech, which was received with loud cheers by the assembled crowd.

Then Mr. G. Reiche delivered an address in German; he was followed by Mr. John Cosgrove, who delivered the "Oration of the Day."

After this, Mr. N. M. Drake read a sketch of the history of Cooper county, which had been prepared for the occasion in accordance with the request of the Committee of Arrangements.

It was then, on motion of Major H. M. Clark, Chairman of the Committee of Arrangements, unanimously resolved by the assembled multitude, that Messrs. H. C. Levens and N. M. Drake, by whom the above mentioned sketch was written, be granted further time to prepare a complete history of Cooper county, and that they be requested to have the same published in book or pamphlet form. At the close of each of the above exercises an appropriate chorus was sung, by a choir composed of 100 voices; also frequently during the afternoon, the dull boom of the cannon was heard, seemingly to remind the forgetful of our citizens that that was indeed the "Centennial Fourth."

On the night of the 4th, the citizens were called together to witness the display of fireworks, which had been prepared at great expense. And it is not exaggeration to say, that this was the finest display which has ever taken place in Central Missouri. At ten o'clock the last "bouquet of flowers" was fired into the air, and the heavy boom of the cannon notified the assembled multitude that the great celebration of the 4th day of July was over, and the people retired to their homes satisfied with the success of their endeavors to make memorable, the birthday of three millions of "Sons of Liberty."

At the request of many of the citizens of this county, the poem which was composed by Col. H. A. Hutchison, of Boonville, and read by him at the celebration on the 4th day of July, 1876, is here appended in full.

JULY FOURTH, 1876.

BY H. A. HUTCHISON.

THE goddess of liberty, sent from above,
On mission of mercy, on errand of love,
Rejected of empire, discarded by throne,
Through kingdoms and monarchies wandered alone,
Till taking her flight to a land o'er the sea,
She found there a people who sighed to be free.

She breathed on the hearts of our patriot sires,
And kindled within them those burning desires
Which ne'er would be quenched or would slumber again,
Until the fair goddess triumphant would reign.
Sustaining the weak and inflaming the cold
She strengthened the doubtful and cheered on the bold,
And giving our banner the stripe and the star,
She bade them go forth in her service to war!

The mother and sister, and fond hearted wife,
Restrained not their dear one from joining the strife;
The maiden surpressing a sorrowful sigh,
Her lover sent forth with a "cheerful good bye,"
And though they were few and their enemies strong,
Yet striking for freedom, and maddened by wrong,

They struggled and suffered thro' dark weary years,
Of want and privation, of hopes and of fears,
Till tyranny fled and oppression was past,
And victory perched on our banner at last.

That banner unfurled to the sun and the breeze,
As proudly it floats o'er the land and the seas,
The beautiful emblem of freedom and right,
To-day we will hail with a shout of delight!
And let the grim cannon be brought forth once more
Not death from its red mouth in anger to pour,
But only to blend the deep tones of its voice
With shouts of the people who meet to rejoice
O'er this the return of the glorious day,
On which, just a century now passed away,
Our patriot fathers proclaimed them prepared
To die, or sustain Independence declared!

From England and Scotia and Erin so fair,
From Germany's shore, from the Alps bold and bare,
From sunny Italia and beautiful France,
From Spain whose fair daughters win hearts with a glance,
From regions of snow and from tropical isle,
Where summer time reigns with perpetual smile,
Our country's adopted, from all o'er the earth,
To-day will rejoice with her children by birth;
And though they oft dream of the fatherland yet,
Sometimes it may be with a sigh of regret,
Beneath our proud flag to the breezes unfurled,
They'd stand by our country against the whole world!
Tho' memory brings up, in dreadful review,
The armies of gray and the legions of blue,
The heroes who once met in hostile array,
Will mingle together as brothers to-day;
And if the invader should come to our shore,
I know they would rush to the battle once more,
Each veteran's heart to our whole country true,
Though one wore the gray and another the blue!

Now let the wild tones of the jubilant bells,
Be mingled with music, as sweetly it swells!
And may the soft winds, as they wander afar,
Breathe gently to-day, on each stripe and each star,

And bear the glad tidings all over our lands,
There's UNION OF HEARTS, there is joining of hands,
In north and in south, in the west and the east,
Where gather the people, at church or at feast,
On liberty's altar their garlands to cast,
And cover with roses the thorns of the past.

May heaven protect, as in days that are gone,
The old ship of state riding gallantly on,
And be we united, whatever befall—
OUR COUNTRY! OUR COUNTRY! the watchword of all.

HISTORY OF COOPER COUNTY.

CHAPTER XIX.

PRESENT CONDITION OF COOPER COUNTY.

Present Boundaries of Cooper County.—Population of the County at Each Census.—Character of the Soil.—Chief Kinds of Wood, Grain, &c., Produced.—Woodlands Settled First.—Present Condition of the Schools and Churches of the County.—Men Hung in County, &c., &c.

COOPER COUNTY as it now exists, is bounded as follows: On the north by the Missouri river, on the east by Moniteau county; on the south by Moniteau and Morgan counties, and on the west by Pettis and Saline counties, and contains 567 square miles, or 355,172 acres of land.

Since its first settlement it has increased very rapidly in population and wealth. Although during the first few years after the Coles arrived, they lived here almost alone, their only neighbors being the Indians, on the south side of the Missouri river, and the Whites, in what is now Howard county. Yet about the close of the war of 1812, settlers commenced arriving very fast, for by this time, reports of the rich and almost unsettled country lying south of the Missouri river, had reached the thickly settled portions of the United States, in the north and east. The flattering reports of the fertility of the soil and the healthfulness of the climate, caused many persons to leave a home where they were from year to year, barely obtaining the necessities of life, and seek a country which promised abundant harvest with little labor.

The population of Cooper county in 1828, was 6,959; in 1830, 6,904; in 1840, 10,484; in 1850, 12,950; in 1860,

17,356; and in 1870, 20,692. In taking the census of 1870, twelve square miles of the county were omitted by mistake, so that, had the census for that year been taken correctly, the inhabitants of the county would have been found to number at least 23,000. It contains by estimation on the 4th day of July, 1876, 25,000 inhabitants.

The reason of the *seemingly small* increase of population, between the dates of taking the census for the first few times, is explained by the fact that every year or two some new county was cut off from Cooper, thus taking away some part of her territory and population. So that, in fact, from the time of the taking of one census to that of another, the increase must have been very great, as notwithstanding the fact, that large portions of the county were detached from it, each census shows an increase in population over the preceding one.

Some of the main advantages which Cooper county holds out to the persons seeking homes, are the excellence of its educational institutions, the fertility of its soil, the healthfulness of its climate, the splendid facilities which it offers for the erection of manufacturies, and the fact, that being crossed by three railroads through its central portion, and skirted on the north by the Missouri river, the products of the county can be placed upon the markets with small cost to the producer.

The soil of most parts of the county is well adapted to the cultivation of almost every kind of grain, as also tobacco and everything of that kind which any country with this climate could produce. Of all the counties of Missouri, and Missouri is noted for having as rich soil as can be found anywhere, Cooper stands in the front rank as to quality and quantity of grain, &c., raised, as also for having the greatest amount of soil adapted to cultivation, for there is hardly any part of its soil but what can be cultivated with advantage.

The face of the country is divided between prairie and woodland, about one-half prairie, balance woodland. The southern portion of the county is mostly prairie, and as it nears the Missouri river, the country gradually rises into heavily wooded hills.

The western portion of the county is drained by the Lamine and Blackwater rivers; the central portion by the Petite Saline creek and its numerous tributaries, and the southeastern part by the Moniteau creek. There are many mineral and fresh water springs in the county. Among the former, the most noted are the Choteau Springs, situated about ten miles west of Boonville. Although there are no improvements there, yet they are resorted to by many persons, for the water of these springs are noted for their fine medicinal qualities.

The chief kinds of wood which grow in Cooper county, are walnut, hickory, oak of all kinds, ash, cottonwood, redbud, and many others.

The soil of the county is generally very fertile, being well adapted to agricultural pursuits. Nearly every species of grain can be raised here with profit, as has been abundantly proven in the past.

The bottom lands are well adapted to the cultivation of corn and hemp; the uplands to the cultivation of corn, wheat, oats, rye, &c. Peaches, apples, and all kinds of small fruits grow in the greatest abundance. Grapes are cultivated extensively, especially around Boonville, and a great deal of excellent wine is manufactured here every year. It is estimated that at least three-fourths of Cooper county is under cultivation.

Coal is found in the county in the greatest abundance. Also lead and iron, which appear in heavy deposits in the northwestern portion.

The wealth of the county, as appears from the census of 1870, was about $10,000,000.

There are three railroads running through the county; one a branch road, called the Osage Valley and Southern Kansas railroad, connecting Boonville with the Pacific Railroad at Tipton; the Missouri, Kansas and Texas railroad, running diagonally across the county from Boonville to the Pettis county line; and on the south, the Pacific railroad runs about six miles through the county, making in all, fifty-four miles of railroad within the limits of Cooper county.

The exports of the county are corn, wheat, oats, flour, tobacco, stoneware, wine and woolen goods, which are produced here in the greatest abundance.

From 1820 to 1830 the population of the county increased very rapidly, consisting mostly of settlers from Kentucky and Tennessee, also from Pennsylvania and New York; from 1830 to 1840, mostly from Virginia and North Carolina; since which time the emigration has mainly come from the eastern and northeastern states. From the time of the first settlement until 1830, the cultivated lands were confined exclusively to the timbered parts of the county, the settlers not deeming prairie lands fit for cultivation. Another reason for not settling the prairie, was on account of the lack of water, it then being considered necessary to settle by the side of a spring—cisterns, ponds, and even wells not having been much used. When the people commenced making ponds and cisterns, the prairies settled very rapidly, thus proving that they were better civilizers than even steamboats or railroads.

Education in Cooper county is now in a very flourishing condition, there being in the county about 102 schools, 90 white, and 12 colored, which are taught from four to ten months in every year. Education is more generally diffused among the masses, and receives more attention in this county than in most any county in the State.

The churches throughout the county are very numerous, have their pulpits filled with able ministers, and are well attended by the greatest part of its citizens. The prevailing denominations are the Baptists, Methodists, Presbyterians, Christians and Episcopalians.

There have only been two men hung in Cooper county by a due process of law, which speaks well for her good morals. They were both negroes; one named Luke, and the other Jack. Luke was hung in 1826, at Boonville, for killing his master, named Harris, who lived in what is now Lamine township; Jack was hung about the year 1830, for killing a man named Gabriel, who kept a distillery on Haw Creek, about six miles from Florence, which is now Morgan county, but was then in Cooper county.

CHAPTER XX.

Complete list of State officers, who have served from the organization of the State to the present time.

STATE OFFICERS OF MISSOURI.

GOVERNORS.

NAMES.	DATE OF ELEC'N OR APPOINTMENT	TIME FOR WHICH ELECTED, ETC.
Alexander McNair...	Sept., 1820....	For 4 years...................
Frederick Bates.....	Nov. 21, 1824..	For 4 years. Died Aug. 4, 1825.
Abraham I. Williams	Aug. 4, 1825...	Vice, F. Bates, deceased........
John Miller.........	Jan. 20, 1826..	V'e A. I. Williams, abs't f'm St'e.
John Miller........	Nov., 1828.....	For 4 years....................
Daniel Dunklin......	Nov. 21, 1832..	For 4 years....................
Lilburn W. Boggs....	Oct. 1, 1836...	Vice, D. Dunklin, resigned......
Lilburn W. Boggs...	Nov. 23, 1836..	For 4 years.....................
Thomas Reynolds....	Nov. 18, 1840...	For 4 years. Died Feb., 1844...
M. M. Marmaduke...	February, 1844.	Vice Reynolds, deceased........
John C. Edwards....	Nov. 20, 1844..	For 4 years....................
Austin A. King......	August, 1848..	For 4 years....................
Sterling Price........	August, 1852..	For 4 years....................
Trusten Polk.......	August, 1856..	For 4 years....................
Hancock Jackson...	February, 1857.	Vice, Polk, resigned...........
Robert M. Stewart...	Oct. 22, 1857...	....
C. F. Jackson........	1861...........	4 years. Vacated by conv'n ord.
Hamilton R. Gamble.	July 30, 1861..	Elected by convention..........
Willard P. Hall.....	....	Vice, Gamble, deceased........
Thomas C. Fletcher..	Nov. 8, 1864....	For 4 years....................
Joseph W. McClurg..	Nov. 3, 1868....	For 2 years....................
B. Gratz Brown.	Nov. 8. 1870....	For 2 years....................
Silas Woodson.......	Nov. 5, 1872....	For 2 years....................
Charles H. Hardin...	Nov. 3, 1874....	For 2 years....................

MISSOURI STATE OFFICERS.

LIEUTENANT-GOVERNORS.

NAMES.	DATE OF ELEC'N OR APPOINTMENT	TIME FOR WHICH ELECTED, ETC.
William H. Ashley...	August, 1820..	For 4 years..................
Benjamin H. Reeves.	August, 1824..	For 4 years..... ....
Daniel Dunklin.......	August, 1828..	For 4 years..................
Lilburn W. Boggs....	August, 1832..	For 4 years..................
Franklin Cannon.....	August, 1836..	For 4 years..... ....
M. M. Marmaduke...	August, 1840..	For 4 years.............. ....
James Young.......	August, 1844..	For 4 years...................
Thomas L. Price.....	August, 1848..	For 4 years..................
Wilson Brown.......	August, 1852..	For 4 years..... ....
Hancock Jackson....	August, 1856..	For 4 years..................
Thomas C. Reynolds.	August, 1860..	For 4 years.................
Willard P. Hall......	August, 1861..	Elected by convention.........
George Smith........	Nov. 8, 1864...	For 4 years..................
E. O. Stanard........	Nov. 3, 1868...	For 2 years...................
J. J. Gravelly.......	Nov. 8, 1870...	For 2 years..................
Charles P. Johnson..	Nov. 5, 1872...	For 2 years....... ....
Norman J. Coleman..	Nov. 3, 1874...	For 2 years..................

SECRETARIES OF STATE.

NAMES.	DATE OF ELEC'N OR APPOINTMENT	TIME FOR WHICH ELECTED, ETC.
Joshua Barton.......	1820..........	For 4 years..................
William G. Peters....	1821..........	Vice J. Barton, resigned.......
William G. Peters....	1822..........	For 4 years..................
Hamilton R. Gamble.	1824..........	For 4 years..................
Spencer Pettis.......	1826..........	Vice H. R. Gamble, resigned....
Spencer Pettis.......	1826..........	For 4 years..................
Priestly H. McBride..	1829..........	Vice, S. Pettis, resigned........
John C. Edwards....	1830..........	Vice, P. H. McBride, resigned. .
John C. Edwards....	1830..........	For 4 years................ --
Henry Shields.......	1835..........	....
John C. Edwards....	1837..........	Vice, H. Shields, resigned......
Peter G. Glover......	1837..........	Vice, J. C. Edwards, resigned...
James L. Minor.....	1839..........	Vice, P. G. Glover, resigned....
James L. Minor.....	1843..........	For 2 years..................
Falkland H. Martin..	1845..........	For 4 years..................
Ephraim B. Ewing...	1849..........	For 4 years..................
John M. Richardson.	1853..........	For 4 years..................
Benjamin F. Massey.	1856..........	For 4 years..................
Benjamin F. Massey.	1860..........	For 4 years. Rem'v'd by conv'n.
Mordacai Oliver.....	1861..........	Elected by convention.........
Francis Rodman....	1864..........	For 4 years..................
Francis Rodman.....	1868..........	For 2 years..................
Eugene F. Weigel....	1870..........	For 4 years..................
Eugene F. Weigel....	1872..........	For 4 years..................
Michael K. McGrath.	1874..........	For 4 years..................

MISSOURI STATE OFFICERS.

STATE AUDITORS.

NAMES.	DATE OF ELECT'N OR APPOINTMENT	TIME FOR WHICH ELECTED, ETC.
William Christie,	1820	For 4 years
William V. Rector	1821	Vice, W. Christie, resigned
Elias Bancroft	1823	Vice, W. V. Rector, resigned
Henry Shields	1833	For 4 years
Peter G. Glover	1835	Vice, H. Shields, resigned
Peter G. Glover	1837	For 4 years
Hiram H. Baber	1837	Vice, P. G. Glover, resigned
Hiram H. Baber	1839	For 2 years
Hiram H. Baber	1841	For 4 years
William Monroe	1845	For 4 years
James R. McDearmon	1845	Vice, Monroe, resigned
James R. McDearmon	1847	For 4 years. Died.
George W. Miller	1848	Vice, McDearmon, deceased
Wilson Brown	1849	Vice, Miller, resigned
Abraham Fulkerson	1852	Vice, Brown, resigned
William H. Buffington	1856	For 4 years
William S. Mosely	1860	For 4 years
Alonzo Thompson	1864	For 4 years
Daniel W. Draper	1868	For 2 years
Daniel W. Draper	1870	For 2 years
George B. Clark	1872	For 2 years
Thomas Holladay	1874	For 2 years

STATE TREASURERS.

NAMES.	DATE OF ELECT'N OR APPOINTMENT	TIME FOR WHICH ELECTED, ETC.
Peter Didier	1820	For 2 years. Resigned in 1821
Nathaniel Simonds	1821	Elected until 1828
James Earickson	1829	For 2 years
James Earickson	1831	For 2 years
John Walker	1833	For 2 years
John Walker	1835	For 2 years
John Walker	1837	For 2 years. Deceased
Abraham McClellan		Vice, J. Walker, deceased
Abraham McClellan	1839	For 2 years
Abraham McClellan	1841	For 2 years
Peter G. Glover	1843	For 2 years
Peter G. Glover	1845	For 2 years
Peter G. Glover	1847	For 2 years
Peter G. Glover	1849	For 2 years
Peter G. Glover	1851	For 2 years. Died
Alfred Morrison	1851	Vive, P. G. Glover, deceased
Alfred Morrison	1852	For 4 years
Alfred Morrison	1856	For 4 years
Geo. C. Bingham	1861	Appointed till August, 1864
William Bishop	1864	For 4 years
William Q. Dallmeyer	1868	For 2 years
Samuel Hayes	1870	For 2 years
Harvey W. Salmon	1872	For 2 years
Joseph W. Mercer	1874	For 2 years

REGISTERS OF LANDS.

NAMES	DATE OF ELECT'N OR APPOINTMENT.	TIME FOR WHICH ELECTED, ETC.
John Heard..	1841..........	For 4 years ....
George W. Houston..	1845..........	For 4 years ....
Allen P Richardson.	1849.......	For 4 years ....
George W. Houston..	1856..........	For 4 years ....
John F. Houston....	1860..........	For 4 years ....
Sample Orr..........	1861..........	Vice, J. F. Houston who failed to qualify ....
Jared E. Smith......	1864..........	For 4 years ....
Joseph H. McGee....	1868...... ...	For 2 years ....
Frederick Salomon...	1871..........	For 2 years ....
Frederick Salomon...	1873.........	For 2 years ....
George Diegle.......	1874..........	For 2 years ....

SUPERINTENDENTS OF PUBLIC SCHOOLS.

NAMES.	DATE OF ELECT'N OR APPOINTMENT.	TIME FOR WHICH ELECTED, ETC.
Thomas A. Parker...	1866..........	For 4 years ....,......
Llelwellyn Davis	1866..........	Assistant ....
Edwin Clark.... ...	1868..........	Assistant ....
Ira Divall...........	1870.	Resigned ....,..........
John Monteith	....	Vice, Divall, resigned..........
George E. Seymour..	....	Assistant ....
R. D. Shannon ...	1874	For 2 years ....

SUPREME JUDGES.

NAMES OF OFFICERS.	RESIDENCE.	DATE OF APP'T.	HOW APPOINTED, ETC.	TERM OF SERVICE.	REMARKS.
Mathias McGirk	Montgomery Co.	1822	By Governor & Senate	Until 65 years of age	Resigned, 1841.
John D. Cook	Cape Girardeau Co.	1822	By Governor & Senate	Until 65 years of age	Resigned, July 3, 1833.
John Rice Jones	Pike County	1822	By Governor & Senate	Until 65 years of age	Died, April, 1824.
Rufus Pettibone	Pike County	1823	By Governor & Senate	Until 65 years of age	Died, August 1, 1825.
George Tompkins	Cole County	April 27, 1824	By the Governor	Vice J. R. Jones	Until General Assembly.
George Tompkins	Cole County	Feb. 11, 1825	By Governor & Senate	Until 65 years of age	Vice R. Pettibone.
Robert Wash	St. Louis County	Sept. 1, 1825	By Governor & Senate	Until General Assembly	Resigned, May 1, 1837.
Robert Wash	St. Louis County	1837	By Governor & Senate	Until 65 years of age	Not nominated to Senate.
John C. Edwards	Cole County	May, 1837	By Governor & Senate	Until 65 years of age	Vice Robert Wash.
William B. Napton	Saline County	Feb. 19, 1839	By Governor & Senate	Until 65 years of age	Vice M. McGirk.
William Scott	Cole County	At g. 10, 1841	By Governor & Senate	Until General Assembly	Vice M. McGirk.
William Scott	Cole County	Jan. 10, 1843	By Governor	Until 65 years of age	Vice M. McGirk
Priestly H. McBride	Monroe County	March 27, 1845	By Governor & Senate	Vice George Tompkins	His term expires by limitation.
William B. Napton	Saline County	Jan. 27, 1849	By Governor & Senate	For 12 years from Mch. 1, '49	
John F. Ryland	Lafayette County	Jan. 27, 1849	By Governor & Senate	For 12 years from Mch. 1, '49	
James H. Birch	Clinton County	Jan. 27, 1849	By Governor & Senate	For 12 years from Mch. 1, '49	
William Scott	Cole County	Sept. 19, 1851	Elected	For 6 years from Mch. 1, '49	
John F. Ryland	Lafayette County	Sept. 19, 1851	Elected	For 6 years from Mch. 1, '49	
Hamilton R. Gamble	St. Louis County	Sept. 19, 1851	Elected	For 6 years from Mch. 1, '49	
Abiel Leonard	Howard County	Jan. 23, 1855	Elected, Jan. 1855	For 6 years from Mch. 1, '49	Vice H. R. Gamble, resigned.
William B. Napton	Saline County	Sept. 1, 1857	Elected, Aug., 1857	Six years	Vacated by failure to file oath.
John C. Richardson	St. Louis County	Sept. 1, 1857	Elected, Aug., 1857	Six years	Resigned.
William Scott	Cole County	Sept. 9, 1857	Elected, Aug., 1857	Six years	Vacated by failure to file oath.
Ephraim B. Ewing	Ray County	Sept. 1, 1859	Elected, Aug., 1859	To fill vacancy caused by	Resig'n of J. C. Richardson.
John B. Henderson	Pike County	Jan. 15, 1863	Appointed by Gov'r	August, 1863	Declined the appointment.
Barton Bates	St. Charles County	Jan. 15, 1863	Appointed by Gov'r	August, 1863	
Benjamin F. Loan	Buchanan County	Jan. 18, 1862	Appointed by Gov'r	August, 1863	Declined the appointment.
W. V. N. Bay	St. Louis County	Jan. 18, 1863	Appointed by Gov'r	August, 1863	
Barton Bates	St. Charles County	Jan. 5, 1864	Elected, Nov. 3, 1863		Resigned, to take.
John D. S. Dryden	Marion County	Jan. 5, 1864	Elected, Nov. 3, 1863		Effect February 1, 1855.
W. V. N. Bay	St. Louis County	Jan. 5, 1864	Elected, Nov. 3, 1863		
David Wagner		April 10, 1865	Appointed by Gov'r	Vice B. Bates, resigned	
Walter L. Lovelace		May 1, 1865	Appointed by Gov'r	Vice J. D. S. Dryden, de'ed	
Nathaniel Holmes		June 10, 1865	Appointed by Gov'r	Vice W. V. N. Bray, resigned	
Thomas J. C. Fagg		Oct. 1, 1866	Appointed by Gov'r	Vice W. L. Lovelace, res'd	Declined the appointment.
Henry A. Clover		Aug. 3, 1868	Appointed by Gov'r		
James Baker		Dec. 29, 1868	Elected, Nov. 3, 1868	Two years	
David Wagner		Dec. 29, 1868	Elected, Nov. 3, 1868		
Philemon Bliss		Dec. 29, 1868	Elected, Nov. 3, 1868	Four years	
Warren Currier					Resigned, December, 1871.

MISSOURI STATE OFFICERS.

SUPREME JUDGES—Continued.

NAMES OF OFFICERS.	RESIDENCE.	DATE OF APP'T.	HOW APPOINTED, ETC.	TERM OF SERVICE.	REMARKS.
David Wagner		1870.	Elected, Nov. 8, 1870		
Washington Adams	Cooper County	Dec. 27, 1871	Appointed by Gov'r	Vice W. Currier, resigned	
Henry N. Vorhes	Cooper County	Dec. 2, 1872	Elected, Nov. 2, 1872	Six years	
Washington Adams	Cooper County	Dec. 2, 1872	Elected, Nov. 2, 1872	Two years	Resigned
Ephriam B. Ewing	Ray County	Dec. 2, 1872	Elected, Nov. 2, 1872	Eight years	Deceased
Thomas H. Sherwood		Dec. 2, 1872	Elected, Nov. 2, 1872	Ten years	
William B. Napton	Saline County	Jan. 24, 1873	Appointed by Gov'r	Until next General Election	Until suc'sor elected & quali'd
Edward A. Lewis		Sept. 25, 1874	Appointed by Gov'r	Vice Wash. Adams	Resigned
Warwick Hough		Dec. 1, 1874	Elected, Nov. 3, 1874	Ten years	
William B. Napton	Saline County	Dec. 1, 1874	Elected, Nov. 3, 1874	Short term	

CHAPTER XXI.

Complete List of all the County Officers who have served from the organization of the County to the present time.

CIRCUIT JUDGES OF COOPER COUNTY.

NAME.	DATE OF ELECT'N OR APPOINTMENT	DATE OF RETIRING FROM OFFICE.
David Todd	March 1, 1869	January, 1837
William Scott	January, 1837	August, 1841
James W. Morrow	August 14, 1841	August, 1851
George W. Miller	August, 1851	January 1, 1869
T. M. Rice	January 1, 1869	January 1, 1875
George W. Miller	January 1, 1875	Still in office. Term will expire January 1, 1881.

STATE SENATORS,

From the District of Missouri in which Cooper County is situated.

YEAR OF ELECTION	NAMES OF SENATORS.
1820	Cooper and Clark
1824	George Crawford
1828	John Miller
1832	John Miller
1836	David Jones
1840	Reuben A. Ewing
1844	Jordan O'Bryan
1848	David Jones
1852	Wm. Dunlap
1856	James B. Harris
1860	Thomas Monroe
1862	Frank W. Hickox
1866	George W. Boardman
1869	M. McMillen, to fill vacancy
1870	John Pappin
1873	S. S. Abney, to fill vacancy
1874	S. S. Abney. Term expires November, 1878

REPRESENTATIVES.

YEAR.	NAMES OF REPRESENTATIVES.
1820....	Thomas Rogers, Thomas Smiley and Wm. Lillard..........
1822....	B. F. Hickox, Jordan O'Bryan and A. K. Langon..........
1824....	B. F. Hickox and G. W. Wright.............................
1826....	M. Dunn and Jordan O'Bryan...............................
1828....	A. Kavanaugh and D. Jones................................
1830....	A. Kavanaugh and D. Jones................................
1832....	D. Jones and Joseph S. Anderson..........................
1834....	D. Jones and Jordan O'Bryan..............................
1836...	William Calvert and John H. Hutchison....................
1838....	John Miller, B. F. Hickox and L. Hall.....................
1840....	J. O'Bryan, John G. Miller and L. C. Stephens............
1842....	Wm. Shields and John G. Miller...........................
1844....	A. S. Walker and A. K. Langon............................
1846....	Thornton P. Bell..
1848....	Benjamin Tompkins and David Jones........................
1850....	L. C. Stephens and Benjamin Tompkins.....................
1852....	A. K. Langon and Benjamin Tompkins.......................
1854....	Robert C. Harrison and W. C. Ewing.......................
1856....	John M. McCutchen and Robert C. Harrison.................
1858....	A. J. Barnes and Reuben A. Ewing.........................
1860....	G. G. Vest and A. S. Walker...............................
1862....	W. G. Wear and Harvey Bunce..............................
1864....	Henry Elliott and Alfred Mathews.........................
1866....	J. A. Eppstein and D. K. Steele...........................
1868....	Daniel Clark and D. K. Steele.............................
1870....	M. McMillan and D. K. Steele.............................
1872....	Daniel Hunt...
1874....	J. G. Roberts. Term will expire November, 1876...........

CIRCUIT CLERKS OF COOPER COUNTY.

NAMES.	DATE OF ELECT'N OR APPOINTMENT	DATE OF RETIRING FROM OFFICE.
Robert P. Clark......	Mar. 1, '19....	November, 1841..................
Bennett C. Clark.....	Nov. '41......	September, 1853.................
Benjamin Tompkins..	Sept. '53......	January, 1860...................
Justinian Williams..	Jan. '60......	January, 1867...................
W. W. Taliaferro....	Jan. '67......	January, 1875...................
Horace A. Hutchison.	Jan. '75.......	Still in office, term ex. Jan. '79.

COUNTY CLERKS OF COOPER COUNTY.

NAMES.	DATE OF ELECT'N OR APPOINTMENT	DATE OF RETIRING FROM OFFICE.
Robert P. Clark.....	Jan. 8, '21....	January 8, 1836.................
Samuel S. Kofield....	Jan. 1, '36....	August 1, 1837..................
Benj. Emmons Ferry.	Aug. 8, '37....	January 8, 1854.................
Henry C. Levens....	Jan. 1, '54....	January 3, 1875.................
Jackson Monroe.....	Jan. 3, '75....	Still in office, term ex. Jan. 1, '79

COOPER COUNTY OFFICERS.

*SHERIFFS OF COOPER COUNTY.

NAMES.	DATE OF ELECT'N OR APPOINTMENT.	DATE OF RETIRING FROM OFFICE.
William McFarland..	March 1, '19..	July 24, 1819...............
William H. Curtis...	July 24, '19...	July 22, 1822...............
James L. Collins.....	July 24, '22...	November 24, 1822...........
Sylvester Hall.......	Nov. 24, '22...	July 26, 1824...............
Marcus Williams.....	July 26, '24...	August 1826.................
William H. Anderson	August '26...	August 1828.................
Joseph S. Anderson..	August '28...	August 1832.................
John H. Hutchison..	August '32...	August 1836.................
Joel E. Woodward..	August '36...	August 1838.................
James Hill..........	August '38...	August 1842.................
Isaac Lionberger....	August '42...	August 1846.................
James Hill..........	August '46...	August 1850.................
Harvey Bunce.......	August '50...	August 1854.................
B. E. Ferry.........	August '54...	August 1858.................
Harvey Bunce......	August '58...	November 5, 1861............
C. B. Combs........	Dec. 1, '62...	January 6, 1863.............
A. J. Barnes........	Jan. 6, '63...	September 5, 1864...........
Wm. J. Woolery.....	Jan. 11, '65...	May 2, 1865.................
Thos. E. Rochester...	May 2, '65...	June 23, 1870...............
R. B. Newman.......	July 1, '70...	November 1872...............
F. A. Rogers........	Nov. '72.....	November 1874...............
F. A. Rogers........	Nov. '74.....	Term will expire Nov. 1876...

COUNTY COLLECTORS OF COOPER COUNTY.

NAMES.	DATE OF ELCT'N OR APPOINTMENT.	DATE OF RETIRING FROM OFFICE.
Andrew Briscoe.....	April 11, '21...	February 19, 1822............
John C. Rochester...	Feb. 9, '22....	February 18, 1824............
William H. Anderson	Feb. 18, '24...	August 2, 1826...............
David P. Mahan.....	Aug. 2, '26...	June 11, 1829................
Joseph S. Anderson..	June 11, '29...	February 6, 1832.............
Martin Jennings.....	Feb. 6, '32....	February 11, 1833............
John H. Hutchison..	Feb. 11, '33...	August 14, 1836..............
J. E. Woodward.....	Aug. 14, '36...	August 9, 1838...............
James Hill..........	Aug. 9, '38...	August, 1842.................
Isaac Lionberger.....	Aug '42.......	August, 1846.................
James Hill..........	Aug. '46.......	August, 1850.................
Harvey Bunce.......	Aug. '50.......	August, 1854.................
B. F. Ferry.........	Aug. '54.......	August, 1858.................
Harvey Bunce......	Aug. '58.......	November 5th, 1861...........
C. B. Combs........	Dec. 1, '62....	January 6th, 1863............
A. J. Barnes........	Jan. 6, '63....	September 5th, 1864..........
Wm. J. Woolery.....	Jan. 11, '65...	May 2nd, 1865................
Thomas E. Rochester.	May 2, '65....	June 23d, 1870...............
R. B. Newman.......	July 1, '70....	....
Robert McCulloch...	Nov. 3, '72....	February 3d, 1875............
Robert McCulloch....	Nov. '74.......	Still in office, term exp's Feb. '77

JUSTICES OF THE COUNTY COURT OF COOPER COUNTY.

NAMES	DATE OF ELECT'N OR APPOINTMENT	DATE OF RETIRING FROM OFFICE.
A. S. Walker	Nov. 21, '42	May 16th, 1844
Lawrence C. Stephens	Aug. 5, '44	September 24th, 1844.
Benj. F. Hickox	Sept. 24, '44	November 2d, 1846
John H. Hutchison	Apr. 14, '45	August 7, 1848
John S. McFarland	Nov. 2, '46	November 4th, 1850
Robert Stuart	Aug. 3, '47	February 19, 1850
Philip A. Tutt	Sept. 13, '48	November 4th, 1850
Jeremiah Rice	Apr. 5, '50	August 28th, 1854
Ignatius Hazell	Nov. 4, '50	August 16th, 1858
William R. Butler	Nov. 4, '50	August 28th, 1854
Thomas L. Williams	Aug. 28, '54	August 16th, 1858
Leonard Calvert	Aug. 28, '54	February 16th, 1856
Jesse Odgen	May 5, '56	August 16th, 1858
Bennett C. Clark	Aug. 16, '58	February 3d, 1862
Isaac Lionberger	Aug. 16, '58	February 3d, 1862
James H. Baker	Aug. 16, '58	November 2nd, 1866
William E. Baird	Apr. 7, '62	December 19th, 1862
John A. Trigg	June 2, '62	November 6th, 1864
Wm. J. Woolerly	Dec. 19, '62	December 19th, 1864
C. W. Sombart	Dec. 19, '62	November 27th, 1866
Jesse G. Newman	Dec. 16, '62	November 30th, 1868
Jacob Baughman	Nov. 27, '66	December 16th, 1872
Joseph Feland	Nov. 27, '66	December 5th, 1870
Constantine Heim	Nov. 30, '68	December 14th, 1874
James Bruffey	Jan. 8, '21	January 10th, 1822
Archibald Kavanaugh	Jan. 8, '21	August 16th, 1824
James Miller	Jan. 8, '21	May 2nd, 1825
James D. Campbell	Jan. 10, '22	February 6th, 1326
Robert F. Howe	Aug. 16, '24	May 6th, 1825
John Briscoe	May 2, '25	February, 6th, 1826
Charles Woods	May 2, '25	February 6th, 1826
Thomas McMahan	May 2, '25	February 6th, 1826
Joseph Byler	May 2, '25	February 6th, 1826
James L. Collins	Feb. 6, '26	May 7th, 1827
Green Seat	Feb. 6, '26	May 7th, 1827
David Jones	Feb. 6, '26	May 7th, 1827
Samuel Turley	Feb. 6, '26	May 7th, 1827
William Bryant	Feb. 6, '26	May 7th, 1827
John Briscoe	May 7, '27	May 17th, 1832
Marcus Williams	May 7, '27	June 17th, 1830
Joseph Byler	May 7, '27	August 3d, 1829
Rice Hughes	Aug. 3, '29	May 2nd. 1831
Robert Hood	June 17, '30	May 2nd, 1831
Anthony F. Read	May 2, '31	September 8th 1834
Green Seat	May 2, '31	September 8th, 1834
Joseph Patterson	Nov. 6, '32	August, 1836
George W. Weight	Sept. 8, '34	November 21st, 1842
John Briscoe	Sept. 8, '34	November 21st, 1842
C. H. Smith	Feb. 7, '37	June 5th, 1847
A. H. Neal	Nov. 21, '42	September 24th, 1844

JUSTICES OF COUNTY COURT---Continued.

JAMES H. WALKER, present presiding Justice of County Court, elected November, 1870; term will expire November, 1876.

JOHN M. MCCUTCHEN, at present Associate Justice, elected November 1872; term will expire November, 1878.

ROBERT A. MCCULLOCH, present Associate Justice, elected November, 1874; term will expire November, 1880.

COUNTY TREASURERS.

NAMES.	TIME ENTERING OFFICE.	DATE OF RETIRING FROM OFFICE.
Robert P. Clark	Jan. 8, '21	January 4, 1833
Jacob Wyan	June 4, '33	February 17, 1842
C. D. W. Johnson	Feb. 17, '42	August 10, 1853
Wm. P. Speed	Aug. 12, '53	August 10, 1856
James Thomson	Aug. 11, '56	December 19, 1872
Wm. P. Speed	Dec. 19, '62	July, 1863
H. E. W. McDearmon	Aug. 3, '63	February 7, 1865
Christian Keill	Feb. 10, '65	January 5, 1870
*Wm. E. Baird	Jan. 5, '70	November 15, 1870
C. Keill	Nov. 15, '70	November 14, 1872
James Thomson	Nov. 14, '72	November 7, 1874
James Thomson	Nov. 7, '74	Still in office, term ex. Nov. '76.

* William E. Baird was appointed County Treasurer in the place of Christian Keill, on account of his being rendered unfit to discharge the duties of his office, by what afterwards proved to be temporary insanity. But in the suit which Keill brought after his recovery, for his salary as County Treasurer while the office was occupied by Baird, the Supreme Court decided that the office was illegally held by Baird, because Kiell had not been declared insane by the proper tribunal. But at the time of the appointment of Baird, the interests of the county would have greatly suffered by the office being left vacant.

COUNTY ATTORNEYS OF COOPER COUNTY.

NAMES.	DATE OF ELECT'N OR APPOINTMENT	DATE OF RETIRING FROM OFFICE.
Wm. S. Brickey	March 3, '19	June 26, 1840
James Winston	June 26, '40	May 9, 1851
J. L. Stephens	May 9, '51	July 25, 1864
Wm. Douglass	July 25, '64	May 30, 1865
John Trigg	Ap'nt'd pro t'm	During term Circuit Court
D. W. Wear	June 5, '65	November 10, 1866
D. A. Millan	Nov. 28, '66	January 1, 1873
John Cosgrove	Jan. 1, '73	January 1, 1875
James H. Johnston	Jan. 1, '75	Still in office. Term ex. Jan. 1, '77

There was, we think, a small space of time between 18---, and 18--, during which time William D. Muir acted as County Attorney for Cooper county, ex-offieio, he being at that time State Circuit Attorney for this district of Missouri; but the records of the county do not show the facts.

COUNTY ASSESSORS OF COOPER COUNTY.

NAMES.	DATE OF ELECT'N OR APPOINTMENT	DATE OF RETIRING FROM OFFICE.
Geo. Crawford, for Co.	April 9, '21...	February 20, 1822.............
J. Dixon, Boonville T	Feb 20, '22...	February 19, 1823.............
J. Briscoe, Clear Creek	Feb. 20, '22...	February 19, 1823.............
S. D. Reavis, Moniteau	Feb. 20, '22...	February 19, 1823.............
L. Cropper, Saline T..	Feb. 20, '22...	February 19, 1823.............
John C. Rochester...	Feb. 19, '23...	February 18, 1824.............
William Allison......	Feb. 18, '24...	February 22, 1825.............
Lawrence Hall.......	Feb. 22, '25...	February 6, 1826.............
Joseph B. Steele......	Feb. 6, '26....	February 6, 1828.............
Joseph Patterson....	Feb. 6, '28....	February 9, 1832.............
Howard Chism......	Feb. 9, '32....	February 6, 1833.............
George Crawford.....	Feb. 6, '33....	February 6, 1835.............
A. S. Walker...	Feb. 6, '35....	February 6, 1836.............
W. H. Anderson.....	Feb. 6, '36....	February, 1837.............
John Ogden..........	Feb. 6, '37....	February. 1838.............
Thomas L. O'Bryan..	August, '38...	August, 1840...... ....
William R. Butler...	August, '40...	August, 1841.... ....
George Crawford.....	August, '41...	August, 1846................
A. H. Roads.........	August, '46...	August, 1848................
Harvey Bunce.......	August, '48...	August, 1850................
George Crawford.....	August, '50...	August, 1851................
James Hill..........	August, '51...	August, 1852................
Robert H. Turner....	August, '52...	February 16, 1853.............
Thomas McCulloch..	Feb. 16, '53...	December 22, 1853.............
Josiah E. Eubank....	Dec. 22, '53...	December 8, 1856.............
James T. McCulloch.	Dec. 8, '56....	January 5, 1858.. ....
Joseph C. Koontz....	Jan. 5, '58...	February 6, 1860.............
Thomas E. Rochester.	Jan. 5, '58....	February 6, 1860.............
Jesse McFarland.....	Jan. 5, '58....	February 6, 1860.............
R. B. Stoneman......	Feb. 1, '58....	January 3, 1859.............
James L. Bell.......	Jan. 5, '58....	January 3, 1859.............
N. T. Allison........	Jan. 5, '58....	February 6, 1860.............
D. R. Drake..... ..	Jan. 3, '59....	February 6, 1860.............
J. E. Eubank........	Jan. 3, '59....	February 6, 1860.............
B. R. Waller........	Feb. 6, '60...	August, 1860........ ....
Thomas E. Rochester	August, '60...	October 6, 1862 ....
D. A. Melvin........	Oct. 6, '62.....	February 21, 1865.............
Thomas E. Rochester.	Feb. 21, '65...	May 1, 1865................
M. F. Kemp.........	May 3, 1865...	September 4, 1865.............
R. B. Newman.......	Sept. 4, '65...	July 1, 1870................
R. W. Whitlow......	July 2, '70....	January 1, 1873.............
J. H. Orr............	Jan. 1, '73 ...	January 1, 1875.............
James F. Adams.....	Jan. 1, '75....	Still in office. Term ex. Jan. 1, '77

PUBLIC ADMINISTRATORS.

NAMES.	DATE OF ELECT N OR APPOINTMENT	EXPIRATION.
John M. McCutchen.	Jan. 6, '48...	May 4, 1857..................
H. A Hutchison.....	May 4, '57....	February 13, 1860.............
Elisha N. Warfield...	Feb. 13, '60;..	October 18, 1862..............
Harvey Bunce......	Oct., '62......	November 20, 1872............
Viet Eppstein.......	Nov. 20, '72...	El'ted 4 y'rs. Term ex. Nov., '76.

COUNTY SURVEYORS OF COOPER COUNTY.

NAMES.	TIME OF ENTERING OFFICE.	TIME OF RETIRING FROM OFFICE.
William Ross	March 1, '19	—— 2, 1829
Baxter M. Ewing	July 9, '21	February 22, 1822
John Dixon	Feb. 22, '22	September 11, 1833
George T. Boyd	Sept. 12, '33	February 3, 1836
George W. Weight	Feb. 3, '36	August 3, 1843
P. A. Tutt	August 3, '43	November 8, 1859
C. H. Allison	Nov. 8, '59	December 8, 1868
Charles Atkinson	Dec. 1, '61	December 18, 1872
W. W. Trent	Dec. 8, '72	December, 1874
W. W. Trent	Dec., '74	Still in office. Term ex. Dec. '78.

Those to Whom we are under Obligations for Assistance.

The greater part of the information concerning the "History of the Boone's Lick Country" south of the Missouri river, was obtained from Capt. Samuel Cole, who, with the exception of his sister, Mrs. Jennie Davis is the only living witness of the events which transpired from the first settlement of the county to the year 1815. They, at the age of nine years, came to the county with their mother, and have resided within the same ever since.

The information concerning that part of the country lying north of said river, was mostly obtained from Col. N. G. Elliott, who is now living in Howard county. His history, which is no doubt reliable, was obtained from the first settlers when living.

We also acknowledge assistance from the "Annals of the West," "Campbell's Gazetteer of Missouri," and other able histories.

The next living witness is William Gibson, who emigrated to this county in the year 1815. In 1816 we have Mr. Jesse McFarland, who was in 1819, Deputy United States Surveyor of Cooper county, Judge John S. McFarland and Mrs. Margaret Stephens; in 1817, Joseph Stephens, son of Joseph Stephens, Sr.; in 1818, Mr. and Mrs. John Kelly, Mr. and Mrs. Jesse Homan, Jonathan and Miss Mary Reavis, all of Boonville. Also at later dates, Messrs. William L. Scott, N. T. Allison, Sr., Peter H. Ferrel, Judge Bennett, C. Clark, and Dr. Waid Howard.

Those who rendered assistance in compiling the history of the different townships of the county, were Messrs. Thomas J. Starke, William G. Pendleton, David Schilb,

Dr. T. H. Winterbower, William Lamm, and Rev. N. T. Allison, Jr. Those who assisted us in the war history of the county, were Col. Joseph A. Eppstein, David Schilb, Marcus Williams, Capt. Joseph L. Stephens, and some few others, to all of whom we return our sincere acknowledgments.

We are also under many obligations to Mr. John W. Pattison, Clerk in the department of the Secretary of State at Jefferson City, from whom we obtained much valuable information, and who was untiring in attending to our simplest requests.

Also Col. H. A. Hutchison, Circuit Clerk, and Jackson Monroe, County Clerk of Cooper county, for their kindness extended during our examinations for record history in their respective offices.

POPULATION OF COOPER COUNTY, AS SHOWN BY EACH CENSUS, FROM THE YEAR 1820 TO THE PRESENT TIME.

Year.	White Population.	Colored Population.	Total Population.
1820	6,307	652	6,959
1830	5,876	1,028	6,904
1840	8,312	2,172	10,484
1850	9,837	3,113	12,950
1860	13,528	3,828	17,356
1870	17,340	3,352	20,692

The reason of the seemingly small increase in population between the dates of the taking of the census for the first few times, is explained by the fact that every few years some new county was cut off from Cooper, thus taking some part of its territory and population. In taking the census of 1870, twelve square miles of the county were left out by mistake, so that, had the census for that year been taken correctly, the population would have been found to have been several thousand more.

ABSTRACT OF APPORTIONMENTS TO THE CHILDREN OF COOPER COUNTY FROM THE DIFFERENT SCHOOL FUNDS.

Year.	Children in County	State Apportionm't	Township Appor'm't	County Appor'm't	Total Appor'ment.
1854	3,850	$3,722.58	$1,154.14	$ 729.80	$5,606.52
1855	4,085	2,737.04	2,882.58	699.16	6,318.78
1856	4,185	3,246.70	699.46	264.80	4,210.96
1857	4,498	3,508.44	2,057.30	1,089.76	6,655.50
1858	4,787	3,350.90	2,450.47	1,214.50	7,015.87
1859	5,005	3,494.85	2,356.60	566.50	6,037.95
1860	5,068	3,461.88	2,740.21	362.01	6,564.10
1861	5,104		1,164.73	467.20	1,631.93
1863	3,698		2,992.27	521.36	3,513.83
1864	5,635	2,240.13	1,966.41	531.55	4,738.09
1865	3,971		2,816.26	1,165.58	3,981.84
1866	4,599	594.44	2,679.82	495.99	3,770.25
1867	5,024		2,416.81	1,002.90	3,419.71
1868	7,028	3,720.78	17,550.35	844.47	22,105.60
1869	7,177	4,148.31	1,876.21	1,066.14	7,090.63
1870	6,94	3,758.00	2,592.30	2,144.63	8,494.93
1871	7,198	4,747.03	3,113.48	2,385.10	9,245.61
1872	7,436	3,961.97	3,482.43	1,599.13	8,043.56
1873		3,901.19	2,428.76	2,407.58	8,737.53
1874		4,477.89	2,684.64	3,633.95	10,796.48
1875		5,154.93	2,462.29	731.62	8,348.84
1876	6,211	4,796.52	2,421.69	638.40	7,856.11

In the above abstracts, from 1866 to 1876, both years inclusive, the number of colored children and the apportionment of the above funds to them, is included in that of the white children.

ABSTRACTS OF THE SCHOOL TAX BOOKS OF COOPER CO.

Year.	District Tax.	Township Tax.	Total Taxes.
1870	$39,343.89	$2,687.51	$42,031.40
1871	36,984.67	690.38	37,615.05
1872	56,313.25		56,313.25
1873	32,186.72	1,021.55	33,208.27
1874	29,155.19	410.55	29,565.74
1875	26,787.75	2,162.31	28,950.06
1876	25,406.34	470.85	25,877.19

Previous to the year 1870, the school taxes were levied and collected by the different township clerks, so that the aggregate for years previous to 1870 cannot be given.

ABSTRACTS OF TAXABLE WEALTH AND TAXES OF COOPER COUNTY

Year.	Value of Real Estate.	Value of Pers'l Pro'y	To'l Val'a'n	State Tax.	All County Tax.	To'l Taxes
1819	$	$	$	$	$	$
1820				1,734.04	867.02	
1821				726.32	363.16	
1822						
1823						
1824						
1825						
1826				1,269.06	634.53	
1827				1,242.96	621.48	
1828				1,457.18	728.59	
1829						
1830				1,729.96	864.98	
1831						
1832						
1833						
1834						
1835						
1836						
1837	595,899	571,918	1,167,847	1,189,21	1,189.21	2,878.42
1838	863,153	639,442	1,502,595	1,509.16	2,300.76	3,809.92
1839	918,640	817,073	1,735,722	2,627.41	3,331.08	5,958.49
1840	1,141,775	742,267	1,984,042	2,715.54	4,029.06	6,744.60
1841	1,098,646	1,077,665	2,176,311	3,154.01	3,604.65	6,758.06
1842	1,386,126	1,094,997	2,481,123	3,455.59	3,455.59	6,911.18
1843	1,255,934	700,109	1,956,043	3,691.01	2,318.25	5,409.26
1844			2,012,632	3,749.60	2,812.20	6,561.80
1845			2,095,366	4,227.86	4,227.86	8,455.72
1846			2,216,053	4,103.06	4,103.06	8,206.12
1847			2,062,547	4,833.02	4,720.50	6,561.52
1848	1,288,322	921,494	2,209,810	5,426.62	5,089.91	10,486.53
1849	1,101,795	1,189,188	2,290,983	5,115.85	5,115.85	10,231.70
1850	1,232,740	1,060,518	2,293,258	5,200.04	5,188.16	10,389.10
1851	1,237,905	1,460,437	2,698,342	5,996.36	11,992.72	17,989.08
1852	1,264,695	1,492,532	2,757,227	6,143.72	7,522.46	13,666.18
1853	1,177,850	1,552,778	2,730,628	6,141.11	11,022.51	17,163.62
1854						
1855	1,606,680	1,531,650	3,138,330	7,046.34	12,553.32	19,599.64
1856	2,634,645	2,316,195	4,950,840	10,682.43	19,803.36	20,485.79
1857	2,249,160	2,518,330	4,767,490	10,289,48	10,289.48	20,578.96
1858	3,385,821	3,458,683	6,844,504	15,588.13	21,671.05	37,250.18
1859	3,672,538	3,428,789	7,101,327	23,330.29	18,923.24	42,253.53
1860	3,603,872	3,186,830	6,790,602	22,402.81	21,720.67	44,123.48
1861	2,679,385	2,621,210	5,400,595	18,046.13	17,679.27	35,725.40
1862			3,894,000	12,777.50	13,334,91	26,112.41
1863	1,917,230	1,540,070	3,457,300	20,086.96	12,562.38	32,649.34
1864	1,976,390	1,089,660	3,066,050	22,126.36	35,871.98	57,998.34
1865	2,047,280	909,580	2,956,860	23,507.16	13,812.08	37,319.24
1866	2,662,757	1,027,807	3,690,564	41,219.07	32,291.07	78,510.58
1867	4,588,978	1,366,377	5,955,355	38,609.80	38,609.80	77,219.60
1868	4,929,762	1,164,443	6,094,205	31,243.50	75,580.86	106,832.86
1869	4,782,080	1,074,081	4,856,161	29,280.80	84,035.76	113,316.56
1870	4,787,165	1,069,167	5,856,362	29,281.81	111,684.47	140,966.28
1871	4,384,641	1,164,928	5,549,559	27,747.84	130,325,14	158,072.98
1872	4,275,973	1,252,845	5,528,818	24,879.68	107,956.26	132,835.94
1873	4,226,150	1,370,300	5,596,450	27,542.63½	129,198.91½	156,741.55
1874	4,226,150	1,347,250	5,573,400	25,814.65	113,186.00⅝	139,000.65⅝
1875	3,773,740	1,366,485	5,140,225	23,131.01	71,834.81	94,965.82
1876	3,773,605	1,781,550	5,555,155	22,174.42	92,472.12	114,646.54

CORRECTIONS.

We ask the forbearance of our readers in making the following corrections. It is extremely difficult to get names in type correctly:

On page 31, meat cattle should be *neat* cattle.
On page 53, Amistead A. Grundy should be *Armstead*.
On page 54, Fitsworth should be *Titsworth*.
On page 60, "haloed" should be *hallooed*.
On page 65, Augus*tine* A. Simpson should be Augus*tus*.
On pages 128, 137 and 156 Bo*n*sfield should be Bo*u*sfield.
On page 148, *F*itsworth should be *T*itsworth.
On page 152, William *P.* Reavis should be William *T.* Reavis.
On page 154, William, Jesse *and* Moon should be William *and* Jesse Moon.
On page 181, Elmi*ra* should be Elmi*na*.
On page 181, Julia Collins should be *Jaily* Collins.
On page 184, Wm. *H.* McClanahan should be Wm. *N.*
On page 192, "just before Christmas in 1818," should be 1828.
On page 192, "was taught by a man named Rogers," should be Rollins.
On page 190, in third paragraph, the name should be Mr. Nichols in both places.
On page 197, John S. Buckey should be Brickey.
On page 97, Boemstein should be Boernstein.
On page 104, first line, Kock should be Koc*h*.
On page 216, under the head of Secretary of State :—
    Eugene F. Weigel, 1870, for 4 years, should be 2 years.
    Eugene F. Weigel, 1872, for 4 years, should be 2 years.
    Michael K McGrath, 1874, for 4 years, should be 2 years.
    William G. Peters should be William G. Pettus.

INDEX OF THE HISTORY OF
COOPER COUNTY, MISSOURI

-A-
Abney, S. S. 221
Abstracts 230
Abstracts, School Tax 230
Abstracts, Taxable Wealth 230
Adams, Andrew 201
Adams, David 144
Adams, James F. 226
Adams, John 201, 204
Adams, Josiah 181
Adams, Miss Maria 201
Adams, Washington 220
Adams, William W. 144
Adams, Wm. M. 98
Adams, Wm. W. 79
Advertiser Printing 103
Agricultural 212
Alexander 204
Alexander, Capt. 102
Alexander, Jas. 76
Alexander, John 50
Alexander, Thomas 161
Allcorn, James 172
Allen, Chas. H. 66
Allison, 142
Allison, C. H. 227
Allison, Greenberry 180
Allison, Hugh 79, 80
Allison, Martin 91
Allison, Nathaniel T. 143
Allison, N. T. 226, 228
Allison, N.T.Jr. 143, 229
Allison, William 226
American 82
Amick, Mrs. Abram 161
Amick, Wesley 3rd. Corporal 91
Anderson, 51, 111
Anderson, Bill 186
Anderson, James 50

Anderson, James H. 144
Anderson, Jos. S.(Jackson) 80
Anderson, Joseph S. 152 181, 222, 223
Anderson, W. H. 79,226
Anderson, William H. 223
Anderson, Wm. 61, 96
Anderson's 115, 116
Anderson's Branch 110
Anderson's Bushwhackers 110
Anderson's Men 117
Andrew, Col. 180
Andrew, James 177
Andrew, Geo. W. 177
Andrew, W. M. 177
Andrews, Mrs. 93
Arkansas, Militia 117
Arni's, Frank 172
Artillery 110, 113
Arrow Rock 13, 106
Arrow Rock(Township) 66, 72, 73, 75
Asberry, Frank 160
Ashcraft, Jesse 144
Ashley, William H. 216
Ashley, Wm. H. 76, 78
Atkinson, Charles 227

-B-

Babbitt, John 70
Baber, A. G. 4th. Corporal 91
Baber, Hiram H. 217
Bacon, Thomas 91
Bailey, 142
Bailey, Herman 150
Baird, William E. 224
Baird, Wm. E. 225

Baker, James 219
Baker, James H. 224
Bancroft, Elias 217
Bank 82
Baptist, 36,58,59
Baptism (First) 60
Barnes, A. J. 222,223
Bartlett, John M. 144
Bartlett, William 50,52 127
Bartlett, Wm. 49, 144
Bartlett's, William (Boardinghouse) 54
Barton Convention 128
Barton, David 78, 196
Barton, David Judge 40
Barton, Joshua 40, 216
Barton, Judge 39,40,41
Basil (Negro) 44
Bass, Radford 194
Bates, Barton 219
Bates, Edward (Adams) 80
Bates, Edward 40,79,201
Bates, Frederick 78,79,215
Battle, 96,99,100,101 105, 108,110,114,117
Battle, New Orleans 89
Baughman, Jacob 224
Bay, W.V. N. 219
Bayse, Alfred 199
Bazars, 107
Beihle, Capt Charles 104, 107
Bell Air 112,117,135
Bell Air Road 113
Bell, James L. 226
Bell, Jas 138
Bell, John 83
Bell, Mr. 148
Bell, Thornton P. 222

Bell, T. P. 138
Bell, Zepheniah 49,52
Bellingsville 113, 135
Benedict, Scott 32
Bennett, Judge 228
Bernard, Joseph W. 144
Berry, Charles R. 150
Berry, Finis E. 150, 151 161
Berry, James 161
Berry, James C. 57
Berry, Jas 158
Berry, Joshua 148
Berry, Ragan 151
Best, Annie 181
Best, Thomas 180
Big Lick 61
Billingsley, Jeptha 151
Billingsley, Joe 79
Bingham, Geo C. 217
Birch, James H. 219
Birney, Alexander 166
Birney, James 166
Bishop, William 217
Black, Gerhardt 195
Black, William 54
Blackhawk 18
Blacksmith, (First) 129
Blackwater River 212
Black Water Township 14, 142
Blair 97
Blair's Col 98
Blair Gen. 100
Blair Milo 67
Blevens Dr. M. D. 188
Bliss, Philemon 219
Blundo Chiefs 18
Boarding Houses 127
Boardman, George W. 221
Boemstein Col. 97
Boggs, Lilburn W. 215, 216
Boggs, Lilburn W. Gov 88
Boogs, T. J. 64
Bohannon's 109
Bolin, Delany 20,25,49
Bombs 98
Bombshells 98
Bonsfield 128
Bonsfield, Richard D. 137, 156
Bonne Conty 112
Boone, Daniel 11, 166
Boone, Daniel M. 13

Boone Femme Creek 35
Boone's Lick Country 11, 29 30, 33, 39
Boonville 13, 16, 27, 32, 33 35, 39, 40, 41, 49, 64, 66 67, 70, 78, 83, 88, 89, 90 91, 92, 95, 96, 97, 98, 99 100, 101, 102, 103, 104 105, 106, 107, 109, 110 111, 112, 113, 114, 115 116, 118, 126, 129, 130 131, 132, 143
Boonville Advertiser 66
Boonville County Seat 125
Boonville Daily Advertiser (Newspaper) 67
Boonville Eage(Newspaper) 67
Boonville(First Court) 49
Boonville Herald 64
Boonville Observer 64, 66
Boonville Patriot(Paper) 66
Boonville Township 143
Boundaries 11
Bowis 65
Bowler T. T. 91
Bowles, Jesse 155
Bowles, Robt H. 91
Bowlin, Delany 143
Box, Muke 20, 25, 143
Boyd, George T. 227
Boyle, Judge John 201
Bradley, Edward 76
Braynum, Gray 40
Breastworks 105
Breckenridge, James C. 83
Brent, Robert 64
Brickey, John S.(Prosecuting Attorney) 49,50,53,144
Brickey, Wm. S. 128, 225
Bridge 22, 97, 106, 126
Bridges, James 180
Bridgewater, Nathaniel 143
Brigadier General 89
Briscoe, Andrew 57, 223
Briscoe, J. 226
Briscoe, John 76, 224
Briscoe, John M. 181
Briscoe, Judge John 138, 180
Briscoe, Mary 181
Briscoe, Patsy 181, 182
Briscoe, Tobe 181
British 17, 19

British(Officer) 46
Broch, James 143
Brown, Alexander 150
Brown, Capt. 104
Brown, Col 104,105,107,102
Brown, Ellis 150
Brown, Gen 113
Brown, Gratz B. 215
Brown, Hugh 150
Brown, Isaac 150
Brown, James 166
Brown, Samuel 33
Brown, Thomas 53
Brown, Wilson 216, 217
Brownfield, Thomas 186
Bruce, Horatio 91
Bruce, John B. 91
Bruffee, James(Blacksmith) 62
Bruffee, James 50, 52,56 72, 144, 224
Bruffy, James 129
Bryan, J. O. 22
Bryant, William 53, 164 224
Bryant, Wm 77
Buchanan, James 83
Buchanan,R. J. 173
Buckner, Alex 80
Buckey, John S. 197
Buffington, William H.217
Bull Ride 39
Bullock, David 196
Bunce, Harvey 84, 177, 222 223, 226
Bunceton, 111, 134
Buness, David 33
Burial 105
Buried Vine or Concord Church 112
Burk Wm 54
Burke, Samuel 160
Burkhart, Nicholas S. (Sheriff) 40, 199
Burkhart's Mr. 33
Burnam, Hiram 91
Burnett, sam'l D. 91
Burns, John 159, 161
Burns, Laird Rev. 159,161
Burr, Mr. 104
Burr, Wm. E. 104
Burress, David 20, 155
Burress, Hawking 155

Burress, Waiter 20, 143
Burton, Julius 154
Bushwhackers 106, 110
  115, 190
Butler, William 224, 226
Butler, Wm. R. 173
Butler, W. R. 172
Butler's Judge 172
Byler, Joseph 145, 224

-C-

Calaboose 94
Caldwell County 88
Caldwell, Elverton 191
Caldwell, F. M. 64,66
Caldwell, F. W. 66
Caldwell, Noding 191
California 108, 110
Calvert, John 191
Calvert, Leonard 191,224
Calvert, William 191,222
Camp 39
Camp-Bacon 99
Campbell 27, 28
Campbell, George W. 91
Campbell, James D. 46
  151, 152, 179, 198, 224
Campbell(Potter) 27
Campbell, Rhoda 181,182
Campbell, Robert Gen 93
Campbell, Samuel 20
Campbell, Susan 181
Campbell, Thomas M. 128
Campbell's 27, 228
Canale, Charles 48
Cannon, Franklin 216
Cannon, Zollinger 175
Capitol 97, 102
Captain 89, 93
Carpenter, Jacob 184
Carpenter, Peter 148
Carpenter, Samuel 184
Carr, Dabney 53
Carr, Wm. C. 79
Carroll, Charles 41
Carroll, Henry 127
Carter 127
Cason, Pemberton 198
Castell, Frederick 158
Castle Rock 108
Cathey, George 49, 52
Cathey, James 180

Cathey, John 49, 49, 52
  180
Cathey, Joseph 180
Cathey, Michael 180
Cathey, William 180
Caton, John 167
Cattle 32
Cavalry 107
Cedar Creek 39
Celebration of July Fourth
  203
Cemetery(Walnut Grove) 78
Central Missourier
  (Newspaper) 67
Challis, Rice 151, 153
Chamberlain 129
Chambers, Benjamin 50
Chambers, James 49, 144
Chambers, William 144
Chandler, Timothy 193
Chapman, George 143
Chariton River 30
Chenoweth, J. W. 173
Children 36, 65, 120
Chilton, Van Tromp 172
Chism, Howard 226
Chism, Jacob 59, 144
Chism, Mike 169
Christie 142
Christie, William 14, 143
  217
Christmas 125, 129
Church 36, 56, 59, 110
  134, 135, 188
Church, Concord(First) 58
Church, First 58, 128
Church, Nebo New 59
Church(Old Nebo) 59
Church, Presbyterian 60
Churches, 132, 134, 214
Circuit Court 55
Circuit Judges 221
Clark, 221
Clark, Benjamin 51
Clark, Benj. L. 144
Clark, Bennett C 222,224
Clark, C. 228
Clark, Daniel 222
Clark, Edwin 218
Clark, George B. 217
Clark, Major H. M. 206
Clark, Jewell(Captain) 91
Clark, John B. 128

Clark, John B. Gen Sr. 89
Clark, John J. 144
Clark, Robert P. 56,72
  75, 85, 128, 222, 225
Clark & Reed 174
Clark, Robert 143
Clark, Robert P. 144,196
Clark, R. P. 49, 52
Clark, Hon. R. P. 128
Clark, William 12
Clark, Wm. 76
Clark's Fork 106, 136
Clark's Fork Township 147
Clay County 90
Clay, Henry 77, 82
Clear Creek 136
Clear Creek Township 149
Clifton 137
Cline, Absalom 165
Cline, James H. 158,165
Cloney 174
Clover, Henry A. 219
Coal, William 155
Cobb, Edmund M. 143
Coffee 167
Coffee, Joel 91
Colbert, John 91
Colburn's 172
Cole 41
Cole A.B. 2nd.Corporal 91
Cole, Captain 20, 99
Cole County 77
Cole, Dikie 16
Cole, Hannah 16, 33
Cole, Hannah Mrs. 20
  127
Cole, Holburt 16
Cole, James 16,24,33
  136
Cole, Jennie 16
Cole, Mack 37
Cole, Mattie 16
Cole, Nellie 16
Cole, Phoebe 16
Cole, Miss Rhoda 197
Cole,Sallie 179
Cole,Samuel 11,16,17,18
  20,22,25,26,33,34,39,42
  43,44,45,77,145,179,180
Cole, Samuel Capt 228
Cole, Stephen 16,21,25,34
  37,39,40,52,143
Cole,Stephen Major 34,40,197

Cole, William T. 2nd.Sergeant 90
Cole, William 16
Coleman, Norman J. 216
Coles 210
Collins, Andrew 181
Collins, James L. 79,223 224
Collins, J. S. 64
Collins, Julia 181
Collins, Thomas 180
Colony 37
Colored Men 124
Colored People 125
Combs, C. B. 223
Combs, Wm. E. 173
Commercial Point 133
Concord Church 36
Confederate 104,111,113
Congress 78,80,100,72,76
Congress(1822) 77
Conner, Frederick 191
Conner, James F. 191,194
Conner's Mill 136
Constable 77, 79
Constitution 78
Cook, Edmond G. 91
Cook, Heli 91
Cook, John D. 219
Cook, Nathaniel 76
Cook, Nath'l 78
Cook, Wesley 160
Cooper 28,29,30,190,221
Cooper, Benjamin 12,15,17
Cooper, Col. Benjamin 15 16, 27
Cooper, Braxton Jr. 30
Cooper, Captain 32
Cooper County 16,29,32,36 48,50,77,83,84,88,89 90,93,95,101,108,111 112,114,118
Cooper, Jr. 29
Cooper Sarshell Captain 31
Cooper, Thomas 190
Cooper, William 50
Cooper's & McLean's Fort 26
Corn 19, 29
Corn-Shuckings 124
Cornwell, L. S. 173
Coroner 40,79,80
Corrections 231
Corum, Harden 180

Corum, Heli 180
Corum, Henry 77, 180
Corum, Hiram 180
Corum, James 181
Corum, John 76
Cosgrove, John 206,225
Council Bluffs 22
County 40
County Assessors 226
County Attorneys 225
County Clerks 222
County Collectors, 223
County Court 49, 71
County Court(First) 56
County Officers 76
County Seat 40,56,57,58
County Surveyors 227
County Treasurers 225
Court 39,40,63
Court(First County) 56
Court House(Building) 52, 57
Court(Justices) 56
Courtships 121
Cox 168
Cox, Tarleton T. 173
Coxes, Mathew 50
Cramer, John 154
Cranmer 167
Cranmer, George 167
Cranmer, T. C. 166, 174
Cranmer, Thomas C. 158 167
Crawford 174
Crawford, George 56,79, 148, 221, 226
Crawford, John 58, 85
Creek 87
Crimes 37
Crittenden, Col 113,114
Crockett, Robert 143
Cropper, L. 226
Cropper, Levin 191
Crowther, Henry 81
Crowther, Henry W. 89
Cully, Maj. 100
Currier, Warren 219
Curtis H. Wm. 76
Curtis, Rev. 206
Curtis, W. 141
Curtis, William 51,54
Curtis, William H. 223
Curtis, Wm. 56

Custom 121

-D-

Dade, John 128
Dallas, Dikie Mrs. 145
Dallias, Dikie 17
Dallmeyer, William Q. 217
Davis, Gen. Jeff C. 103
Davis, James 24,136,166
Davis, Jennie 17
Davis, Jennie Mrs. 228
Davis, John 49
Davis, Llelwellyn 218
Davis, Philip E. 151
Day, Darius 141
Declaration of National Indep. 62
Deitrick, Bernhard 195
Delegates to State Constitution 75
Dellis, Joshua 151
Democrat 83, 86
Democratic Paper 65
Devine, Wm. 173
Dial, Hiram 151
Dickson, Alexander 54
Dickson, Alexander R. 191
Dickson, Alpha 198
Dickson, Andrew J. 198
Dickson, Miss Catherine 198
Dickson, George 191
Dickson, George D. 198
Dickson, Harriet 198
Dickson, Isabella 198
Dickson, John 76
Dickson, John D. 198
Dickson, Josiah 191
Dickson, Lee Ann 198
Dickson, Margaret 198
Dickson, Robert 191
Dickson, Thomas H.B. 198
Didier, Peter 217
Diegle, George 218
Diehl, John 190
Diehl, Peter 195
Dillard, James 144
Dillard, Joseph 144
Dillard, William 144
Divall, Ira 218
Dix, Larkin T. 143
Dixon J. 226

Dixon, John 227
Dobbins, Mrs. 128
Documents 40
Dodge 28
Dodge, Gen 27, 28
Donaldson, James 61
Donaphan's Expedition 93
Donaphan's, General 93
Donelson, James 155, 156
Douglass, Stephen A. 83
Douglass, William 84
Downs, John P. 161
Draffen, J. W. 104
Drade, 85
Drake, Charles 84
Drake, D. R. 226
Drake, N. M. 185, 188, 206
Draper, Daniel W. 217
Drennan, Mrs. A. M. 134
Drinkwater, Robert 148
Drinkwater, Samuel 148
Drinkwater, William 148
Drury, Mr. 66
Dryden, John D. S. 219
Dugan, Daniel 49
Dunklin, Daniel 215, 216
Dunlap, Wm. 221
Dunn, Kyra 144
Dunn, M. 222
Dunn, Michael (Adams) 80
Dunn, Michael 79
Durklin, Daniel (Jackson) 80
Duvall, Jacob 91

-E-

Earickson, James 217
East Boonville 33
Easton, Lucius 40
Easton, Rufus 79
Eckhard, Adam 56, 197
Eder, Jacob 195
Edgar, James 76
Edgar, Russell 144
Edger, Lewis 77, 144
Edwards, Cyrus 53
Edwards, John C. 215, 216, 219
Election (First in Cooper County) 72
Elizabeth, Miss 180
Elliott, Col. N. G. 228
Elliott, Henry 222

Elliott, Samuel 91
Ellis, William 151
Ellis, Willis 151
Ellison, Ephraim 144
Embree, George 173
Embree, Geo. W. 173
Embree, George W. 173,175
Emmons, Julius 48, 50
Epperson, Hiram 91
Epperson, Jesse 91
Epperson, Joel 91
Eppstein, Col. 103, 104, 106, 107,108,109,110
Eppstein, J. A. 222
Eppstein, Joseph A. 103
Eppstein, Joseph A. 102
Eppstein, Joseph A. Col. 167, 229
Eppstein, Major Joseph A. 100
Eppstein Viet 226
Estes, Joel 50
Estill, Benjamin 40
Eubank, Edmond 91
Eubank, J. E. 226
Eubank, Josiah E. 226
Evans, Alexander 138,141
Evans, Elisha 50
Evans, James 79
Evanks, John 50
Ewing, Baxter M. 227
Ewing, Ephraim B. 216,219
Ewing, Finis 169
Ewing, Finis (Paston) 60 158,159,160, 162,164
Ewing, Irving 161
Ewing, Mr. 162
Ewing, Reuben 158
Ewing, Reuben A. 80,156 161,221, 222
Ewing, W. C. 222

-F-

Factory 131
Fagan, General 108,109, 110, 117
Fagg, Thomas J. C. 219
Fantastic Company 68,69,70
Farris, James Jr. 191
Farris, John 191
Farris, Thomas 191
Fashions 130

Fayette 31,40,111
Feland, Joseph 224
Ferrel, Geo. W. 66
Ferrel, Peter H. 228
Ferry 51, 127
Ferry B. E. 85, 223
Ferry, Benjamin E. 89
Ferry, Benj. Emmons 222
Ferry, Benj. E. 64
Ferry Gen. 90
Fessler, John,Lieutenant 2nd 104
Fetzer, John Major 107
Fifth Division 90
Fillmore, Millard 82,83
Fine, David 53, 191
Finley, Henderson 170
First Newspaper 47
Fisher, John 154
Fisher, Joseph 154
Fisher, Peter 154
Fisher, Samuel 154
Fitsworth, Gabriel 54,148
Flat Creek 45
Fletcher, Thomas C. 215
Florence, 101
Forbes, Jeremiah 151
Forbes, Martin G. 151
Forbes, Phillips 151
Forbes, Rubeys 151
Forbes, Sam 169
Forbes, Samuel 151
Forbes, William G. 151
Force, Charles 191,194
Ford, Benj. P. 91
Ford, Nathaniel T. 91
Ford, Oliver G. 91
Forsythe, J. L. 68
Forsythe, Logan J. 89
Forsythe, Major 71
Forsythe, Major J. Logan 69, 70
Fort, 20, 27, 33, 34, 37,38 39, 41
Fort, Hannah Cole's 29, 34 35, 40, 43
Fort Sumpter 100
Foster, Andrew 161
Foster, Pethnel 154
Foxes 27
Fox Indians 17
Frame, George W. 66
Francis, Henry 91

Franklin Bottom 35
Franklin Clunty 16
Frederick, Rev. 161
Fremont, John C. 83
French, Charles 197
French, Charles R. 201
Frontiersman 27
Fulkerson, Abraham 217

-G-

Gabriel 214
Gabriel, John 170
Gale, 130
Gallagher, James 179
Gamble, Hamilton R. 53, 201
  215, 216, 219
Garten, Nat 167
Gazetteer 228
George, Carrol 49, 155
George, Long 160
George, Martin 155
George, Reuben 144, 148
George, William 51, 106, 148
Georgetown 110, 117
Georgetown Road 113
Gibson 42, 181
Gibson, Abram 144
Gibson, William 42, 49, 74, 77
  78, 127, 143, 144, 128
Gibson, Wm 39, 61
Gilbert, Ben 167
Gill, Mr 66
Givens, Alexander 144
Givens, James 144
Givens, Robert 144, 191
Glasgow, James H. 167
Glover, John 145, 147, 179
Glover, Peter G. 216, 217
Governor, 78, 80, 96, 97
Governor Lieut Nathaniel Cook
  76
Governor, Alex McNair 76
Governors 215
Gooche's Mill 136
Good, Jacob Sr. 195
Good, Jerry Jr. 195
Graham, Noah 167
Grand Jury 49
Grand Jury Cooper County 52
Grand River 17
Grant, Col U. S. 103
Graveley Col. 109

Gravelly, J. J. 216
Graveyard 129
Great Salt Lake 90
Grundy, Arinstedd A. 53
Guard 106
Guarding Bridge 109
Guards 96, 105
Guards Home 101, 102
Guyer, Henry 49, 52

-H-

Haas' Brewery 102
Haas, Emil, 1st Lieutenant
  102
Haas, Major Emil 103
Haffenburg, Franz 195
Hain, John A. Sergeant 102
Hall, Col. 195
Hall, Lawrence 226
Hall, Sylvester 77, 223
Hall, Willard P. 215, 216
Hambrich, Enoch 143
Hamilton, 204
Hammer, 138
Hammond, Allen 64, 65
Hammond, Samuel 72
Hancock, Stephen 12
Hardin, Charles H. 215
Harlan, Chris 175
Harlan, John 166
Harlan, Wm. B. 164
Harper, Harvey 179
Harris 214
Harris Dr. N. W. 136
Harris. Mr. E. H. 185
Harris, Hezekiah 154
Harris, James B. 102, 221
Harris, Peter B. 144
Harris, Reuben B. 170
Harrison 82, 136
Harrison, Jason 76
Harrison, Robert C. 81, 222
Hart, George C. 57, 130
Hasbrook, Chas. E. 66
Hatfield, Manty 185
Hatwood, John 168
Haupe, Rudolph 154
Hayden, Adams 202
Hayden, Emmett R. 202
Hayden, Henry C. 202
Hayden, Peyton R. 52, 53
  128, 144, 197, 201, 202

Hayes, Samuel 217
Hayne, John A. 103, 105
Hazell, Ignatius 224
Hazell, Judge J. 138
Head, William 40
Headquarters 106, 116
Heard, John 218
Heath, 142
Heath, John G. 14, 143, 40
Heath's Salt Lick 14
Hedrick, Bill 138
Hedrick, Isaac 154
Heim, Constantine 224
Hemenway, Anson 160
Hempstead, Fort 22
Henderson, John B. 202, 219
Hendricks, Littleberry 128, 144
Henry, Eli N. 49
Henshaw, William 194
Herndon 106
Hickerson, Alpheus D. 91
Hickerson, Daniel 141
Hickox, Benjamin 50
Hickox, Benjaman F. 52
  62, 92, 145
Hickox, Benj. F. 77, 79, 144
  224
Hickox B. F. 81, 222
Hickox, Mrs. B. F. 145
Hickox, Charles 155
Hickox, Frank W. 221
Hickox, Truman V. 62
Higby, 90
Higgerson, Mr. Wm 106
Hill, Benjamin 194
Hill, James 85, 179, 180
  223, 226
Historians 96
History of Cooper County 119
History of All Newspapers
  of Cooper County 64, 65
  66, 67
History Early 127
Hitherto 20
Hoecher, Fred 110
Hogan, General 172
Holladay, Thomas 217
Holmes, Nathaniel 219
Homan, Harrison 173
Homan, Jesse 62, 129, 144
Homan, Mrs Jesse 145, 228
Homan, Jessie 144
Homan, Samuel M. 173

Home Guards 103, 105, 115, 116
Hood, Robert 224
Hook, Elijah 166
Horace, Capt 115
Hornbeck, Michael 54,184
Hotel 127, 128
Hough, Warwick 220
Houses (First) 128
Houston, George W. 218
Houston, John F. 218
Houx, Frederick 49,54,144
Houx, Mrs. Frederick 75, 145
Houx, Mathias 185
Houx, Nicholas 54
Howard 156
Howard County 12, 16,27,31 33, 39, 40, 83, 110, 112, 113
Howard Shore 113
Howard, Stephen 155
Howard, Waid 155
Howe, Robert F. 224
Hubbard, Daniel 12
Huff, Mr. 181
Hughes, James S. 4th Sergeant 90
Hughes, Rice 151, 224
Hughes, Samuel 151
Hulett, Richard 91
Humes, Joel F. 84
Hunt, Daniel 222
Hupp, Aaron 173
Hurt, Acrey 148
Hurt, Clayton 49, 148
Hutchison, Ann 181, 182
Hutchison, Ardell 181,182
Hutchison, David 180,181
Hutchison, Elizabeth 181
Hutchison, Elmira 181, 182
Hutchison H. A. 66,203,226
Hutchison, Col H. A. 206 207, 229
Hutchison, Horace A 222
Hutchison, James 180, 181
Hutchison J. H. 79
Hutchison, John H. 60, 85 79, 180, 181, 222, 223, 224
Hutchison, Col. John H. 177
Hutchison, Margaret 181,182
Hutchison, N. 130
Hutchison, Sarah 181,182
Huth, David 195

-I-

IIall. L. 222
Illinois Regiment 103
Indian 30,32,87
Indians 19,21,26,29,30,31 32,33,34,37,39,88
Indian(Territory) 75
Indian(War) 33
Infantry 107
Infantry Company A.B. 103
Inspector General 89
Iowa Cavalry 110
Iowa Regiment 100, 105
Ish, Jacob 50

-J-

Jack, 214
Jackson, 200, 199
Jackson, Andrew 77
Jackson County 88
Jackson C. F. 215
Jackson Gen. 89, 154, 162 164, 167
Jackson, Gov 96, 97, 99
Jackson, Hancock 215, 216
Jackson, Stephen 12
Jackson's Gov 101
Jeffreys, James M. 91
Jeffreys, William J. 91
Jefferson, 204
Jefferson Barracks 93
Jefferson City 93,96,97,102 103,105,107,116,117
Jefferson Township 66
Jennings, Martin 57, 148 223
Jennings, William 58, 151 152
Joachimi, L. 67
Jobe, Abram 76
Johnson, C.D.W. 225
Johnson, Charles P. 216
Johnson, Col. William Preston 206
Johnson, John R. 91
Johnson's Factory 24
Johnston H.A.B. 173
Johnston, James H. 225
Johnston, James John Robert 148
Johnston, James H. 200

Johnston, John S. 173
Johnston, Mr. 200, 201
Jolly, John 190, 191
Jolly, Joseph 20,23,190
Jolly, William 190,191
Jonesborough 89
Jones 110, 112
Jones, Caleb 143
Jones. D. 222
Jones, David 40,76,80,81 154,155,221,224
Jones, Hon. David(First Settler) 137
Jones, James 155
Jones, James H. 91
Jones, John 155
Jones, John Rice 219
Joseph, 155
Justices of County Court 224

-K-

Kaiser, John B. Lieut Col. 107
Kavanaugh A. 222
Kavanaugh, Archibald 56,224
Kavanaugh, Archie 80,128
Kavanaugh, William Rev. 159 164
Keill, Christian 225
Keiser, John B. 103
Kelly, Caperton 151
Kelly, James 148,151
Kelly, John 151, 154, 179 198
Kelly, John M. 91
Kelly, Mr. John 145
Kelly, Mrs John 228
Kelly, Mrs. 130
Kelly, Parthena 181
Kelly, Miss Sally 148
Kelly, Tibitha Mrs 145
Kelly Township 151
Kelly Wm. 76
Kelly, William J. 151
Kelly's 99
Kemp, M. F. 226
Kemp Mr. 164
Keokuk Chiefs 18
Kerr, George W. 51
Kimball (Private) 105
Kincaid, David 40

Kincaid's Fort 25,27,29
  22, 30
Kine, Charles F. 91
King, Austin A. 215
King, Samuel 159
Kirkpatrick, David 161
Kirkpatrick, Jim 167
Kirkpatrick, Robert 158,160
Knob Noster 45
Kock, Charles 2nd Lieut 104
Kofield, Samuel S 222
Koontz, Joseph C. 226

-L-

Labbo's, Mr. 114
Lafayette 204
Lamine, 136
Lamine River 51, 106, 212
Lamine Township 32,73,74,75
  76,77,154
Lamm, Mr. 194
Lamm, William 191, 229
Lamm, Wm. 194
Lampton, Benj. C. 91
Lampton, Joshua 112
Land Office 39
Land Sales 41
Landers, Mr. 179
Landers, William 155
Langon, A. K. 222
Larnd, Samuel 154
Law Congress 107
Lawless, Miss 130
Lawless, Bradford 154
Laws, 37
Lawton, Edward Dr. 129
Lawyers, 128
Leathern, 36
Leatt, Felix 80
Legislature 78, 96
Lemons, Samuel R. 91
Leonard, Abiel 35, 53,144
  201, 219
Leonard, Judge Abiel 129
  197
Leonard, Major 112,113,114
Leonard, Nathaniel 112,180
Leonard's Major 111
Levens, B. W. 51, 57, 76
  181, 191, 193, 198
Levens, Dr. B. W. 180
Levens, Emarins 181

Levens, Messrs. H. C. 185,
  188
Levens, Lieutenant 92
Levens, H.C. 2nd Lieut 90
Levens, H. C. 206
Levens, Henry 191,192
Levens, Henry C. 182, 191
  222
Levens, Zerilda 181, 182
Lewis and Clark 13
Lewis, Edward A. 220
Lewis, Jas. P. 91
Lewis, Merriwether
  (Governor) 15
Lewis, Wm. 51
Lexington, 89,99,103,105
Liberty, 90
Lillard, William 50.75,76
  144, 155
Lillard, Wm. 222
Lilly's Branch 35
Lincoln, Abraham 83
Linn Tree 33
Lionberger, Isaac 85,138
  223, 224
Loan, Benjamin F. 219
Lockhart, Bird 51, 127
Lone Elm 136
Longan, Augustus K. 155
  156
Longan, Austin K. 77
Longan, George 156
Longan, John B. 59, 155
  156, 192
Longden, Rev. John B. 137
Loutre Island 15
Lovelace, Walter L. 219
Lowery, Wm. C. 180
Lucas 57
Lucas, Charles 40, 126
Lucas, J.B.C. 77
Lucus, John B. 144
Ludwig, F. W. 67
Luke, 214
Lyongens, 97, 98, 99
  100, 101
Lyon, Gen Nathaniel 100

-Mc-

McAdam, Samuel 159
McBride, Priestly 216
McBride, Priestly H. 219

McCampbell, James 79
McCarty, James 144
McCarty, Nicholas 144
McCarty's, Mrs. 109
McClain, James 184
McClanahan, Absalom 184, 191
McClanahan, Adam 184,191
McClanahan, Joshua 191
McClanahan, Lacy 184, 191
McClanahan, Wm. G. 184
McClanahan, Wm. H. 184
McClellan, Abraham 217
McClellan, Geo. B. 83
McClurg, Joseph W. 215
McCord, Adam 27
McCoy, Dr. M. 128
McCulloch, 166
McCulloch, James T. 226
McCulloch, Robert A. 153
  225
McCulloch, Robert Col 204
McCulloch, Robert 153, 223
McCulloch, Thomas 226
McCutchen 101, 130
McCutchen, John 185
McCutchen, John M. 222, 225
  226
McCutchen, Judge John M.
  185
McDaniel, William 154
McDearmon, H.E.W. 225
McDearmon, James R. 217
McDearmon, Mayor 112
McDowell, John 91
McFall, August 191
McFarland 177
McFarland, Jacob 144, 178
McFarland, James 144, 159
McFarland, Jas 77
McFarland, Jesse 52,144
  226
McFarland, Mr. Jesse 228
McFarland, John S. 144, 224
McFarland, Judge 127
McFarland Judge John S. 228
McFarland, Justinian 91
McFarland, Samuel 155
McFarland, Mr. 179
McFarland, William 50,144
  178, 223
McFarland Wm. 76, 145
McFarland, William(Sheriff)
  49

McGee, David 33, 54
McGee, Joseph H. 218
McGirk, Andrew 53
McGirk, Mathias 219
McGrath, Michael K. 216
McGravock, Robert 53
McKenzie, 128
McKenzie, K. 144
McLane, Ewing 31
McLane, Wm 29, 31
McLane's Fort 31
McMahan 29, 33
McMahan, James 154
McMahan, Thomas 57,154,224
McMahan, Samuel 32
McMillen, M. 221,222
McMillan, Nalcolm Mr. 205
McNair, Alex 76, 215
McNair, James 56

-M-

Macafferty, Green 50
Mahan, David P. 77,79,80
Mahan, James 151
Mahan, Patrick 155, 156
Mahan, Samuel 151
Majors, Mr. 160
Manufactories, 132
Mann, Jesse 53
Mark, 38
Marmaduke, General 97
Marmaduke, M. M. 215,216
Marmaduk's, Col.98,99,101
Marshall, 114
Marshal, Chief 204
Marshall, Fleming 143
Martin, Falkland H. 216
Martin, Henderson C. 91
Martin, Joe 155
Martin, Valentine 155
Martyn, 130
Masonic Hall 134
Masonic Lodge 173
Massey, Benjamin F. 216
Mathews, Alfred 222
Matthew, 168
Maxey, James W. 155
Mayo, Mr. Wm. 186
Mayor, 99
Megguire, 90
Megguire, Joseph 89
Melvin, D. A. 226

Mercer, Joseph W. 217
Merchants, 128
Methodist,(First) 128
Metzger, Prof. J.P. 206
Mexican, 87
Mexican War 90
Mexicans, 93
Mexico, 90, 116
Miami Townships 72,73,75,76
Middleton, James O. 64
Mike, 170
Milam, Tom 172
Militia, 107
Militia Law 68
Millan, D. A. 225
Miller, 99
Miller, Edward S.D. 91
Miller, George Capt 204
Miller, George W. 217,221
Miller, G. W. 99
Miller, James 56,79,224
Miller, John 79,185,196
   199,200,201,215,221,222
Miller, John G. 81, 222
Miller, Judge George W.
   185, 199
Miller, John(Jackson) 80
Miller, Mr. 200
Miller, Mrs 200
Miller, Samuel 164
Miller's and Murphy's 109
Milo Blair Co, Messrs 67
Minerals 142
Minister, 36
Minister(First) 58
Minor, James L. 216
Minteer, Joseph 166
Mitchell, John S. 53
Mississippi River 39
Missouri Pacific Railroad
   134
Missouri Register 65
Missouri River, 29,31,34,41
   42,53,89,94,97,98,102
Mitchell, Charles B. 144
Mitchell, Fleming G. 144
Mitchell, Thomas 144
Mitchell, William 144
Mitzell, 190
Mitzell, Peter 189
Mock, George 91
Modern History Boonville 130
Moniteau County 110

Moniteau Creek 31,108
Moniteau Township 155
Monroe, Jackson 222
Monroe, James(President)
   78
Monroe, Thomas 221
Monroe, William 217
Monroe's 26
Monteith, John 218
Moon, Jesse 154
Moon, William 154
Moore, Andrew B. 181
Moore, Chas. F. 138
Moore H. Wm. 76
Moore, John H. 74, 144
Moore, Joseph H. 177
Moore, Margaret 177
Moore, Mary 177
Moore, Robert 177
Moore, Sallie 177
Moore, Wm. H. 129
Moore, William Dr. 61, 139
Moore, William 177
Moore, William H. Dr. 181
Moore, William H. 181
Moreau Creek 108
Moreau Township 75, 76
Moreland, John S. 53
Morgan, 57
Morgan and Lucus 127
Morgan Asa 51,53,126,128,144
Morgan County 84,101
Morgan, Stanley G. 52,54
Mormon, 87,89
Mormons 90
Mormon War 88
Morris, Hugh 151
Morrison, Alfred 217
Morrison, Hugh 170
Morrow, James W. 221
Mosely, William S. 217
Muir, Mrs Maria 25
Muir's Mrs. 116
Muir, William D. 225
Mulligan Col. 103
Muroe, John 40

-N-

Napton, William B. 219
Nash, Ira P. 12, 13
Nash, William 12
Nashville, 92

Nathan, 13
Nauvoo, Illinois 89
Neal, A. H. 224
Neal, Nathan 167
Neale, Minor Rev 161
Neef and Boiler 117
Negro 117
Negro, Joe 33
Negro(Man) 29
Negroes, 88
Nelson, Jesse 91
Nelson, J. M. 117
Nelson, T. W. 99
New Franklin 11,30,110
Newman, Jacob 144
Newman, Jesse G. 224
Newman, R. B. 223, 226
New Mexico 93
New Nebo Church 110
New Palestine, 135
Newspaper(First) 64
Newspaper(Caldwell & Stahl) 66
Newspaper(Drury & Selby) 66
Nicholas, George 185
Nicholas, John 185
Nicholas, Mr. 190
Nolan, Bryant T. 57
Noland, William 49
Nolin, 127
Norris, Richard 3rd Sergeant 90
Nortwick, Ira Van 65

-O-

O'Bryan, James H. 99
O'Bryan, Jordan(Adams) 80
O'Bryan, Jordan 77,79,81,150 221,222
O'Bryan, Thomas L. 226
Odd Fellows 134, 135
Odgen, Jesse 224
Ogle, Daniel 181
Ogden, John 226
Ogden, Judge Jesse 194
Old Fort Field 16
Old Franklin 39,40,41,111 129, 130
Old Palestine, 137
Oliver, Mordacai 216
Organization, 120
O'Rourk, Strawther 173

Orr, J. H. 226
Orr, Sample 218
Osage River 39, 42, 53,108
Osage Township 76
Ostermeyer, Peter 104
Otterville, 102, 112, 134
Otterville & Lebanon Township 157
Overton, 136
Owens, Abel 50, 76
Owings, Ignatius P. 199

-P-

Painter, H. N. Ells.(Rev.) 104
Palestine, 89, 90
Palestine township 177
Pangborn, J. G. 66
Pappin, John 221
Parker, Thomas A. 218
Parks, 130
Parks, Captain 96,110,111
Parm, Wyant 154
Parrish, R. J. 138
Parsons, General 93, 101
Parson, John W. 158
Parsons, Mr. 165
Parsons, Thomas 165
Patrick, Bonaparte 181
Patrick, Thomas 179, 181
Patten, Nathaniel 47
Patterson, Joseph 224, 226
Patterson, Lovel 141
Pattison, John W. Mr. 229
Payne, John 53
Pendleton W. G. 188
Pendleton, William G. 185 228
Perry, Samuel(Adams) 80
Peters, Katie 179, 181, 182
Peters, Newton C. 181
Peters, Sallie 181, 182
Peters, Samuel 49,54,179,180
Peters, William G. 216
Petibone, Rufus 219
Petite Saline Creek 25,109
Pettis County 87, 101
Pettis, Spencer 216
Pettis, Spencer(Jackson) 80
Phoebe, James 16
Phoebe, Mark 16
Phoebe, Nellie 16

Phoebe, Polly 16
Phoebe, Rhoda 16
Physicians, 130
Pierce, Franklin 82
Pilot Grove 134, 135
Pisgah, 137
Pleasant Green 135
Poem, 207,208,209
Poem of Hutchison 203
Poindexter, Major 104, 105
Political History of Cooper County 72, 73, 74, 75, 76, 77, 78, 79, 80, 81, 82, 83, 84, 85, 86
Polk, James K. 82
Polk, President 200
Polk, Trusten 215
Poor, William 77
Pope, Col. 111, 112
Pork, 174
Porter's John Capt. 116
Porter, Wm. C. 79
Poston, William 144
Potter, George 144
Potter, John 50,51,57,144
Potter, Oscar F. 173
Potter, William 144
Prairie Home, 136
Prairie Home Township 184
Prairie Lick 101
Presbyterian, 128
President, 103
Prewitt, 12
Price, 65, 107
Price, Gen 96,97,99,105,106 107,108,109,116,117
Price, Sterling 215
Price, Thomas L. 216
Price's 96
Price's Army 118
Price's Raid into Cooper County 115
Prior, Tipton 1st. Corp. 91
Prisoners, 27,28,37,90,100 105, 116
Privates, 90
Probate Courts 55
Proclamation, 97
Prosecuting Attorney 140
Provost, Marshall 110
Public Administrators 226
Pursley, Joseph 191

Putnam, D. E. 141

-Q-

Quapa Indians 27
Quarles, Dr. 101
Quashgami, Chief 17
Quiltings, 124
Quisenberry, 65

-R-

Race, 30
Raid, 96
Railroad 126,134,135,213
Railroad Bridge 112
Railroad, M.D.&T. 33
Railroad Pacific 130
Railway, 97
Railway M. H. & T. 133
Ramsey, Miss 181
Ray County 90
Read, Anthony F. 180,224
Read, A. J. 118
Read, Joseph 105
Read, William 148
Reatherd, Captain John 104
Reavis, 51
Reavis, Andrew 61, 144
Reavis, Mrs. Bartlett William 127
Reavis, David 54, 144
Reavis, Jackson 152
Reavis, Johathan 144,152,228
Reavis, Joseph 105,152,153
Reavis, Lieut.Col. 111
Reavis, Lewis 152
Reavis, Miss Mary 145,228
Reavis, Mrs. Mary 144
Reavis, Sam D. 76, 77
Reavis, S. D. 226
Reavis, William T. 152
Rebellion 96
Rector, William V. 217
Redd, William J. 53, 199
Reed, A. M. 165
Reed, John 159
Reed, William 54, 165
Reed, Wm. A. 173
Reeves, Benjamin H. 216
Regdon, Sydna 90
Registers of Lands 218
Reiche, Mrs. G. 206

Reid, Capt 94
Reid, David 154
Reid, John Rev. 162
Reid, John 154
Reid, William 154
Religious, 88
Renfro, Isaac 53
Republican 84
Reubadeaux(First Store) 127
Reynolds, Thomas 215,216
Rhea, Robt 91
Rhoda, Miss 180
Rice, Charles E. 166
Rice, Jeremiah 224
Rice, T. M. 221
Rice, Judge T. M. 204
Richardson, Allen P. 218
Richardson, John C. 8,219
Richardson, John M. 216
Richmond, 90
Riggs, Thomas 77
Rio Grande River 34
River 36,97,106,111,112 133, 212
Rivers
  Blackwater 142
  Bonne Femme 13
  Ceder Creek 11
Femme Osage 13
  Gasconade 15
  Heath's Creek 14
  Lamine 12, 142
  Missouri 75
  Moniteau Creek 13
  Osage 10
  Rock 17
Roads, A. H. 226
Robbers 115
Roberts, 90
Roberts, J. G. 222
Roberts, John 49, 144
Robertson, Charles 148
Robertson, Edward Andrews 148
Robertson, William Mr. 153
Robinson, Edgar A. 65
Rocheport 81, 98, 110
Rochester, Bell 147
Rochester, J. C. 76
Rochester, John C. 147, 223 226
Rochester, Thos. E. 223,226
Rochester, Zepheniah 147

Rockport, 92
Rockeport, 97
Roe, J. W. 187
Roe, Samuel Sr. 185, 186 187
Rodgers, Mr. 181
Rodman, Francis 216
Roeschel, Ernest 2nd Lieutenant 102
Rogers, 192
Rogers, F. A. 223
Rogers, Thomas 127, 144 155, 222
Rogers, Thos 76, 77
Rolla District 107
Rollins, 61
Rose, Muke 49
Ross, Dr. J. W. H. 188
Ross, James C. 91
Ross, J. P. 84
Ross, William 46, 51, 77 127, 144
Ross, Wm. 45, 51
Roupe, Gilliard(First) 127
Roupe's Branch 127
Rubey, Bill 167
Rubey, Thomas 158, 161
Rubey U. E. 91
Rubey W. B. 91
Ruble, Owen 79
Rupe, Giliad 143
Rupe, Gillard 20
Rubels, Andrew 50
Rupe's Brance 52
Ruppe, Gillard 50
Russelville 108
Ryland, John F. 53, 201 219

-S-

Saline County 77,87,89,104 105
Saline Township 190
Salmon, Harvey W. 217
Salomon, Frederick 218
Salsman, Charles 91
Salt Lake 90
Samuel 29
Samuel, Cole 39
Sanborn Gen. 107,108,110
Sanborn's 109
Sanborn's Gen. 117

Sanders, Bryant 76
Santa Fe 34
Santa Fe Traders 41
Sarshell 29, 30
Sauk Indians 17
Sauks, 27
Saunders, S. H. 173
Savage, 21
Savage, James 20,36,49 143
Savage, John 20,35,49,51 143
Savage, William 20, 143
Savages, 29, 34
Schilb, David 195, 228 229
Scholars, 35
School 29,34,126,134,188
School, Catholic 126
School, Colored 126
Schools 183, 192
Schools(First) 56, 61
School House(First) 128
Schutler, Jacob 138
Scott, 82
Scott, General 82
Scott, John 72, 76, 77, 78 79
Scott, Kemp 137, 156
Scott, William 219, 221
Scott, William L. 228
Scouts 98, 106
Seat 126
Seat, Green 224
Seat, Green B. 144
Seat, John B. 144
Seat of Justice 48
Sebrom, 138
Secongost, Mr. 128
Secretaries of State 216
Sedalia, 174, 175
Seigel, Albert Col. 107
Seivers, Thompson 91
Selby, Mr. 66
Seth, 155
Settled, 39
Settlers, 24,29,30,31,32,33 38, 40
Settlers, Cooper County 119
Seymour, George E. 218
Shaefer's, Col. 98
Shannon, R. D. 218
Sharp, John V. 56, 63

Shelby, Gen. 113
Shelby, Gen. Joseph 112
Shelby's, 96
Shelby's Command 116
Shelby's Gen. 114
Shelby's(Men) 113
Shelby's Raid 112
Shellcraw, David 143
Sheriff, 79, 80,85
Sheriff, Wm. H. Curtis 76
Sheriffs of Cooper County 223
Sherwood, Thomas H. 220
Shields, Henry 216, 217
Shields, William 85, 148,222
Shoemaker, 115
Shoemaker, Capt. 116
Shouse, C. Q. 143
Shurley, Frederick 167
Shurley, Robert 167
Sifers, Joseph 189
Simonds, Nathaniel 217
Simons, Jake 56, 60
Simms, James 180
Simpson, Augustine W. 65
Skirmish, 108
Skofield's 107
Slaughter, Prof. 136
Slavery, 78, 85
Slaves, 120
Sloan, Alexander 158,160 166
Sloan, Robert Rev. 160
Sloan, William 160,165,166
Sloan's Alexander
Small, Henry 161
Small, Moses B. 173
Smallwood, Russell 180
Smelser, Harmon 154
Smelser, John 154
Smiley, Mr. 161
Smiley, Thos. 76
Smiley, Thomas 222
Smiley, Thomas B. 155, 198
Smith, 21, 164
Smith A. J. Gen. 117
Smith, C. H. 224
Smith, Judge C. H. 128, 156
Smith, George 216
Smith, George R. 175
Smith, George W. 158, 165 166
Smith, Hiram 90
Smith, Jared E. 218

Smith, Jeremiah 184
Smith, Joseph 49,89,90
Smith, Luther 181
Smith, Mr. 164
Smith, Thomas 20,23,181
Smith, Thomas A. Gen 41
Smith, Mr. Wm. 129
Smith, Geo. W. 172
Snodgrass, James 155
Snodgrass, Samuel 155
Society, 124
Soldiers, 27, 94
Sombart, C. W. 224
Son, Michael 137, 138
Southern Troops 115
Speed, Wm P. 225
Spillers, Peter 160
Springfield, 100
Stanard, E. O. 216
Stanford, Richard 51
Staples, Dr. Thomas E. 143
Starke, Milton 173
Starke, Thomas J. 176,228
Starke, Thomas J. Mr. 157
State Auditirs 217
State Officers 76, 215
State(Senator) 79,80,221
State Treasurers 217
State Troops 97,99,101 106
St. Clair County 17, 37
Steamboat 102
Steamer, L. F. Linn 91
Steel, D. K. 222
Steele, Elizabeth 158
Steele, Joseph B. 226
Steele, William 167
Stephen, Maj. Cole 178
Stephen Cole's 34
Stephens, 44
Stephens, Captain 93, 94
Stephens, George H. 182
Stephens, James M. 198
Stephens, J. L. 16, 225
Stephens,John D. 1st Sergeant 90, 182
Stephens, Joseph 39,43,44 46,177,198,228
Stephens, Joseph Jr. 179
Stephens, Joseph L. 182
Stephens, Joseph Sen. 178
Stephens, Joseph L. Captain 90

Stephens, Joseph Sr. 46, 179, 180, 196, 197
Stephens, Larry 44
Stephens, J. Lawrence 138
Stephens, Lawrence C. 81, 181, 222, 224
Stephens, Judge Lawrence C. 177
Stephens, L. C.)Judge) 59, 61
Stephens, Margaret 182
Stephens, Mrs Margaret 228
Stephens, Mrs. 43, 178
Stephens, Mrs. L. C. 75
Stephens, Nelly 198
Stephens, Peter 179
Stephens, W. H. 91
Stephens, William 151, 179
Stephens, Zilpha 198
Stephenson, Col. John D. 101
Stevens, Joseph 45
Stevens, Joseph Sr. 59
Stevens, Mrs. 44
Stevens, William 59
Stewart, Alex 77
Stewart, Robert M. 215
Still, Joseph 29, 30
Stillman, 192
Stillson, William A. 155
Stinson, James 155
St. Louis, 28, 41, 92, 93, 94, 107
Stone, William 158, 161
Stoneman, Colin 158, 169
Stoneman, Colin C. 161
Stoneman, R. B. 226
Store, 128
Strain, John D. 173
Stringtown, 108
Strother, G. F. 78
Stuart, Alex 80
Stuart, Robert 224
Sullans, William 91
Sulphur Springs 113, 114
Summers, Jacob 180
Summers, Phillip 91
Superintendents of Schools 218
Supreme Judges 219
Surgeon, 103, 107
Surveyed, 127
Surveyor, 52
Swap, Franklin 1st Lieutenant 110
Swearinger, William 151

Syracuse, 101, 102

-T-

Tabeaux Township 72, 75, 76
Taliaferro, James 138
Taliaferro, W. W. 222
Tate, Stephen 53
Taylor, 82, 138
Taylor, Elijah 154
Taylor, Gen 93
Taylor, James 149, 150, 163
Taylor, James Jr. 149, 185
Taylor, Jas. 159
Taylor, John 149
Taylor, Mr. 150
Taylor, Robert M. 173
Taylor, William 149, 185
Territorial, 39, 40
Territorial(Laws) 29, 37
Telegraph, 97
Tevis, Mr. 180
Tevis, Simeon Capt 180
Thomas, Dr. F. W. G. 84
Thomas, Jesse 144
Thomas, John B. 50
Thomas, John D. 76, 144
Thomas, John 177
Thomas, Peyton 144
Thomas, Silas 159, 163
Thompson, 172
Thompson, Alonzo 217
Thompson, Gibeon R. 171
Thompson, harrison Capt. 115
Thomson, James 225
Thompson, James Capt. 127, 197
Thompson's James 190
Thornton, Col. 128
Tipton, 103, 105, 106, 116
Tippecanoe(Battle) 81
Todd, Capt. 189
Todd, C. W. 64
Todd, David 49, 50, 79, 196, 221
Todd, Jonathan 20, 23
Tompkins, Benjamin 84, 222
Tompkins, George 51, 53, 219
Toole, John 167
Totten, Capt. 98
Towns, Cooper County 126

Townsend, Saunders 154
Trade, 130
Trading Posts, 12
Trail, 30
Travis, Francis 51
Traveled, 121
Travillian, T. M. 174
Trent, W. W. 188, 227
Trigg, John A. 224
Trigg, John 225
Trigg, Stephen 199
Trigg, William H. 44
Triggs, Dr. 128
Trigg's Dr. Wm. II 101
Tri-Weekly Observer 66
Trotter, David 51
Troops 90, 96, 97, 98, 102
Tucker's, Thomas 111
Turley, Col. 70, 71
Turley, Col. Jesse J. 69
Turley, Jesse 154
Turley, Jessie J. 89
Turley, Samuel 154, 224
Turley, Stephen 51, 154
Turley's, Col. 70
Turner, James 191
Turner, John 191
Turner, Robert H. 226
Turner, Robert 85
Tutt, Dr. Samuel J. 138
Tutt, P. A. 227
Tutt, Philip A. 181, 224
Tutt, William 84
Twentyman, Thomas 49, 144
Tyler, 81, 82, 173

-U-

Umphrey, 143

-V-

Van Buren 66
Van Buren, Martin 80, 82
Van Odell, Henry E. 173
Verian, John 50
Vermont, 137
Vest, G. G. 222
Virginia 83
Vollmer, 190
Vollrath Place 109
Vorhes, Henry N. 220

Vote Cast (First) 74

-W-

Wachter Am Missouri(Newspaper)
    German Language 67
Wadley, Jennie Mrs. 145
Wagner, David 219
Waid, Dr. 228
Walker, Anthony 163
Walker, A. S. 151, 222, 224 226
Walker, Green 164
Walker, H. R. 151
Walker, James G. 165
Walker, James H. 225
Walker, John 217
Walker, Samuel 151
Walker, Vincent 161, 169
Walker, William 160
Wallace, Andrew 180
Wallace, John 180, 181
Wallace, Robert 50, 52, 75
Waller, B. R. 226
War 34,39,87,89,90,93,95
Ward, 65
Ward, John 193
Ward, Parker 51
Ward and Parsons 138
Ward, William 199
Warden, 145
Warden, William 53
Warfield, Elisha N. 226
War History 87
War History of Cooper
    County 96
War Mexican 82
Warren, Edward V. 199
Warren, George W. 199
Warren, Mr. 199
Wash, Robert 219
Wash, Robt. 78
Washington, 100, 204
Washington, Judge 201, 202
Water Springs 212
Waynesville, 107
Wear, Bennett Wm. Rev. 163
Wear, D. W. 225
Wear, Col. D. W. 111
Wear, George 172
Wear, Hugh 159, 163
Wear, James H. 160, 172
Wear, James L. 159

Wear, John 158,159,160
Wear, Rev. James L. 158,160
Wear, Samuel 158,160 173
Wear, Samuel Jr. 160
Wear, Samuel Mr. 162
Wear, Sr. 160
Wear's W. G. 172,173,174 175, 222
Wear, William 48
Wear, William G. 172
Wear Wm. 50
Wear Wm. G. 160
Weatherford, Archibald 198
Weatherford, Frances 198
Weatherford, James 198
Weatherford, Johanna 198
Weatherford, Joseph 198
Weatherford, Lawrence C. 198
Weatherford, Madison 198
Weatherford, Mary 198
Weatherford, Nancy 198
Weatherford, Nelly 198
Weatherford, Peter 198
Weatherford, Rhoda 198
Weatherford, William 198
Weatherford, Zilpha 198
Weaver, Abner 170
Weber, Henry 195
Weber, Joseph Lieut. 104
Webster, Daniel 81
Weddings, 121
Weigel, Eugene F. 216
Weight, George W. 148,224 227
Weight Geo. W. 79, 80
Weite, Gen. 89
Weite, Lyman 90
Werthumer, M. J. 113
Westbook, Joseph 191
Western, The Emigrant
    (Paper) 64
Whig, 65,82,85
Whigs, 80,81,83
White, Green 181
White, Hartley 151
White, Jenus 61,174,177
White, Jesse 151
Whitesides, James H. 12
White, Spague 91
Whitler, Paul 50
Whitley, John 91
Whitlow, R. W. 226

Wholesale, 130
Wier, William 76
Wilcox, George 52
Wilcox, Paul 97
Wilcoxson, J. R. P. 91
Wilkerson, James G. 166
Wilkerson, John Mrs. 164
Williams, Abraham 12, 15
William Bartlett's
    Boarding House 42
Williams, Britton 49
Williams, Miss Elizabeth 148
Williams, Ezekiel 154
Williams, James 53
Williams, Joseph 128, 197
Williams, Justinian 128,144 146, 222
Williams, Luke 36,48,59 129, 144, 146, 167, 178
Williams, Rev. Luke 58 180
Williams, Marcus 79, 146 223, 224, 229
Williams, Marcus Jr. 89
Williams, Newton 1st
    Lieutenant 90
Williams, Samuels 52
Williams, Thomas L. 224
Williams, William 128, 197
Wilson, W. D. 144
Winston, James 225
Winter of 1818, 130
Winterbower, Dr. T. H. 195, 229
Wood, Jesse 191
Woods, Adam 26
Woods, Alexander 155,191
Woods, Charles 224
Woods, Gen. Charles 151, 152
Woods, Peter 59
Woodson, Silas 215
Woodward, J. E. 223
Woodward, Joel E. 89 223
Woolerly, Wm. Jr. 224
Woolery, Ewing E. 91
Woolery, Henry 180
Woolery's Henry Mill 59
Wooley's Mill 87

Woolery, Wm. Jr. 223
Woolsey, Wm. 91
Wrench, Joseph 138
Worthington, Col. 102, 103
 105, 106
Worthington, Gen. 66
Wright, G. W. 222
Wyan, Jacob 128, 225

-Y-

Yarnell, Joseph 20
Yeoman, William T. 65
Young, James 216
Young Married 123
Young Readers 123

-Z-

Zeller, 190
Zeller, Otho 189

www.ingramcontent.com/pod-product-compliance
Lightning Source LLC
Chambersburg PA
CBHW020646300426
44112CB00007B/266